RITES OF THE
NEW HUMANITY

Rites of the New Humanity: Essays on Sacramental Theology
Copyright © 2025 by Peter J. Leithart

Theopolis Books
An imprint of Athanasius Press
715 Cypress Street
West Monroe, Louisiana, 71291
athanasiuspress.org | (318) 323-3061

Cover design and typesetting: Rachel Rosales

ISBN: 978-1-957726-24-3

Printed in the United States of America.

RITES OF THE NEW HUMANITY

Essays on Sacramental Theology

PETER J. LEITHART

DEDICATION

This book is dedicated to our grandson Duncan Emilio, third child and second son of Christian and Tara Leithart, the first of a barrage of grandsons born in the spring of 2025. As Duncan's first pastor, I had the privilege of baptizing him during Easter season. I forgot to prepare water for the occasion, so I baptized him from the styrofoam cup I had drunk from earlier in the service. An Augustinian object lesson there: The rites of the new covenant are fewer, simpler, and more powerful than the rites of the old. Jesus uses even the humblest water to draw us into the life of the regeneration. Duncan shares this enacted parable with the Ethiopian eunuch: "Look! A styrofoam cup with water! What prevents me from being baptized?"

TABLE OF CONTENTS

PREFACE

My theological obsessions seized me early on and haven't let go over four decades (and counting) of writing theology. Sacramental theology has been one of my main manias—not sacramental theology as an almost-forgotten addendum to systematic theology but as a central concern of all theology, ecclesial and pastoral practice, and cultural and political mission. My agenda was to rethink theology back-to-front, from sacramental theology through the loci of systematics all the way back to theology proper. Given the fact that Jesus left His church with rites of water and wine, what must the church be, what is the shape of salvation, what is the relation of old and new, what is creation, and who is God?

If our understanding of salvation makes it impossible for me to echo Peter's "baptism now saves you" (1 Pet 3:21), we need to revise our understanding of salvation. If our doctrine of God pressures us to minimize or deny our *koinonia* with Jesus in bread and wine, we need to change who we think God is, because if there's one thing we know about the living God, it's that He gives us a cup and a loaf for communion in the body and blood of His Son (1 Cor 10:16-17). One of the questions that's guided my writing to this day has been: What would theology look like if we took "This is My body, this is My blood" and "be baptized . . . for the remission of your sins" (Acts 2:38) as rubrics governing *all* theology? What would happen if we did theology as if we believed what Jesus and Peter say?

The essays collected here, most of them previously published, represent some of the early results of this obsession. I hope they edify Christians of all traditions, for my aim has been to edify the *church*, not merely to challenge and edify my tribe. I hope these indicate, though they can hardly prove, that a theology guided by the reality of sacraments is more biblical, more concrete, more creational and visceral, more political than traditional theology, Protestant, Catholic, Orthodox, or other.

And that leads me to the more specific, tribal context for these essays. During the early 2000s, the American Reformed world was roiled by yet another tempest in a thimble—the debate over the "Federal Vision" or the "Auburn Avenue Theology." As thimble-tempests go, FV was Category 4, leading to several heresy trials (mine included), formal denunciations from conservative Presbyterian churches (the PCA and OPC among them), split churches, swirling polemics against and for FV.

It was not an edifying spectacle. The "Federal Vision" Conference had barely folded its last table when someone tossed an "H" bomb into that space of dispassionate contemplation we call the internet. FV was soon conflated with the "New Perspective on Paul," and FV heretics were accused of flirting with Arminianism or Roman Catholicism. The storm has died down, but it's not over. There's a Presbyterian seminary in Kyiv, Ukraine, that used some of what I imagine are scarce resources to translate and publish a book-length attack on FV. In September of this year (2025), I plan to teach at a conference in Porto Allegre, Brazil, and I'm told anti-FV vultures are already circling, eager to pick over my lectures. In some parts of the world, straight-line winds are still bending trees and pulling down power lines.

I *do* understand what the fuss is about. At its clearest and most rigorous, when it's not dodging and feinting and double-speaking to appear innocuous or blandly traditional, FV *does* challenge fundamental instincts and convictions of much contemporary Reformed theology. FV rehabilitated some themes in older Reformed theologians, but it was never a *ressourcement* project. While FV advocates are contentedly at home in the Reformed Confessional tradition, it *is* a new iteration, offering a revised and, I think, refreshed theology. And if there's one thing Reformed folk don't much appreciate, it's novelty.

To press the point: Reformed churches reacted to FV in the way they did because they're in the grip of Baptistic Evangelicalism. That quintessentially American brand of Christianity is the target, usually hidden, of most of my polemics here. Its main flaws are three: It has dislodged the Old and New, with the result that sacramental theology floats free of the rich liturgical setting of Torah and temple. As much as classical liberalism, it rests on a "semi-Marcionite" reading of Scripture. Further, and partly for this reason, it has, at best, an anemic conception of sign, symbol, rite, and ritual. At worst, it is allergic to liturgy. Behind both of these tendencies is, finally, an adherence to an understanding of creation and grace that owes more to late medieval theology than to Augustine or Aquinas or the original Reformed. FV was an effort to purge semi-Marcionite semiotics and nature-supernatural dualism from the Reformed churches. It was *nouvelle theologie* for Protestants. Despite some progress, that task mostly remains to be finished.

I came to "FV" convictions in the decade before FV existed, my outlook forged at Biblical Horizons conferences, in conversations with Jim Jordan, Jeff Meyers, and others, and during my doctoral studies at Cambridge. The papers collected in this volume represent my deepest explorations of the issues. As I reviewed them for publication, I was reminded what FV was for. It's an *Augustin-ian* refinement of Reformed sacramental theology, and in that regard a friendly amendment and enhancement. It's a *catholic* revision, an attempt to incorporate insights and ways of speaking from other traditions—from the best of medieval sacramental theology, including Aquinas, modern Catholics like Henri de Lubac and Yves Congar, and Orthodox thinkers like Alexander Schmemann. It's an *ecumenical* effort to move beyond the heavily-armed barricades that separate church from church. It's, finally, a *multi-disciplinary* revision, drawing on the resources of cultural anthropology and other social sciences to set the sacraments smack-dab at the center of a Christian theolo-gy of culture—not to mention at the heart of soteriology.

If you followed the FV debates online or in the var-ious General Assemblies, that last paragraph may sound odd. Very few of those topics ever came up, or come up. Nor did most of the other issues I elaborate in these es-says: a relational, Trinitarian ontology and anthropology; the central importance harmonizing Old and New in the-ology, especially sacramental theology; signs as constitu-tive of communion, rather than pointers to a mystical, interior communion that transcends signs; sacraments as ritual actions; disciplined attention to the *surface* of sacramental practice, exploring the theological import of bread, wine, and water, of washing, eating, and drinking;

obsession with the cultural and political import of the sacraments.

Most of these essays are decades old, but I have left them more or less as they were when I first published them. They mostly hold up, but in the interim I have continued to refine my thinking. If I were to write them again, I'd put more stress on the gift-character of the sacraments, on God's agency as self-Giver, on the action of the Spirit. At certain points, I'd emphasize the political character of the church. I'd be harder on Calvin and Rahner and a bit easier on Aquinas, and I would repeat Robert Jenson's "revisionary metaphysics" like a mantra, rather than dismiss, as I sometimes do here, metaphysics as such.

Younger readers in search of research topics might discover some trails to blaze: A history of the rhetoric and theology of the "Judaizer" epithet in the early church, medieval Christendom, and the Reformation; a full-scale study of Augustine's wonderful, underexplored *contra Faustum*; an appreciative Protestant primer on medieval sacramental theology. The Big Idea I'd still like to pursue (given world enough and time): Investigate how changes in sacramental theology and practice contributed to the complex we know as modern civilization.

Rites of the New Humanity may be long past its sell-by date. Who reads essays from the early 2000s, much less the 1990s—a decade from *the last century*? Perhaps, but I hope for better. In the somewhat calmer thimble of the present day, when Reformed folk are distracted by ever-fresh cyclones, these essays may spark or contribute to a renewed, more charitable, more intelligent debate about the truth of the matter. Perhaps too, these essays will make a contribution to the larger aim of formulating a more *catholic* theology that helps to overcome the theological effects of our unhappy divisions.

Beth-Elim
Gardendale, Alabama
Pentecost 2025

ACKNOWLEDGEMENTS

Most of the essays in this volume have been published previously. Though they have been edited and corrected for this collection, I have made no substantive revisions. Portions of these essays also appear in my dissertation, *Priesthood of the Plebs* (Wipf & Stock, 2003).

Chapter 1, "'Framing' Sacramental Theology" was first published in the *Westminster Theological Journal* 62.1 (2000). Both chapter 2, "Embracing Ritual," and chapter 3, "Conjugating the Rites" first appeared in the *Calvin Theological Journal* (2004 and 1999, respectively). Thanks to the *CTJ* for their permission to reprint here.

"More Than a Dainty Sip," a study of Augustine's treatise against Faustus the Manichean, is previously unpublished. "Semiosis and Social Salvation" was first published as a chapter in Wayne Cristaudo and Heung Wah Wong, eds., *St. Augustine: His Relevance and Legacy* (ATF Press, 2010).

Three essays appeared in *Pro Ecclesia*: Chapter 5, "Old Covenant and New in Sacramental Theology New and Old," 14.2 (May 2005); "Marcionism, Postliberalism, and Social Christianity," 8.1 (1999); and "Modernity and the 'Merely Social'" 9.3 (2000). "Womb of the World" was first published in the *Journal for the Study of the New Testament* 22.78 (2000), and "Christs Christened into Christ" in *Studia Liturgica* 29.1 (1999). All of these are Sage journals, which grants permission to authors to reuse published material.

The final chapter, "What's Wrong with Transubstantiaiton," is the oldest of the bunch, beginning life as a seminar paper at Westminster Seminary and then appearing in the *Westminster Theological Journal* 53.2 (1991).

I'm grateful to Rev. Steve Wilkins and Rev. Zach Parker for their interest in publishing this collection, and to Zach, Jeremy Bennett, and the rest of the Athanasius Press team for polishing the essays. Stephen Long read through the essays, spotted many errors and inconsistencies, and posed characteristically penetrating questions.

"FRAMING" SACRAMENTAL THEOLOGY: TRINITY AND SYMBOL

J. P. S. Uberoi has argued that modern culture emerged from Reformation disputes about the nature of the eucharistic presence. According to his account, the "modern concept of time in which every event was either spiritual and mental or corporeal and material but no event was or could be both at once" was a product of the "double monism," the separation of symbol from reality, inherent in Zwingli's eucharistic theology. Implicitly, all sides in the Reformation debate accepted Zwingli's assumption of "two separate and distinct spheres of spiritual and mystical versus material and corporeal presences." Even the Tridentine doctrine of transubstantiation was "no longer a normal transaction of God and man in this world" but a "kind of miraculous transference by God's agency between two separate places and two different times." Modernity, in short, was born at Marburg in 1529.[1]

---

1. J. P. S. Uberoi, *Science and Culture* (Delhi: Oxford University Press, 1978), 25–34. E. Brooks Holifield begins his history of Puritan sacramental theology with a reminder of the two-front war that the Reformation bequeathed to its successors: "In 1520 Martin Luther sharply challenged the entire sacramental system of medieval Christendom, but within five years he was struggling to save the sacraments themselves from radical reformers who wished to push beyond externals into a realm of pure spirit" *(The Covenant Sealed: The Development of Puritan Sacramental Theology in Old and New England, 1570–1720* [New Haven, CT: Yale University Press, 1974], 1). Particularly in the Reformed wing of the Protestant church, various theological emphases have conspired to produce a pronounced anti-sacramental tenor. Among the important factors have been an emphasis on the primacy of the intellect that exalted verbal communication above non-verbal forms; a sharp metaphysical distinction between spirit and flesh, which shaped a metaphysical interpretation of Jesus' statement that the "flesh profits nothing" (John 6:63); the related principle that *finitum non capax infiniti;* and the doctrine of election, which implies that sacraments could be assuring signs of God's favor and means of grace only to the elect, a circle within the circle of the church. The dominical authority for the sacraments has been too weighty for Reformed churches ever to consider abandoning the sacraments, and there have been periodic outbreaks of strong sacramental piety, informed more by Calvin than by Zwingli, yet the Reformed churches have never escaped profound ambivalence toward the use of material objects, symbols, and rites in worship. On this question generally, see Carlos M. N. Eire, *War Against the Idols: The Reformation of Worship from Erasmus to Calvin* (Cambridge: Cambridge University Press, 1986). On Calvin, see B. A. Gerrish, *Grace & Gratitude: The Eucharistic Theology of John Calvin* (Minneapolis, MN: Fortress, 1993); Ronald S. Wallace, *Calvin's Doctrine of the Word and Sacrament* (Tyler, TX: Geneva Divinity School, 1982).

Henri de Lubac places the rupture between reality and symbol several centuries earlier, noting that during the medieval eucharistic debates, the orthodox gained a monopoly on "truth" while the heretics retained symbol: *"Au mystice, non vere respond, non moins exclusif, un vere, non mystice."* In de Lubac's detailed retelling, Berengar rather than Zwingli is the harbinger of the future.[2] Alexander Schmemann agrees.[3] Similarly, Henning Graf Reventlow finds the origins of modern critical biblical studies in late medieval Spiritualism, which placed such stress on the possession of the Spirit as to render "superfluous both the letters of Holy Scripture and all external forms of the communication of salvation . . . above all the sacraments and the clergy." Antipathy to external ceremony among English Puritans was likewise a "stimulus in later biblical interpretation for the denigration of all that

---

2. *Corpus Mysticum L'eucharistie et l'église au moyen age: Étude historique*, 2nd ed. (Paris: Aubier, 1949), 251, 254. On medieval eucharistic controversies, see also Gary Macy, *The Theologies of the Eucharist in the Early Scholastic Period: A Study of the Salvific Function of the Sacrament According to the Theologians, c. 1080–c. 1220* (Oxford: Clarendon, 1984); Charles E. Sheedy, *The Eucharistic Controversy of the Eleventh Century Against the Background of Pre-Scholastic Theology* (S. T. D. Diss., Catholic University of America Studies in Sacred Theology, 2nd series, no. 4; New York: AMS Press, 1980); N. M. Haring, "Berengar's Definitions of *Sacramentum* and their Influence on Mediaeval Sacramentology," *Medieval Studies* 10 (1948).

3. Alexander Schmemann, *For the Life of the World* (Crestwood, NY: St. Vladimir's Seminary Press, 1973), 128, 138.

was priestly," and for the notion that Hebrew religion declined from "a pure and natural form to a final form distorted by ritualism," a notion later developed into a basic hermeneutical principle by Julius Wellhausen.[4]

Colin Gunton, by contrast, traces the origins of various dilemmas of modern theology and culture to an incipient Unitarianism in the western doctrine of God. Paradoxically, while modernity has presented itself as a Heraclitean assertion of the rights of the many against the monistic Parmenidean past, it has produced forms of oppression of the many to the one far more brutal than anything the premodern world could have imagined. Once they had rejected the conviction that the universe finds its coherence in God, modern thinkers embarked on a search for an immanent unifying principle. Modern individualism, collectivism, and postmodern anarchism are all incapable, however, of sustaining a vision of "otherness-in-relation" or a sufficient appreciation for particulars. In sum, "Parmenides and Heraclitus have called the tune and so have obliterated the trinitarian categories which enable us to think of the world—and therefore also culture and society—as both one and many, unified and diverse, particular and in relation." Western theology, with its tendencies toward monism, homogenization,

---

4. Henning Graf Reventlow, *The Authority of the Bible and the Rise of the Modern World*, trans. John Bowden (London: SCM, 1984), 17, 412.

and authoritarianism, bears significant responsibility for this situation. There is hope only in a revival of a robust trinitarian theology and practice.[5]

Both of these narratives attribute the rise of modern thought and culture to theological sources and therefore raise the question whether the two accounts might be integrally related, two aspects of a single, complex development. Is there some inner connection between Zwinglian anti-sacramentalism and the implicit Unitarianism of western theology? One possibility is that both tendencies are traceable back to Augustine, whom Gunton holds responsible for the unitarian trajectory of western theology. For Gunton, Augustine's "neoplatonic assumptions of the material order's incapacity to be really and truly the bearer of divinity" raise difficulties for Christology and support an ontological trinitarianism disconnected from the revelation of the Trinity in the economy of salvation. As a result, personality never quite attains full ontological status in Augustine. Gunton supports his interpretation by citing Augustine's claim in *De Trinitate* (5.12): "The particulars in the same Trinity that are properly predicated of each person are by no means predicated of them as they are in themselves *(ad se ipsa),* but in their relations either to one another or to the creature, and it is therefore man-

---

5. *The One, the Three and the Many: God, Creation and the Culture of Modernity,* The Brampton Lectures, 1992 (Cambridge: Cambridge University Press, 1993), 124.

ifest that they are predicated relatively, not substantially."[6] As a result, the particular persons, Gunton says, "tend to disappear into the all-embracing oneness of God," and he endorses H. A. Wolfson's conclusion that Augustine "identifies the substratum [of the Godhead] not with the Father but with something underlying both the Father and the Son."[7]

On this reading, it is no accident that Augustine employs psychological, rather than social, models for the Trinity. To say that the persons are analogous to functions of the human mind suggests that the persons are only formally distinct. Psychological models, furthermore, are consistent with Augustine's neoplatonic tendency to separate salvation from history. As Gunton says, "*The crucial analogy for Augustine is between the inner structure of the human mind and the inner being of God, because it is in the former that the latter is made known, this side of eternity at any rate, more really than in the 'outer' economy of grace.*"[8] Person, and hence community, are relegated to a secondary and even epiphenomenal level, both in the nature of God and in the history of salvation.[9] Here Augustine's

---

6. Quoted by Gunton, *The Promise of Trinitarian Theology* (London: T. & T. Clark, 1991), 41.

7. Ibid., 42.

8. Ibid., 45.

9. Ibid., 53. Gerald Bray repeats this criticism of western theology and attempts to redress it by insisting, in a discussion of Calvin's

trinitarianism intersects with the concerns of sacramental theology, for if Augustine locates the primary divine-human encounter in the human mind he can be expected to have problems carving theological space for the "external" operation of sacraments.

Gunton's critique of Augustine has been challenged by Rowan Williams,[10] and F. Bourassa defends Augus-

---

trinitarian theology, on the primacy of persons over essence (*The Doctrine of God*, Contours of Christian Theology [Downers Grove: InterVarsity Press, 1993], 167,197–224). Bray's discussion is unfortunately vitiated by his fairly rigid distinction between the "levels" of person and substance. The distinction itself is of course unobjectionable, but Bray employs it in singular ways. It appears, for example, in his classification of God's attributes: incommunicable attributes are "attributes of the divine essence," while communicable attributes are "attributes of God's personal character" (213–14). Even posing the question of "priority," however, is based on the false assumption that the divine essence exists anhypostatically. If, by contrast, the divine essence *is* only as it is in the Father, Son, and Spirit, then the issue of priority simply evaporates. Moreover, Bray's use of this distinction in the end either collapses or undermines his effort to give due prominence to God's personal character, as the impersonal pronoun in the previous sentence illustrates. The point can be made less abstractly if we ask whether God's "omnipotence," which Bray classifies as an attribute of essence, is a personal omnipotence. If not, then what has happened to the primacy of persons? If so, then how is it not an attribute of personal character?

10. *"Sapientia* and the Trinity: Reflections on the *De Trinitate"* in B. Bruning, *Collectanea Augustiniana* (Leuven University Press, 1990), 317–32; and "The Paradoxes of Self-Knowledge in the *De Trinitate"* in Joseph T. Lienhard, et al., eds., *Collectanea Augustiniana* (New York: Peter Lang, 1993), 121–34.

tine against the charge of ignoring redemptive history.[11] Against Gunton, it is difficult to see how Augustine could have emphasized the economic revelation of the Trinity more strongly than he does in the early books of *De Trinitate,* which give detailed attention to OT theophanies, the incarnation, and the Spirit's descent. Suffice it to say that there is a great deal more discussion of biblical history in Augustine than in any of Gunton's works on the Trinity. At least, the case against Augustine must be judged not proven; it is likely that the search for the origins of western Unitarianism would be more fruitfully pursued along other pathways.

It is not my purpose to locate these pathways. Rather, with this historical suggestion lingering unanswered in the background, I attempt in this essay a constructive theological account of the relations between a fully trinitarian doctrine of God and sacramental theology; practically, the conclusion is that a vigorous sacramental theology and practice requires a renewed trinitarianism, and vice versa. This effort is particularly relevant to the Reformed churches, since Reformed theology has never been able to fit sacramental theology convincingly into its overall system. Even when the importance of the sacraments has been affirmed, it has often taken the form of concession rather than implication: *In spite of who* God

---

11. "Theologie trinitaire chez saint Augustin," *Gregorianum* 58 (1977), 675–725.

is, and *in spite of his* sovereign distribution of grace in
salvation, and *in spite of his* normal way of operating, God
also communicates his presence to his people in signs and
seals.[12] Yet the very idea of a systematic theology suggests
that there can and should be demonstrable consistency
among various truths, in particular some consistency
between the nature of God and how he makes himself
known in the church. Therefore, there must be some way
to show the consistency of theology proper and sacra-

---

12. In his classic statement of Reformed soteriology, *The Plan of Salvation*, rev. ed. (Grand Rapids, MI: Eerdmans, 1984), B. B. Warfield
first distinguishes between naturalistic and supernaturalistic notions
of salvation, that is, between those that claim that God saves and
those that teach some form of self-salvation. Within supernatural religion, he distinguishes between those in which God operates "indi-
rectly" on the soul through mediators and a sacramental machinery
(sacerdotalism) and those that teach that God works "directly" (evangelical). Finally, within the "evangelical" category, he distinguishes
between those that introduce some form of universalism and the
one, Calvinism, that is consistently particularist. True and consistent
Christianity, he says, teaches that salvation is by a supernatural operation of God directly on the souls of particular human beings. It is
not clear how the sacraments, church, or even the "external" preaching of the gospel can fit into this scheme. If room can be made for
sacramental mediation, it will be *in spite of* the overall thrust of soteriology. And, since the nature of salvation reflects the nature of God,
Warfield will affirm sacramental means of grace in spite of what we
otherwise affirm about God. In criticizing Warfield on these points,
I am not affirming a "sacerdotal" view of salvation, but suggesting
that the antithesis between sacerdotal and evangelical is a false one
that a trinitarian account of sacraments (and salvation) will help us
to escape.

mental theology in order to develop a trinitarian theology of Christian symbols and rites.

John Frame has underscored the importance of this kind of consistency in his exposition of the thought of Cornelius Van Til. Van Til, Frame points out, does not relate doctrines to one another with an "in spite of" formula, but with a more boldly paradoxical "because of" formula. Thus, Van Til formulates the classic Reformed problem of relating God's sovereign control with human responsibility by insisting that human beings are morally responsible creatures *because of* divine sovereignty.

> As Christians we hold that determinate human experience could work to no end, could work in accordance with no plan, and could not even get under way, if it were not for the existence of the absolute will of God.
>
> It is on this ground then that we hold to the absolute will of God as the presupposition of the will of man. Looked at in this way, that which to many seems at first glance to be the greatest hindrance to moral responsibility, namely the conception of an absolutely sovereign God, becomes the very foundation of its possibility.[13]

---

13. John Frame, *Cornelius Van Til: An Analysis of His Thought* (Phillipsburg, NJ: Presbyterian and Reformed Publishing, 1995), 83; cf. 162–63.

The argument that follows is this: God's trinitarian character is the "very foundation of the possibility," or the "foundation of the inescapability," of sacraments. Sacraments are not "exceptions" to God's typically "non-symbolic" means of communicating and communing with creatures. Rather, the Creator, because he is Trinity in Unity and Unity in Trinity, draws his people into fellowship with himself through symbols, of which the sacraments are a particular kind. To develop this thesis, I draw on two modern theologians outside of the Reformed tradition: the Roman Catholic theologian, Karl Rahner, and the Greek Orthodox writer, John Zizioulas. Despite the problems that arise in their theologies, these theologians offer biblically sustainable formulations that assist a constructive trinitarian sacramental theology.

Theology of Symbol

In his essay, "The Theology of the Symbol," Karl Rahner offers a trinitarian ontology of symbol. In the initial section of the essay, entitled "Ontology of the Symbol," Rahner defends the thesis that "all beings are by their nature symbolic, because they necessarily 'express' themselves in order to attain their nature."[14] Beings, Rahner ar-

---

14. "Theology of Symbol," in *Theological Investigations, Volume IV: More Recent Writings*, trans. Kevin Smyth (Baltimore: Helicon Press, 1966), 224–52. Page numbers will appear in the body of the text. To avoid unnecessary confusion, I am taking "beings" here to refer to "human beings." Rahner may intend it more broadly, but the sym-

gues, are not fundamentally simple but multiple: "a being is, of itself, independently of any comparison with anything else, plural in its unity." Even the unity of a being is a unity that "unites the plural," so that the unity that is ontologically ultimate is the unity of a unified plurality, not a "hollow, lifeless identity" (227). As a unified entity "emerges into a plurality," it is not alienated from itself, because the "plural is in agreement with its source in a way which corresponds to its origin," and therefore the plurality is an "'expression' of its origin by an agreement which it owes to its origin." Plurality thus is the way that a being fulfills its unity (228–29).

Given the correspondence between plurality and unity, the plurality has the character of a symbol of the origin, and this symbolic expression is essential for the realization of the being's unity and self-knowledge. Rahner claims that being is known only insofar as it is *in actu,* and hence a being comes to knowledge of itself only in the act of expression. A being knows itself through its symbols:

> It expresses itself and possesses itself by doing so. It gives itself away from itself into the "other," and there finds itself in knowledge and love, because it is by constituting the inward "other" that it comes to (or from) its self-fulfillment, which is the pre-

---

bolic expressions of arachnids or primates fall outside the scope of this paper.

supposition of the act of being present to itself in knowledge and love (230).

A being is "'symbolic' in itself," not merely in expressing itself to others. By constituting itself as "other," it "communicates itself to itself" (230).

Mutual knowledge of one being and another, further, is dependent on this same dynamic of symbolic expressiveness. This is not simply because the inner being is inaccessible to us, and must be externally expressed. Rahner does argue that a being's symbolic projection outside itself is a condition for the possibility of being known by another, but this kind of symbolic expression is "in addition" to the symbolic expression that is present in the depths of the thing known. Thus, knowledge depends not only on the reception of symbols by the knower, but on the internal symbolization of the object known. To be known, the object must be in act, which is to say, the object must be symbolically expressing itself to itself. Somewhat cryptically, Rahner states that "a being can be and is known, in so far as it is itself ontically (in itself) symbolic because it is ontologically (for itself) symbolic" (231). Putting these two dimensions of symbol together, Rahner concludes that the primordial meaning of symbol is that

> as a being realizes itself in its own intrinsic "otherness" (which is constitutive of its being), retentive

of its intrinsic plurality (which is contained in its self-realization) as its derivative and hence congruous expression, it makes itself known (231).

To sustain this thesis about the ontology of symbol, Rahner has to show that God himself "expresses himself in symbol," and he thus moves on to the "Theology of the Symbol," where he focuses on the relation of Father and Son. According to Rahner, "the theology of the Logos is strictly a theology of the symbol, and indeed the chief form of it" (235). The Logos is the self-expression and image of the Father, and, since the Father is never without his word, he eternally expresses himself in and through his word and image. It is in the Son that the Father comes to know himself: Without the generation of the Son, "the absolute act of divine self-possession in knowledge cannot exist" (236). Thus, "the Father is himself by the very fact that he opposes to himself the image which is of the same essence as himself, as the person who is other than himself; and so he possesses himself." The Logos is thus a "symbol" in the sense described above: "the inward symbol which remains distinct from what is symbolized, which is constituted by what is symbolized, where what is symbolized expresses itself and possesses itself" (236). The Father's self-expression in creation and redemption is grounded in this eternal and essential symbolic act. "It is because God 'must' 'express' himself inwardly that he can also utter himself outwardly; the finite, created utterance *ad extra* is a continuation of the immanent constitution of 'image and likeness' in the Logos" (236). Rahner applies this model also to the incarnation, so that the humanity of the incarnate Christ is the "self-disclosure of the Logos," the symbolic exteriorization of the second person of the Trinity (239). From the incarnation as symbolic expression Rahner derives the further principle that created things in general are symbolic expressions of the Father (239).

In particular, the church is the continuing symbolic expression of the Logos in the world. Because it is the expression of the Logos in real human life, it goes "with the grain" of human existence, and thus takes an institution, juridical, and social form. But the church is not merely social and juridical, but the "primary sacrament," possessing and not merely signifying the "irrevocable eschatological grace of God which conquers triumphantly the guilt of man" (240–41). Specific sacraments make the symbolic reality of the church concrete, and are thus, like the church itself, symbols in Rahner's sense. Because the sacramental signs are "symbols," it is impossible that they can be seen "apart from what is signified" (242).

There are several problems with Rahner's argument, but first a pseudo-problem needs to be addressed: Is it true that the Father "realizes" his nature in generating the Son? At first blush, this seems problematic, since it appears to make the Father a being in process who has not fully attained his nature until he has expressed himself in the Son. But Rahner is speaking of the ontological Trinity, so that the Father "realizes" his nature in the Son eternally and essentially. Rahner's formulation does highlight the fact that the Father is not the Father, and hence not fulfilled in his personal subsistence, except as he eternally generates the Son, and also puts emphasis on the "dynamism" of the relation of Father and Son. Neither of these emphases, however, violates orthodox formulations of the Trinity. To say that the Father is dependent on the Son for his fatherhood is simply to restate the doctrine of aseity in a trinitarian frame: God (the Father) depends only on God (the Son and the Spirit). And the notion that the relation of Father and Son is dynamic is consistent with a long tradition that defines God's *esse* as *moveri* (movement).[15]

Second, a genuine difficulty: while Rahner may be able to show that the Father realizes himself in the generation of an "image," the same cannot be said for the Son and Spirit, neither of whom "generate" a symbol. It is not, therefore, true without qualification that beings realize their nature by expressing themselves through symbols. To press this claim without showing how it is true for the Son and Spirit leaves Rahner open to serious

---

15. Bray, *Doctrine of God*, 169–70.

trinitarian difficulties, suggesting that only the Father is fully a "being," or that he alone is God. One might suggest in response that there is a reflexive "image-making" on the part of the Son. In the economy of redemption, the Son does only what he sees the Father doing; he is realized as incarnate Son by his "imitation" or "imaging" of the Father (John 5:19). If we can press this relation back into the ontological Trinity, it would imply that the symbolic expressiveness of the Father in generating the Son does not reduce the Son to passivity, for the Son eternally and actively "symbolizes" the Father. Rahner's thesis that every being realizes its nature in symbolizing can be preserved, so long as "symbolizing" is broadened to include not only "generation of an image" (the Father) but also "actively imaging" (the Son).

This leads to another genuine problem. Despite his claim that the unity of a being is fundamentally a unity in plurality, Rahner's language sometimes suggests that divine plurality is secondary to a prior unity: "Being as such, and hence as one *(ens* as *unum)* for the fulfillment of its being and its unity, emerges into plurality—of which the supreme model is the Trinity" (227). The term "emerges" is problematic, indicating that first there is unity, and then the plurality that comes at some secondary stage by the Father's expression and projection. In the case of the Trinity, Rahner hints at a unity logically prior to and "behind" the plurality of persons, a view that either implies subordinationism or a quaternity in which there is some undifferentiated essence anterior to the three persons. That Rahner's statements imply this is very odd, given Rahner's complaint elsewhere that western theology has illegitimately separated the treatises on the unity of God from treatises on the Trinity, unduly privileging God's oneness to the detriment of a full trinitarian theology.[16]

Despite these and other problems, one of Rahner's main points is a true and fruitful insight, namely, that God is by nature a "speaker" and a "producer of symbols." Rahner is especially focusing on John's title for the Son (John 1:1). The fact that the Word is eternally with God means that the Father eternally expresses himself, eternally "speaks," eternally produces uncreated "language." The eternal divine speaking is not, however, limited to the Father. To be sure, the Father alone generates Word but the Word is also a person who has personal fellowship and communion with the Father and the Spirit. He is "toward God"; the Word spoken by the Father speaks back to the Father. This intertrinitarian communication is the uncreated original of human communication, and is reflected in the intertrinitarian communication revealed in the economy of redemption (e.g., Matt 11:25–27; John 17). Thus, both the Son and the Spirit also eternally "speak" or

---

16. *The Trinity*, trans. Joseph Donceel (New York: Crossroad, 1997), 15–21.

"communicate," and in this sense, the Son and Spirit are also employing "symbols."

"Word," moreover, is not the only way that the New Testament describes the Son's relationship to the Father. The Son is also the "express image of his nature" (Heb 1:3), a description already implicit in the name "Son," which is sometimes interchangeable with "image" (cf. Gen 5:1–3). To say that the Father has a Son, therefore, is to say that he has and generates an eternal "image." Thus, we can say not only that the Father eternally speaks and eternally generates the Word, but also that the Father eternally generates his image, an uncreated "symbol" of himself, and this insight was the basis for medieval view that the Logos, or Word, is the "Art" of God. For the Father, symbol-making, like speaking, is a primordial eternal activity.

These trinitarian reflections can be brought to bear on sacramental theology by an anthropological route. Insofar as we are made in the image of the Son, we are created images as the Son is an uncreated image of the Father, created to actively symbolize the Father as creatures. Insofar as we are made in the image of the Father, we are symbol-makers who generate other humans and cultural artifacts "after our own image, according to our likeness." Since we are made in the image of a trinitarian God, a God who eternally speaks and symbolizes, a God who eternally is spoken and is symbolized, generation of symbols is inseparable from human existence. Semiosis is a basic human, and uniquely human, process.

Rahner says that the "expression" of beings in symbols is the means by which beings attain their natures. In trinitarian context, this means that the Father's eternal generation of the Son is the basis of his personal character as Father. As Rahner points out, it is not merely that the Father eternally generates the "symbol" of himself, but that the Father is Father only because he does so. Since there is no Father without a Son, the Father's personal particularity is constituted by his generation of an image.[17] The image is what makes the Father Father. Hence, the Son is the "generator" of the Father, for the symbol made makes the symbol-maker. It is impossible to apply this directly to human nature. Being creatures in time, we do not eternally generate "images" and we are not eternally what we are. Analogically, however, human beings become what we are through the generation of symbols, images, and words. Scripture says, for example, that the words have a formative effect on the speaker. According to Prov 12:14, "a man will be satisfied by the fruit of his mouth," and Prov 13:2 adds "from the fruit of a man's mouth he enjoys good." Our words not only "feed" and "water" others but also produce fruit for us. If we speak good words, the fruit we receive back will be good. If

---

17. "Theology of Symbol," 235–36.

there is poison under our tongues, we will suffer its effects. The symbols and words we generate become distinct from us, turn toward us, and make us. Our words and symbols, like the eternal Word and image, speak back "toward" their "father."[18]

We thus generate symbols not in spite of who God is, but because of who he is, and this leads us to expect that in communicating his life to us, he will also employ symbols. Thus, we move from a trinitarian (and semiotic) anthropology to sacramental theology proper. Rahner builds a bridge from a trinitarian theology of symbol to sacramental theology by positing that the church is a continuation of the incarnation or the "sacrament" of Christ. Unfortunately, this bridge lacks adequate support. Both of Rahner's ecclesiological conceptions are problematic. If the church is a continuation of the incarnation, the NT's distinction between head and body is blurred; instead of submitting to her head, the church, or some sector of it, is competitive with it.[19] As Miroslav Volf notes, the notion that the church is the sacrament of Christ leaves unanswered the question of the nature of a "sacrament":

---

18. Perhaps a Trinitarian response to the Marxist idea of alienation lies along these lines.

19. This is the burden of G. C. Berkouwer's still-relevant discussion of Roman Catholicism in *The Conflict with Rome,* trans. David H. Freeman (Philadelphia, PA: Presbyterian and Reformed Publishing, 1958), esp. 20–37.

"is the church an instrument in God's hands in such a way that Christ remains the sole subject of saving grace, or not?"[20] By contrast to Rahner, I do not wish to build a bridge with the materials of Christology but with the materials of anthropology, and that will require rather different engineering. Still, if Rahner does not take us to a satisfying trinitarian sacramental theology, his efforts toward a semiotic anthropology bring us several steps closer to our goal.

Being and Communion

The second theologian whose work helps "frame" sacramental theology is John Zizioulas, a Greek Orthodox theologian. In *Being As Communion*,[21] he argues that the early Greek Fathers broke decisively with Greek metaphysics and ontology and invented, through their reflection on the doctrine of the Trinity and their experience of the Eucharist, an ontology in which personhood and interpersonal communion have ontological ultimacy. For the Greek Fathers, then, to be is to be in communion.

As in Rahner, there are difficulties with Zizioulas's account that must be examined before moving to his

---

20. *After Our Likeness: The Church as the Image of the Trinity* (Grand Rapids, MI: Eerdmans, 1998), 164n29.

21. *Being As Communion: Studies in Personhood and the Church* (Crestwood, NY: St. Vladimir's Seminary Press, [1985] 1993). Page numbers appear in the body of the chapter.

more productive claims.[22] First, Zizioulas several times implies that there are inherent flaws in creation, that the human problem is not merely ethical or covenantal but metaphysical. In spite of his insight that Heidegger is a gnostic, Zizioulas himself falls into a form of gnosticism. Discussing what he calls the "biological hypostasis," i.e., man as created and finite, he claims that biological hypostasis limits freedom. All men are born into a state of necessity, situations of givenness, so that the world that confronts us is not a product of our free choice. Moreover, we are subject to a variety of natural instincts and necessities that inhibit our achievement of the absolute freedom of personhood:

> if, in order to avoid the consequences of the tragic aspect of man which we have discussed, the person as absolute ontological freedom needs a hypostatic constitution without ontological necessity, his hypostasis must inevitably be rooted, or constituted, in an ontological reality which does not suffer from createdness (54).

Thus, for Zizioulas, being born from above means receiving a new birth into a life dominated not by necessity but by freedom. Grace does not restore nature but

---

22. See also the penetrating criticism offered by Volf, *After Our Likeness,* 73–123.

elevates it: "True life, without death, is impossible for us so long as our being is ontologically determined by creaturehood" (108).

He explains this whole line of thought briefly in his introduction:

> Between the being of God and that of man remains the gulf of creaturehood, and creaturehood means precisely this: the being of each human person is *given* to him; consequently, the human person is not able to free himself absolutely from his "nature" or from his "substance," from what biological laws dictate to him, without bringing his annihilation. And even when he lives the event of communion either in the form of love or of social and political life, he is obliged in the last analysis, if he wants to survive, to relativize his freedom, to submit to certain natural and social "givens." The demand of the person for absolute freedom involves a "new birth," a birth "from on high," a *baptism.* And it is precisely the ecclesial being which "hypostatizes" the person according to God's way of being (18–19).

Christ has been sent to overcome createdness.

Zizioulas's notion that the givenness of human existence is a flaw sits oddly with his emphasis on the reciprocity of personal relations within the Trinity. On his own premises, it would seem, reception as much as giving characterize the intertrinitarian relations. At this point, the western theologians that, according to Zizioulas, paid insufficient attention to the personal relations within the Trinity actually offer a much stronger account of reciprocity. Augustine's view that the Father and Son are engaged in an eternal *traditio* and *redditio* of the Spirit of love makes it impossible to think of receptivity *per se* as an imperfection.[23]

Doubtless, Zizioulas's failure to recognize the reciprocity of the persons is related to his tendency toward subordinationism. Reciprocity of the type that Augustine describes suggests that the Father is conditioned by the Son even as the Son is by the Father, but this undermines the eastern view that the Father is the causative principle of the Godhead. Some of Zizioulas's reasons for defending this eastern form of subordination are worthy enough. He wants to avoid any implication that there is anything impersonal in God, and he recognizes that positing a divine substance as a "source" of the three persons runs the risk of de-personalizing the Trinity. To ensure that the principle of the Godhead is thoroughly personal, he claims that the Father is this source. Zizioulas concedes that this involves a kind of subordination-

---

23. Augustine, *On the Trinity*, 15.17.29. See also Thomas Aquinas, *Summa theologiae*, I.35.2.

ism, but says that the church accepts this as the price of securing the full personality of God. But this avoids one problem by creating another, equally serious one. In the end, Zizioulas must admit that "God owes His existence to the Father" (18).

Finally, Zizioulas's language is often vague and confusing, though part of this difficulty is doubtless due to differences in the ethos of eastern and western theology. Yet, a reader is put off by undefined discussions of how this is "rooted in" that and how that is "prior to" this. Obscurity of this sort affects Zizioulas's historical judgments. He repeats, for example, the common claim that western trinitarian theology makes the "one God" prior to the Trinity, and complains that Augustine along with the scholastics is responsible for saying that the "ousia" or "essence" of God, rather than the Father, is the "causal" principle of the Godhead. As noted briefly above, this is questionable as a historical judgment, and it is questionable too whether the beginning point of the doctrine of God makes all that much difference. Frame, following Calvin, has suggested that there are many different starting points.[24] Especially with the doctrine of the Trinity, any starting point leads, perichoretically, in several directions.

Yet, Zizioulas offers a number of insights that are useful for "framing" sacramental theology and the theol-

---

24. Frame, *Doctrine of the Knowledge of God* (Phillipsburg, NJ: Presbyterian and Reformed, 1987), 89–90.

ogy of symbol. He does this by developing a trinitarian account of personhood. According to Zizioulas, Greek philosophy could not, given its monistic ontology, ever make personhood and personal relationship an ontologically weighty category. Monism undermines personality in two ways. First, the monist God and the world are locked together in a single chain of being. Not even God is genuinely free and personal, for he does not stand sufficiently outside of the world to "dialogue" with it. If freedom is the essence of personhood, then there is no being that is fully personal in the Greek view, including whatever God there might be. Second, if everything is ultimately one, the multiplicity of the things that we experience is secondary, and even a fall from true, unified being. This makes relationship an effect of a fall from true being, for relationship requires separation and difference. "Person" cannot, on monist premises, be an ultimate ontological category.

Because of their monist assumptions, neither Plato nor Aristotle were able to give full significance to human personhood. Significantly, Zizioulas says, only a doctrine of an eternal person can provide a basis for a full philosophy of personhood, and none of the Greek philosophers conceived of an eternal person. For Plato, the soul, which ensures the continuity of personal identity, is not permanently united to an individual man but can migrate to other men. For Aristotle, the hylomorphic unity is dissolved at death, and thus he too fails to secure personal identity. Zizioulas also sees significance in the linguistic fact that the Greek and Latin terms for "person" originally referred to the mask worn by an actor or to the role one played in legal and social relations. In the context of drama, man struggled against necessity and achieved a measure of freedom, and hence there he was truly "person." But this was only temporary, and it was only a mask or a role. Once he removes his *persona* and steps outside the theater or the court, necessity and fate return. In both the theatrical and the legal usages, a "persona" is something that one adds to a basic underlying substance, as the "persona" is added to the actor (31–34).

The Greek Fathers produced a double revolution in philosophy. By insisting on the doctrine of creation, they broke the links that bound God and the world in a single determined continuum. God is separate from creation, stands over against it, and therefore can relate to it as an "other." The Greek Fathers, therefore, were capable of giving full ontological weight to relation, freedom, and personality. In the doctrine of the Trinity, Christian theology went a step further to claim that personhood is not merely a feature of created reality but ontologically ultimate. The Greek Fathers identified "hypostasis," the concrete entity of the particular being, with "person," an identification never made in Greek philosophy, where "hypostasis" referred to the individual subsistent thing to which a *persona* might be added. Substance, as the name suggests, was something "underlying" the surface appearance, the public "persona." For the Greek theologians, however, God himself is persons in relation; there is no underlying substance because the essence is enhypostatized in the Father, Son, and Spirit, and that without remainder. Instead of separating "being" from "being a person," Christian theology, especially against Sabellianism, taught that, for God, to be is to be personal. Not only is there a difference between God and the world, there is difference and plurality within the being of God, and this inner-divine difference never collapses into a higher or more basic unity. This constitutes a decisive and revolutionary break with Greek monism, for it means that multiplicity is not the product of a tragic fall from primordial unity. Multiplicity is itself primordial.

As a result, love becomes the most ultimate ontological reality. God is eternally love because he is eternally persons in relation. The love and communion of the three persons of the Trinity constitutes the being of God. Relations of one to other also become ontologically ultimate, such that each person is constituted in his individuality by his relation to the others. The Father is the Father only because he has a Son, the Son is Son in relation to the Father, and the Spirit is unique and distinct only by relation with the other two. Relationship constitutes the personal character, the particular uniqueness of each member of the relationship.

For human beings too, personhood, love, and relationship are given full weight in making human beings what they are. Zizioulas's anthropological claims here are as challenging to modern thought as to ancient Greek philosophy. It seems commonsensical to moderns that one first *is* and *then* enters into relation, but this is not true. For God, neither the Father nor the Son have any existence that is not existence-in-relation, and the same is true, analogically, in human life. At a purely biological level, no human being exists except through sexual relations between a man and a woman, and we grow to mature humanity only in relations with others.[25] For Zizioulas, the essence of original sin is trying to cut oneself off from relationship and communion, attempting to live as an individual, autonomous and isolated. In redeeming us, Christ restores true personality by opening us up to communion. Just as the uniqueness of the divine persons is dependent on their relations, so also we achieve personal uniqueness and individuality only in relationship with God, other persons, and the world. It follows that a person's unique identity is not somehow hidden behind his external social interactions. Zizioulas's trinitarian account

25. Zizioulas is ambiguous on this point. He writes at times of the autonomous, separated, independent individual as if such a being could exist.

of personhood challenges the Cartesian dualist conception of the "ego" as a ghost in a machine, as well as the
ancient notion of an inviolable soul lurking behind the
various social roles and masks that we take on. He urges
instead that we actually are what we are-in-relationship.

I have a particular connection with a certain (rather
large) group of children; I am their father. It is not the
case that the real me is an underlying someone that can
be isolated from that particular role, that the *real* me is
not a father. Nor, obviously, is it the case that I am a father whether or not I have children. I am a father because
of my relation to my children, and that relation-defined
role is one among many that constitutes my identity. The
same point applies to other roles and relations, whether
constituted by biology or by covenant. I fulfill the roles
of son, brother, husband, neighbor, teacher, church member, theologian, friend, and the real me is at least the sum
of these roles and relationships. To be sure, there is a sur-
plus beyond these roles since the fundamental relation
that constitutes my identity is my relation with God.
But even my relation with God is mediated through a
relation with others—with Adam and the incarnate Son,
with the apostles and prophets who announced the gospel and wrote the Scriptures, and with the community
of the church in which I first heard the gospel. The inner
and outer me cannot be separated into the "real me" and

the "social self." The "real me" is my social self as much as my inner self.

Zizioulas's recognition that personal identity and existence are constituted by relationships has profound implications for sacramental theology. Let us consider baptism to follow through some of the implications. Despite vigorous disagreements on other matters, there is a consensus across Christian traditions that in baptism one becomes a member of the visible church and is publicly committed to Christ as his servant and disciple. When the question of baptismal efficacy is pressed beyond this, however, the consensus disappears, and, within the Reformed churches, the traditional ambiguity toward sacraments comes to the fore. How can an external application of water affect my "spiritual" standing before God? How can it have any real effect on me? But these questions themselves assume that "I" am separable from the communities of which I am a member and the roles I have been commissioned to play. In Zizioulas's framework, by contrast, it becomes clear that the "external" obligations and relations imposed by the rite of baptism have everything to do with my real self. If I have been baptized, I am a member of the royal priesthood, and that relational fact is part of what constitutes my identity. I may be faithful or unfaithful in that role, but the role has defined me. Since, further, God relates to me as *me,* the fact that I have been baptized into the visible community of believers means that God relates to me differently than before I was baptized. After I pass through the water, I have a standing before God and man that I did not have before. Thus, a trinitarian framework leads to a strong affirmation of baptismal efficacy that is as far as possible from anything "magical" or "sacerdotal."

More broadly, Zizioulas's discussion highlights the necessarily social nature of man made in the image of a "social" God. If redemption means reversing the effects of Adam's sin and re-making humanity as it was created to be, it necessarily implies the gathering of a community of the saved. Were God to redeem isolated individuals, he would not be redeeming man as he actually exists. Redemption is the remaking of man, and therefore the remaking of man in his relationships. Salvation is necessarily social salvation. Thus, the church is necessary to the achievement of salvation because God created man in his image, as "beings in communion."

Once the soteriological necessity of the church is made clear, Rahner's theology of symbol can be brought back into the discussion. For Rahner, semiosis is primordially human, and it is only in and through symbols that knowledge of and fellowship with others can exist. Human beings are external to each other, and the doctrine of the Trinity implies that this differentiation is basic and will never be dissolved into an undifferentiated unity. Yet, the doctrine of the Trinity also implies that we are made for communion. Rahner's argument suggests that the only way for a human to communicate what he thinks, feels, hopes and desires is through external means. If people are to be united in community, therefore, there must be common symbols. It follows that if there is to be a church, there must be sacraments. And since the triune nature of God implies the necessity of the church, the triune nature of God also implies, at a second remove, the necessity of sacraments. In summary: God is triune, three persons in interpersonal communion and love. Made in God's image, we are made for communion. Sin violates community, and redemption necessarily involves God's gathering of a people, the restoration not only of individuals in their unique integrity, but of relationships and the institutional structures that give form to relationships. These relationships among men and between God and men can exist only through the use and exchange of symbols. Therefore, *because* God is triune, sacraments are necessary to the achievement of salvation.

Conclusion

Though I have relied here on two modern theologians, the argument is not a modern, much less a modernist, one. On the contrary, I mean to challenge the modern tendency to disrupt symbol and reality and to collapse the Trinity into unity. And I take encouragement from the fact that this argument is anticipated in a compressed form in one of what Calvin considered the more sober scholastics, Thomas Aquinas. Sacraments are necessary for salvation, Aquinas argues, because, given the nature of God and of man, it is fitting that God makes use of sacramental signs and rites in redemption. In developing his argument, Thomas first quotes Augustine's statement (from *Contra Faustum*, 19.11) that it is impossible to unite men in a religious association without the use of symbols or sacraments. Since it is necessary for salvation for men to be bound in one true religion, Thomas argues, sacraments are essential to the achievement of salvation.[26] While the Reformers rightly rejected many aspects of the mechanistic medieval sacramental system, Thomas's insight is compatible with a Reformed anthropology and soteriology, and points toward the best of Reformed sacramental theology. And it provides support for the "framing" of sacramental theology offered here.

---

26. *Summa theologiae*, IIIa.61.1.

CHAPTER TWO

EMBRACING RITUAL:
SACRAMENTS AS RITES

Over the past century, sacramental and liturgical theology have been growth industries in many Christian traditions,[1] but this explosion of interest and fresh scholarship has had little impact on the Reformed and evangelical churches in America. A few evangelicals, such as Robert Webber, have pressed for renewed attention to historic

---

1. For a very tiny sampling, see the Roman Catholic Bernard Cooke, *The Distancing of God: The Ambiguity of Symbol in History and Theology* (Minneapolis, MI: Fortress, 1990); the Anglican Archbishop of Canterbury Rowan Williams, "The Nature of a Sacrament," in *Signs of Faith, Hope and Love: The Christian Sacraments Today*, eds. John Greenhalgh and Elizabeth Russell (London: St. Mary's Bourne Street, 1987), 32–44; and the Lutheran theologian Robert Jenson, *Visible Words: The Interpretation and Practice of Christian Sacraments* (Philadelphia, PA: Fortress, 1978).

liturgies,[2] and evangelical publishers occasionally release books that explore baptism or the Lord's Supper in a new light.[3] In the main, however, evangelical treatments of sacramental theology do little more than rehash traditional debates about paedobaptism or the real presence[4] and make little use of the anthropological and philosophical insights that have been fruitfully applied to liturgical theology in other traditions.[5] Despite a rich liturgical and sacramental heritage deriving from Calvin and other Reformers, many sectors of the Reformed church have

---

2. See, for example, Robert Webber, *Worship Is a Verb* (Waco, Texas: Word Books, 1985).

3. See, for a recent example, Michael Welker, *What Happens in Holy Communion?*, trans. John F. Hoffmeyer (Grand Rapids, MI: Eerdmans, 2000).

4. For example, Millard J. Erickson, *Introducing Christian Doctrine,* 2nd ed. (Grand Rapids, MI: Baker, 2001), 356–68.

5. One indication of this failure to engage with the wider discussion is the neglect of ritual studies. From a survey of 1,043 articles from a variety of evangelical journals, Gerard A. Klingbeil found that only thirteen contained "important references to ritual" ("Between Law and Grace: Ritual and Ritual Studies in Recent Evangelical Thought," paper presented at the 2001 national conference of the Evangelical Theological Society. I am grateful to Professor Klingbeil for providing me with a copy of this paper, later published as Gerard A. Klingbeil, "Between Law and Grace: Ritual and Ritual Studies in Recent Evangelical Thought," *Journal of the Adventist Theological Society*, vol. 13, iss. 2, no. 4 [2002].)

also ignored contemporary developments.[6] Even where evangelical and Reformed theologians have drawn on the resources of modern liturgical renewal, little seems to have filtered down to the practice of churches or to church members.[7]

Causes for the stagnation of Reformed and evangelical sacramental theology are doubtless deeply rooted in the respective traditions where Puritanism and revivalism have, separately or in conspiracy, vitiated attention to

---

6. See, for example, D. G. Hart & John R. Muether, *With Reverence and Awe: Returning to the Basics of Reformed Worship* (Phillipsburg, NJ: P&R Publishing, 2002), whose authors, despite several welcome emphases, operate completely within the confines of traditional Reformed liturgies and its difficulties and show little awareness of wider ecumenical discussions. The same goes for Michael Horton, *A Better Way: Rediscovering the Drama of God-Centered Worship* (Grand Rapids, MI: Baker, 2002). Keith A. Mathison's treatment of Calvin's eucharistic theology is superb as far as it goes, but it addresses traditional questions in a traditional way *(Given For You: Reclaiming Calvin's Doctrine of the Supper* [Phillipsburg, NJ: P&R Publishing, 2002]). The situation is far worse in Robert L. Reymond, *A New Systematic Theology of the Christian Faith*, 2nd ed. (Nashville, TN: Thomas Nelson, 1998), 917–67. By contrast, Jeffrey Meyers, *The Lord's Service* (Moscow, ID: Canon Press, 2003), presents a Reformed liturgical theology fully in conversation and confrontation with contemporary liturgical scholarship.

7. One piece of evidence in support of this assessment is the widespread adoption of user-friendly worship styles within Reformed and evangelical churches. These forms of worship have developed with little liturgical-theological reflection and with virtually no attention to traditional Christian liturgies.

sacraments. Exploring those historical factors, however, is outside the scope of this article. Instead, I hope to open up fresh perspectives on the sacraments, writing from the conviction that Reformed and evangelical sacramentology must be revised at a fundamental level. I offer, as a first step toward that revision, critical analyses of several common definitions of "sacraments in general." In the course of this critical analysis, I move toward a constructive proposal for the reformulation of sacramental theology, which argues for reconceiving sacraments under the rubric of ritual or rite rather than as means of grace, signs, symbols, or visible words.[8] Most of these latter definitions and descriptions are salvageable but will be useful to future sacramental theology only insofar as they are molded more into the shape of ritual.[9]

---

8. My discussion of these alternative definitions of sacraments in general is admittedly somewhat impressionistic. My goal is less to examine the technicalities of definition than to suggest the general thrust or trajectory of each definition. Thus, while I may not be able to find a theologian who would unpack the notion of *visible word* in the way I have done, I believe that the way I have described it is a fair account of what many Christians understand when they hear the phrase. My evidence for this is rather inchoate, based on impressions from sermons and conversations over many years.

9. I have not here dealt with the terminology of *seal,* but hope to do so later. I avoid discussion of the topic here mainly because of the complications of the historical usage of the term. Patristic writers, for example, normally used *seal* in the sense of "brand" or "tattoo" or "identifying mark," and as such, it has significant value in baptismal

The value of this reconceptualization will, I hope, become evident in the course of my argument, but one illustration is offered at the outset. Many of the specific debates regarding sacraments are fundamentally debates about the nature of sacraments in general. Paedobaptists and Baptists, for example, differ not only about the subjects of baptism but also about the nature of baptism. What kind of event is it? Is it a profession of faith, or is it a rite by which God marks the baptized as a member of his covenant people? Before we can hope to resolve these issues on the surface, deeper consideration must be given to foundational questions about sacraments as such. Conceiving the sacraments as rituals or rites not only provides a more philosophically and theologically coherent account of sacraments but also offers promise for addressing and resolving surface debates that have sorely wounded the unity of the church.

---

theology (though less value as a description of the Supper). Calvin, on the other hand, finds an analogy between the seal of the sacrament and the seal that authenticates an official document, a use of the image that is to my mind far more obscure than the patristic usage. Seal imagery came to play an exceedingly important role in later Reformed sacramental theology, and any sustained treatment of the topic would have to explore that usage. Finally, *seal* functions more as a technical term in sacramental theology, and thus requires a different sort of treatment than I have adopted in this article.

Means of Grace

For centuries, sacraments have been described as *means of grace*, and, of course, this language is not unique to Reformed theology or evangelicalism. According to the Westminster Larger Catechism, God enables us to "escape the wrath and curse of God due to us by reason of the transgression of the law" by making "diligent use of the outward means whereby Christ communicates to us the benefits of his mediation." Among these means are "word, sacraments, and prayer; all of which are made effectual to the elect for their salvation" (Q. 153 and 154). In particular, sacraments "signify, seal, and exhibit. . . the benefits of [Christ's] mediation" and thereby "strengthen and increase . . . faith, and all other graces" (Q. 162).

To the extent that the phrase *means of grace* is intended to highlight the fact that believers receive real benefit from baptism and the Supper, the definition is useful. This language has also been attractive to Protestants as a way of rebutting the (supposed) Catholic claim that the sacramental elements contain virtue in themselves. *Means of grace* has a salutary deflationary effect: If the sacraments are only means, then the real efficacy comes from God who employs the means.

In several respects, however, this definition is misleading. First, talking about the sacraments as *means* tends to mechanize their operation, and obscures the fact that sacraments are places or moments of *personal* encounter with God, trysting places between God and his people, as Luther put it.[10] Historically, the Reformed tradition has defined sacraments as "signs and seals of the covenant of grace," thus emphasizing the covenantal and interpersonal character of sacramental performance, but the personal aspect of this covenantal theology is undercut by the notion of sacraments as *means*.

The phrase *means of grace* further obscures the personal dimension of sacraments when allied with a reification of grace. Shortly after the apostolic period, theologians began to treat grace as a created thing, force, or energy communicated through the sacraments, and in medieval theology this idea was elaborated in the concept of created grace. Imagery of grace as fluid, moving through sacramental pipelines to the sinner, strengthened and reinforced this notion.[11] Ultimately, this model rests

---

10. This becomes more explicit in theologians such as Aquinas who describe sacraments as "causes" of grace, and employ technical analogies to explain God's use of sacraments to distribute grace (e.g., God giving grace through sacraments is like a carpenter driving a nail through the means of a hammer).

11. See T. F. Torrance, *The Doctrine of Grace in the Apostolic Fathers* (Edinburgh: Oliver and Boyd, 1948). Torrance argues that for the apostolic fathers, grace came to be conceived pneumatically but lost its Christological grounding. Thus, it "came to be thought of in sub-personal fashion as pneumatic power" and as "the gift of spiritual energy that ranged itself in the heart of the believer... a phenomenon, a pneumatic energy implanted in the soul." Grace came to be seen as a "ghostly potency" (140). In the scholasticism of the

on a mistaken doctrine of God, for there is no impersonal force in God nor any energy that mediates between God and creation. The God revealed in Scripture and in Jesus is exhaustively and eternally personal, eternally in relationship, and therefore God's relationship to the creation cannot but be a personal one. Grace is not a thing or energy but God's attitude of favor toward us, manifested in his coming near to us through his Spirit to form and renew covenant friendship, to have personal communion with us, and to offer us the gifts and blessings of Word and Sacrament.[12] When the New Testa-

---

thirteenth century, Peter the Lombard's dictum was widely accepted: *quod gratia gratificans nos Deo, vel per quam nos grati sumus Deo, est aliquid creatum in anima* (II Sent. dist. Xvii, q. 1 a. 1, quoted in Alister E. McGrath, *Iustitia Dei: A History of the Christian Doctrine of Justification,* 2 vols. [Cambridge: Cambridge University Press, 1986], 1.231n6). The widespread imagery of an "infusion" of grace supported the notion of grace as an energy or substance, as did Hugh of St. Victor's comparison of the grace of the sacrament to liquid in a vessel *(De Sacramentis* 1.9.4). Reformed theologians have generally not followed these medieval examples, but imagery of sacraments as channels through which grace flows to the recipient is not uncommon (e.g., Charles Hodge, *Systematic Theology,* 3 vols. [Grand Rapids, MI: Eerdmans, 1986], 3:466). Taking note of imagery such as this may seem trivial, but images can and do have a powerful impact on the trajectory of sacramental theology and other loci as well.

12. I have explored the question of why God's personal communion comes to the church in sacramental form in "'Framing Sacramental Theology': Trinity and Symbol," *Westminster Theological Journal,* vol. 62, no. 1 (2000): 1–16.

ment describes graces as being poured out on believers or the church, the Spirit, not some detached divine energy, is the substance being poured (cf. Acts 10:45, Titus 3:5–6, Rom. 5:5). The model of the sacramental operation, thus, should not involve four terms: God, grace, sacraments (as means or channels of grace), and the church, but only three: God (who is gracious), sacraments, and the church. In the sacraments, we engage in a covenantal and personal communion with the Triune God. The Jews marveled at the change that came about in the disciples, and noted that they had been with Jesus (Acts 4:13). Transformation occurs in the same way for us who have not seen Jesus in the flesh: We are transfigured by contact with the Lord who has become life-giving Spirit (1 Cor. 15:45, 2 Cor. 3:17–18).

Understanding sacraments as means of grace has also allied with an overly individualistic concept of sacramental efficacy. When it is asked, "Do sacraments communicate grace?", the underlying question is often, "Do sacraments communicate grace to the individual believers who receive them?"[13] This, however, is a radically minimalist view of sacramental performance. Sacraments are done by

---

13. The individualistic bias is evident in objections to infant baptism: If faith is necessary for baptism to be efficacious, and if the infant cannot exercise faith, then what is the point of baptizing him? The answer is, in part, that baptizing infants is not *only* about the infant baptized.

groups of Christians and are signs and symbols that have their meaning within the community bound together by the Spirit. In the patristic period, the presence of Christ in the Supper was conceived as his presence in the community, not in the elements alone,[14] and when Aquinas asked about the necessity of the sacraments, he answered by citing Augustine's dictum in his treatise *Contra Faustum* (19.11):

> On the contrary, Augustine says, "It is impossible to keep men together in one religious denomination, whether true or false, except they be united by means of visible signs or sacraments." But it is necessary for salvation that men be united together in the name of one true religion. Therefore sacraments are necessary for man's salvation (*Summa theologiae* III, 61.1).

---

14. See Paul H. Jones, *Christ's Eucharistic Presence: A History of the Doctrine*, American University Studies (New York, NY: Peter Lang, 1994). Medieval theologians systematized this view in their claim that the thing itself *(res tantum)* of the Lord's Supper, the thing to which the sacrament and elements ultimately pointed, was the unity of the church. For a historically rich study of the corporate dimensions of the medieval mass in England, see Eamon Duffey, *The Stripping of the Altars: Traditional Religion in England, c.1400–c.1580* (New Haven, CT: Yale University Press, 1992), ch. 3.

For Thomas, the necessity of sacraments does not pertain only to the individual recipient but to the community of the church. New creation takes a social form in the church, the body of the Last Adam, and as there is no social interaction, no common goals and programs without the use of signs and symbols, so there can be no church without sacraments. If understood in this corporate framework, sacraments may be called *means of grace* because they are tools for the formation and strengthening of the bonds among members of Christ's body.[15] Employing *means of grace* in this sense, however, is already stretching the language beyond the boundaries of its normal usage. I believe a superior framework is available, one that secures the positive implications of means of grace but avoids the pitfalls.

Symbols and Signs

Medieval theologians often defined sacraments as "outward signs of an inward grace," and this definition or some variation of it is employed by Protestant theologians to this day.[16] One of the difficulties with this definition

---

15. Cf. the fine discussion of Thomas C. Oden, whose discussion of sacraments is completely embedded in a discussion of the community of believers *(Systematic Theology: Life in the Spirit*, vol. 3 [1994; repr., Peabody, MA: Prince Press, 1998], part 3).

16. See, e.g., Reymond, *New Systematic Theology,* 918, quoting Charles Hodge to the effect that "the two simplest and most generally accepted (definitions of the word 'sacrament') are the one by Augus-

is the striking ambiguity of both *sign* and *symbol*. Philosophers, anthropologists, literary critics, sociologists, and others have expended enormous energy attempting to define *symbol* and to distinguish symbols from signs, indexes, icons, and similar phenomena.[17] Within theology, this ambiguity is evident among Reformed writers who use the same terms in different senses. While Calvin and Turretin, for example, both describe the sacraments in terms of *signum* and *res,* they differ radically in their account of the sacramental union of the two, that is, in their understanding of how and why signs signify things. For Calvin, sacramental union depends on God's ordination that *these* objects convey Christ's benefit to us; for Turretin, by contrast, the thing is made present "to the understanding" through one's perception of the sign, so that the sacramental union takes place in the mind of the recipient.[18]

---

tine and the other by Peter Lombard," the second of which is that a sacrament is "invisibilis gratiae visibilis forma." (Hodge himself goes on to comment that "These definitions are too vague," *Systematic Theology,* 3:487). Similarly, Horton, *A Better Way,* 105: "Both sacraments . . . contain two parts: the sign and the thing signified."

17. A dated but still helpful summary of this discussion may be found in Raymond Firth, *Symbol: Public and Private* (London: George Allen Unwin, 1973). A more recent study, with specifically theological purpose, is Bernard J. Cooke, *The Distancing of God: The Ambiguity of Symbol in History and Theology* (Minneapolis, MI: Fortress, 1990)

18. See the excellent discussion in Keith A. Mathison, *Given For You: Reclaiming Calvin's Doctrine of the Lord's Supper* (Phillipsburg, NJ: P & R Publishing, 2002), 113–19.

For those untouched by scholarly debate, symbols are usually understood in one of several ways. First, signs and symbols work cognitively or didactically, in that they help us to remember or consider nonsymbolic concepts, ideas, and things. On this view, baptism is a reminder of our state of original sin, of our need for cleansing, of the coming of the Holy Spirit, and of the sprinkling of our hearts with the blood of Christ. Baptism teaches us something about ourselves and God's work on our behalf. The Lord's Supper reminds us of the death of Christ, and teaches us that he is our life.[19] We might call this the Augustinian concept of signs as visible things that "bring something else to mind."

Second, symbols are understood as more or less unnecessary adornments or enhancements of real life. Straightforward literal language is thus distinguished from symbolic or metaphorical language: to say God is powerful is literal but to say God has a mighty arm is symbolic. Symbolic language has charm and rhetorical power, but it is no more than a striking way to say something that could as easily be said in literal terms. Similarly, fancy napkins, silverware, candlesticks, and china enhance the

---

19. According to Barth, this "cognitive" or "didactic" model of the sacraments is found in Calvin. Barth accused Calvin of inconsistency when he advocated infant baptism within this "didactic" or "cognitive" general understanding of sacraments (*The Teaching of the Church Regarding Baptism,* trans. Ernest A. Payne [London: SCM, 1948]).

table for a special occasion, but beneath these accoutrements is the literal reality of a meal. Churches drape colored paraments over the pulpit to enhance its beauty and to adorn it for Easter celebrations. The key assumptions in this second view are that natural or literal reality can be isolated from its enhancements, that natural or literal reality is nonsymbolic, and that real life is fundamental and foundational, however much we may dress it up with symbols to punctuate certain occasions. I shall call this the Lady Macbeth view of symbols ("the sauce to meat is ceremony; meeting were bare without it").

Neither of these is helpful in thinking about sacraments. In response to Lady Macbeth, it must be said that any sharp distinction between the sauce and meat, between normal and ceremonial, or between literal and symbolic dissolves on inspection. With regard to language, there is no firm line between literal and symbolic. In an important sense, all language is symbolic because it employs visual symbols or sounds that mean something other than themselves. Even if we put that point to the side, it is still evident that there is a spectrum from less metaphorical to more metaphorical language rather than a clear boundary line. For instance, most readers will have understood the previous sentences as primarily literal, yet I have employed several figures in the course of my argument: No one is *really* drawing lines between literal and symbolic words, distinctions are not *literally* sharp,

I am not making points (as if this were an exercise in pin-production), and no reader is *actually* being asked to put my points to the side.[20] By the same token, there is not a sharp distinction (there I go again!) between everyday activities and those adorned with signs or symbols. Meals are not natural events that can be dressed up by symbol and ceremony; every meal, however simple and unelaborated, is always already symbolic, already points to something. Is there a more poignant symbol of loneliness than a man eating a TV dinner alone in front of the screen? Ceremony is sauce, to be sure; but, even without the sauce, the meat (not to mention the meeting) is full of significance.

Augustinian or cognitive accounts of signs and symbols similarly fail because symbols do not merely teach and appeal to the mind but also *do* things.[21] In the main,

---

20. For a fascinating discussion of how metaphorical language necessarily underlies our speech and thought, see George Lakoff & Mark Johnson, *Philosophy in the Flesh: The Embodied Mind and Its Challenge to Western Thought* (New York, NY: Basic, 1999), ch. 4.

21. In the Bible, the word *sign* is applied to God's actions as well as to objects. Signs may indeed be "aids to memory," whether human memory or God's (rainbow: Gen. 9; Aaron's rod: Num.17; pillars from the crossing of the Jordan: Josh. 4). But *sign* often refers to what God has done, as in the repeated statement that God brought Israel out of Egypt with great "signs and wonders and terrors" (e.g., Deut. 4:34, 6:22) or in the Johannine notion that Jesus' miracles were signs (e.g., John 2:11, 23). These signs were not merely objects that bring remembrance. They were actions that communicated something

symbols enable personal communication and communion. Personal communion involves a union of the desires, thoughts, aspirations, and feelings of two or more persons, but because we cannot know the heart of another, these desires, thoughts, aspirations, and feelings must be brought out into the open, made public, and externalized if a personal union of any sort is to be formed. The way we make them public and external is through symbols.[22] Through the symbolic actions or speech and gesture, we create and maintain personal relationships.

A few examples may help establish the point. Language is, as noted above, a symbolic or semiotic system in a broad sense. In language, we use visual signs on paper or the computer screen, or we use audible signs and meaningful sounds. The sounds and signs that we emit are symbolic in the sense that they are pregnant with meaning beyond their sound or visual appearance. (As medieval sign theorists understood, even a prelinguistic grunt carries meaning—pain, hunger, and anger.)[23] Language is

---

about God's character; through these sign-actions God made himself known and accomplished his purposes in the world.

22. I characterize the situation this way for the sake of simplicity. In actual fact, our desires and aspirations are not inherently presymbolic realities that may at some secondary level be expressed in symbols. On the contrary, even our deepest aspirations and desires are formed by symbols, a truth illustrated by every kid who drinks Gatorade to be like the pros.

23. Peter of Spain distinguished between significant and nonsig-

a system of symbols, and is it possible to imagine personal relationship without language? Using language, further, inevitably, involves physical activity, and that means it is invariably public. When we speak, we make movements with our mouths to control the passage of air and make noises that (we hope) carry significance. When we write, we move a pencil or pen across a page or type with a finger, or several, on a keyboard. Through our bodies, our feelings, desires, fears, and thoughts are externalized, and they are externalized in the form of linguistic signs.

Not only language but other sorts of symbolic acts create, renew, or maintain personal relations. Coming into a party full of strangers, you see a familiar face in a small but lively circle near the hors d'oeuvres. As soon as you enter the circle, you begin to deploy symbols, and are deployed against. You use language: "Hello!" "Bonjour!" "Hola!" "Guten Tag!" You exchange greeting gestures—a handshake, a kiss, a hug, a significant exchange of looks, or a secret fraternity rite. Only by using these linguistic and gestural symbols do you reestablish your acquaintance with the person. Should your friend introduce you

---

nificant utterances, and within the former distinguished between those that signified *naturaliter* and those that signified according to convention *(ad placitum)*. His example of a natural but significant sound was the moaning of a sick person *(gemitus infirmorum)*. See the discussion in Ross G. Arthur, *Medieval Sign Theory and Sir Gawain and the Green Knight* (Toronto: University of Toronto Press, 1987), 22–27.

to the other members of the group, you establish personal communication and the possibility of friendship through the use of symbols. You speak, shake hands, and smile. Without these symbolic actions, these meaningful uses of the body, no personal relationship would be established.

Another example: A young man is desperately in love with a young woman. He thinks about her day and night, dreams about her, imagines what it would be like to hold her hand, to kiss her, and so on. This might go on for years and years without becoming an actual romance. If he is going to move from internal feelings of infatuation and an imaginary romance to the risky but more pleasurable relationship with a real woman, he must go public. He does this through symbols. He speaks or writes to her. Employing linguistic signs; he sends flowers, which he intends as an erotic symbol rather than an encouragement to horticulture. She responds with symbols, words, or significant actions, which will imply some response on the spectrum between invitation and rejection.

One important clarification must be introduced here. In these examples, symbols do not dress up and enhance a relationship that already exists; we are not back to Lady Macbeth and her saucy meats. On the contrary, relationships do not exist at all apart from the symbolic and ceremonial exchanges. We cannot say, except as a joke, "I know him well, we're great friends, but we've never spoken or written or exchanged greetings." Symbolic exchanges create or constitute relationship, and it continues only so long as the symbolic exchanges continue. Moreover, the relationship does not exist behind the symbolic exchanges, as if the real relationship were a hidden spiritual reality of which the symbols are only expressions. The pining lover might find comfort in Lombard's definition: The signs he uses are, he might hope, "Visible signs of an invisible relationship." Oh, that he could at least have an invisible romance! But no; it is false comfort. The intricate fabric of exchanged language, gesture, symbol, and action *is* the relationship, and without them there is no relationship.[24]

For sacramental theology, two implications follow from this discussion. First, evangelicals are defined by freedom in talking about a personal relationship with Christ, but this genuine biblical insight can sometimes imply that the personal relationship with Christ takes place apart from participation in public worship and fellowship with other believers or beyond a believing and obedient response to Scripture. If personal relationship

---

24. There is indeed a mysterious extra in personal relationships. I can anticipate my wife's response to a novel circumstance, even though we have never discussed the circumstance. There is a kind of meeting of minds that surpasses anything that has been or can be explicitly said. However—and this is the point I wish to focus on—this meeting of minds does not take place *without* a background of public symbolic exchange and communication. If I had never spoken to my wife, I could hardly anticipate her future actions.

verges in this direction, it is more aptly described as a mystical relationship, one that bypasses the symbolic means by which God communes with his people. Personal relationships among humans and with God simply do not exist apart from language and signs.[25] Sacraments can be defined as signs in this sense—not as dispensable means for making visible a relationship that is perfectly healthy without the visible means but as constituent elements of the relationship. Second, these considerations make it all the more strange to think of the sacraments as means of grace. If we situate sacramental theology within the context of personal interaction and communication between God and ourselves, then it is as odd to think of sacraments as means of communication as it is to say that the words we speak are means by which we communicate to others. Words and gestures *are the* communication.

It will be noted that my discussion of sacramental signs bypasses the traditional question of the relationship between sign and thing signified. That avoidance is deliberate. This traditional question depends on a prior isolation of the sacramental element from its ecclesiological and liturgical context, and I want to resist that isolation.

---

25. This temptation to ascend beyond signs has plagued sacramental theology through most of Christian history. For more, see my "Old Covenant and New in Sacramental Theology New and Old," *Pro Ecclesia*, vol. 14, no. 2 (May 2005), 174-190 [printed in the present book as Chapter Five].

Far preferable is the nuanced analysis of medieval linguistic theorists who distinguished (anticipating important
moves in modern linguistics) between *significatio* and
suppositio. The former is the meaning that a sign would
have if isolated from all context; with regard to words, the
significance could be determined by a dictionary. However, medieval theorists also noticed that words take on nu-
ances of meaning by keeping company with other words,
and this is the concern of *suppositio* ("standing for"). In
an actual proposition, the word *bread* does not merely
mean "a concept of bread," but may mean particularly
this or *that* loaf of bread. In the phrase, "Bread is made
from grain," bread signifies and supposits the concept;
but, in the proposition, "This bread is moldy," the word
signifies a concept (bread) but also supposits a particular
loaf.[26] An analogous analysis can be fruitfully applied to
the eucharistic rite.[27] Considered by itself, the bread is a
sign of the body of Christ (and *sign* here comes close to
the Augustinian sense), but in the eucharistic action it is
not by itself. Considered as part of the eucharistic action
it has to be dealt with in some framework other than the
dualism of sign-thing. It is not enough to determine the
meaning of the bread in some system of meanings *outside*

---

26. Arthur, *Medieval Sign Theory,* 12–13

27. Admittedly, I have not *performed* this analysis here. The comment
is meant to be suggestive.

the rite; the bread must also be considered as a term within the proposition of the Eucharist.

In short, the symbolism involved in sacramental performance is the symbolism of action, less like the symbolism of a painting or a metaphor (which is made or written and laid out for interpretation) and more like the symbolism of a handshake or a wave or a kiss. When sacraments are conceived as symbolic *acts* (analogous to speaking or shaking hands) rather than symbolic objects, and when we combine this with the earlier point that the sacraments are occasions or moments of personal communion or encounter, then we are in a position to make sense of the logic of the sacraments. As symbolic actions, the sacraments are symbols by and through and in which personal, covenantal relationships are forged and maintained. Thus, the definition of sacraments as "signs and symbols" can be retained, but these names fit the reality only if we simultaneously stress that sign and symbol are personal and active, only if we nudge sign and symbol in the direction of ritual.

Visible Words

Since the time of Augustine, sacraments have been described as visible words. Too often, however, the accent in this formulation falls on the first half, on the visibility of the sacraments. It is often said that the word comes to us through the sense of hearing but the sacrament through sight.[28] This has a subtle and highly unfortunate tendency to move our attention away from receiving the baptismal bath and participating in the sacramental meal toward *viewing* the bath and the meal, a shift of attention that can perpetuate the worst abuses of medieval worship. If the sacrament is a *visible word,* then perhaps the main point is to look at it, to ponder what it shows us, to strive to see Jesus in the celebration. Perhaps we should simply wait for the bell to ring and then strain for a look at the bread-made-Jesus.

If, however, we emphasize that the sacraments are visible *words,* Augustine's terminology can be recovered. Sacraments have a linguistic character and function as words do, but this makes sense of sacraments only when we recognize that words do more than communicate information and appeal to the intellect, though words certainly do both. Language, as I stressed above, is the paradigmatic symbolic system, and like other symbols it not only communicates information but also creates and maintains personal relationship.

---

28. Calvin focuses on the visibility of the sacrament: It is like a "mirror," even an "image," of God's promise, where God's promises are "painted as in a picture from life." Turrctin likewise includes visibility within his definition of sacraments *(Institutes of Elenctic Theology,* 3 vols. [Phillipsburg, NJ: P&R Publishing, 1997], 3:339). The Westminster Larger Catechism (Q. 163) uses the more general but preferable phrase *sensible* signs.

Again, an example will help. When we say to the stranger at the bus stop, "Gee, it sure is cold," or, 'These buses always run late," we are not communicating anything new to him. We say it because speech establishes commonality and puts something out in public space that we can both consider and agree with. Phatic speech such as this communicates virtually no content and certainly no new information, but it is not useless speech. Its use is not cognitive or didactic but rather personal. As visible words, the sacraments are not phatic speech. Baptism and the Supper do have cognitive and didactic content, reminding and telling us what God has done and will do for his people, ritually retelling the story of the world's redemption. Yet, sacraments, as visible words, do not have an *exclusively* didactic function. As speech, they are also forming or continuing personal communion.

Speech act theory is of help here as well. Philosophers such as J. L. Austin and John Searle have shown that language deployed in a particular way by a particular person at a particular time not only communicates information but actually performs actions.[29] Austin thus writes of "doing" things with words. A judge who says, "I sentence you to death," is not merely declaring a decision that has already been rendered in some other forum.

---

29. J. L. Austin, *How to Do Things with Words* (Oxford: Oxford University Press, 1962); John Searle, *Speech Acts: An Essay in the Philosophy of Language* (Cambridge: Cambridge University Press, 1969).

Rather, by his declaration, the judge is passing the sentence. Speaking the words is doing the deed. Similarly, the captain who says, "I now name you the Queen Mary," has actually named the ship.[30] Wittgenstein said it simply: "Words are deeds." Just as words are performative, so the sacraments as visible words actually do things and do not merely tell things. They not only remind us and teach us about Christ's death, but they make promises, issue warnings, and establish or renew covenants.

As with the terminology of signs and symbols, the phrase *visible word* is recoverable as a formulation of sacramental theology. As with *sign*, it is recoverable only insofar as it is reconceived as ritual.

---

30. Austin distinguishes between the "locutionary" and the "illocutionary" force of a speech act. The locutionary force is the actual use of linguistic signs and the sense of the signs: I make these particular sounds or write these particular signs, and I mean something by it. My use of these sounds or signs, however, may be intended to accomplish a number of different things, depending on the context of my speech or writing. What I intend to accomplish through these linguistic signs and sounds is the illocutionary force of my utterance. "That ice is thin" has a particular meaning, but it can have a variety of uses. It can be merely a matter of communicating information or it can serve as a warning. If someone hears me state this sentence but does not catch the illocutionary force of the sentence (the point), he might end up drowning. Wittgenstein uses the example of a mason calling to his fellow for another slab of stone simply by yelling the word *Slab*. In Austin's terms, the locutionary force of the word is simply "flat piece of stone" but the illocutionary force is, "Give me another slab."

Ritual and Rites

Sacraments may also be described as rites or rituals.[31] As is apparent by now, I find this a vastly more satisfying

---

31. The term *ritual* has sometimes been used within Reformed sacramental theology. According to Richard Muller's definition, Reformed orthodoxy defined sacraments as constituted by three realities a visible element (bread, wine, water), which is a sign, an action ordained by God, which is called the *actio ritualis* or *actio sacramentalis,* and the saving benefit of the covenant. At times the rite is defined as the whole action of the sacrament, Muller writes that the *actio sacramentalis* embraces consecration, distribution, eating and drinking *(Dictionary of Latin and Greek Theological Terms: Drawn Principally from Protestant Scholastic Theology* [Grand Rapids, MI: Baker, 1985], 20, 267–68). Yet, there is some ambiguity about the definition of *ritual action.* Some have viewed the *actio ritualis* as consisting solely in "the recital of the words of the institution of the sacrament" that consecrates the elements to a new use. Thus, it is not uncommon to define a sacrament as the combination of the words of institution (the *actio)* and the physical element. "God effects the sacrament by the word of institution, which being added to the element, it becomes a sacrament, not by the infusion of a new quality but by change of use" (Lucas Trelcatius, *Scholastica, et Methodica, Locorum communium, S. Theologiae Institutio* (1610), quoted by Heinrich Heppe, *Reformed Dogmatics,* [rev. ed., ed. Ernst Bizer, trans. G. T. Thomson [London: Wakeman Great Reprints, 1950], 592–94). In this formulation, actions such as pouring water, or taking and breaking bread, or drinking wine are *not* included within the definition of sacrament. Many Reformed theologians and documents ignore even the *actio* of the words of institution, and define sacraments without any reference to a ritual or sacramental action. See the Westminster Confession (27.1): "Sacraments are holy signs and seals of the covenant of grace, immediately instituted by God, to represent Christ and his benefits, and to confirm our interest in him, as also to put a visible difference between those that belong unto the church and the rest of the world."

one-word description of baptism and the Supper than the definitions above. Describing sacraments as rituals, rites, or ceremonies has all the advantages of the other terminology but avoids some of the distortions encouraged by the other definitions.

First, as has already been emphasized in the critical analysis above, some of the other definitions fail because they do not focus on the fact that sacraments are actions. By contrast, rite and ritual connote *action*. Contrary to the impression given by Augustine's dictum, "add the word to the element and it becomes a sacrament," baptism is not merely the element of water plus the word.[32] For a baptism to take place, water must be *used* in a particular way, so that there is action as well as words. The Supper is not merely bread and wine plus the word but bread-and-wine-eaten-and-drunk-by-the-church plus the word.

See also Hodge, *Systematic Theology,* 3:487, who defines sacraments as "ordinances instituted by Christ that are 'significant' of some spiritual reality and perpetual, and are given to 'signify, instruct, seal, confirm and strengthen, convey or apply, and thus sanctify believers.'" Intriguingly, and in my judgment ironically, Hodge immediately quotes the Second Helvetica, which defines sacraments as *symbola mystica, vel ritus sancti, aut sacrae actiones.*

32. Medieval theologians did not understand Augustine's dictum in this way. Peter Lombard defines the element of the sacrament of baptism as the washing with water, not the water alone. Other medieval theologians argued that sacraments were constituted by three features: word, element, and action.

Further, by defining sacraments as rites, we move away from a narrow focus on the physical elements or on the visibility of the elements. To speak of sacraments as rites emphasizes that they are performed by a community and are embedded in the life of that community. This point becomes especially clear against the background of ritual studies, a subdiscipline of cultural anthropology that has explored the communal and political significance of rituals in both primitive and modern communities.[33] Baptism from this angle is seen as a rite of entry that expresses the character of the church—that it is a community where racial, economic, and sexual divisions are dissolved (1 Cor. 12:12–13, Gal. 3:27–29). When we all partake of one loaf, the church is publicly and ritually showing the fact that it is one body in Christ and that its many members are working together for the edification of the whole. The ritual becomes a standard against which we measure the quality of our life together.

Understanding sacraments as rites also helps us to understand the efficacy of sacraments. Puritans (and Lady Macbeth) to the contrary, rites and ceremonies are not

---

33. See, for example, Mary Douglas, *Natural Symbols: Explorations in Cosmology* (New York, NY: Vintage, 1973); Victor Turner, *The Ritual Process: Structure and Anti-Structure* (Chicago, IL: Aldine Publishing Company, 1969). I have raised some theological objections to ritual theory in "Modernity and the Merely Social: Toward a Socio-Theological Account of Baptismal Regeneration," *ProEcclesia,* no. 3 (summer 2000): 319–30 [printed in the present book as Chapter Eight].

mere window-dressing added to an occasion that could take place without ritual and ceremony. Like performative utterances, rites actually accomplish things. As an initiation rite, baptism is analogous to other rites of entry into organizations or groups. When one is admitted to the bar, one has to go through certain formalities; at the end of the ritual process, one becomes an attorney. Going through a wedding ceremony creates a marriage, and forms a single man into a husband and a single woman into a wife. Undergoing an ordination ceremony turns the candidate into an ordained minister, and a swearing-in ceremony makes a person a judge and an inauguration makes a President. In all these examples, the person begins the ceremony having one status and ends the ceremony with another. The rite does not recognize a status that already exists; it actually installs the person into that status. Ceremony is not a sauce covering a bare meeting; without the ceremony, the meeting would simply not be what it is—would not be a wedding, or an ordination, or an inauguration. Without ceremony, the meeting would be something else entirely.

Scripture recognizes the reality of status-changing rites. A child circumcised on the eighth day becomes a child of the covenant, and an unclean person who undergoes the prescribed washings is made clean. In the ordination of priests, to take another example, the priest offers a bull for the sin offering (Lev. 8:14–17). Bulls are used for purifications only for priests or the whole congregation (Lev. 4:3,13–14), so the fact that Aaron uses a bull in the ordination rite is fitting. Other elements of the purification in the ordination rite, however, are not consistent with the purification of priests. In Leviticus 4, the purification of a priest requires the blood to be sprinkled before the veil of the sanctuary and on the horns of the altar of incense (Lev. 4:5–7), but this is not what happens in the ordination rite. Instead, the blood is put on the horns of the altar of burnt offering, and the rest is poured at the base of the altar. Thus, the purification rite is and is not like the purification for priests, and the reason is clearly that at the beginning of the rite Aaron was not yet a priest. During the rite, Aaron's sin offering was performed in one fashion; the next day, it would have to be performed in another fashion. His status changed because he went through the rite of filling.

Importantly, through this rite Aaron's status *before God* changed. To become a priest was not merely to enter a new social status or a new position in a religious organization. Once ordained, Aaron was allowed to approach the tabernacle without being killed, because YHWH had accepted him as a temple servant. Similarly, when two people marry, their status changes from single to married, and what happens through the rite of covenant making is said to be something joined together by God. A week before the wedding, sex between the engaged couple is fornication and a sin; on the wedding night it is no longer a sin.

To call the sacraments rites is to emphasize that they actually accomplish and do things; God recognizes the baptized person as a baptized person, and a church that celebrates the Supper is considered by God as a church that has celebrated the Supper. A sacramental theology conceived in terms of ritual can maintain a high view of sacramental efficacy without giving the least countenance to magic. Such a sacramental theology recognizes the performative character of baptism and the Supper.

The main downside of the language of ritual is that it suppresses to some degree the gift character of the sacraments and might encourage the Pelagian notion that we can sanctify ourselves by performing our rituals or the equally Pelagian notion that sacraments are performed for God's benefit. Protestant theology from the beginning has rightly and severely inveighed against this idea by insisting in the strongest terms that sacraments are gifts *from* God, not works *to* God. It is essential, then, in re-conceptualizing sacraments as rites that this fundamental emphasis not be lost. I suggest two important factors that will head off this danger. First, it must be emphasized that the very existence of the sacraments depends on Christ's ordination. Were it not for God's gracious intention to wash us into his fellowship and feed us at his table, baptism and the Supper would not exist. Second, it must be emphasized that God is giving gifts in, with, and under the performance of the sacramental rituals. Through the ritual of baptism, we are ingrafted into the body of Christ, and, through the meal ritual of the Supper, the Father feeds his children the Bread of Life in the Spirit. To be sure, especially in the Eucharist, the church offers a return gift, an oblation of praise and thanks, but this return gift is a response to the prior gift of life and food. In short, sacraments reconceived as rituals should be reconceived as rituals of gift-exchange.

Conclusion

Transposing sacramental theology into a ritual key has several advantages, both for sacramental theology and for the mission of the church: It emphasizes the crucial role of *action* in sacraments, provides a fresh context for working through questions of sacramental efficacy, highlights the corporate nature of sacraments, and places sacramental theology into direct dialogue with cultural anthropology and its postmodern offspring. I am not able to expound on all of these advantages here, but I hope to have made a plausible case that this revision might reinvigorate a moribund locus of theology and this transposition might help harmonize the cacophony of evangelical and Reformed sacramental theology.

CHAPTER THREE

CONJUGATING THE RITES: OLD AND NEW IN AUGUSTINE'S THEORY OF SIGNS

In his much-cited essay on "Art and Sacrament," the poet David Jones noted that both defenders of a sacramental economy of grace and those who attack it often share the assumption that interior grace is "what matters" and differ only in their evaluation of the usefulness of external signs for achieving this internal state. Sacraments are thus understood as accommodations to our (defective) physicality designed to draw us beyond signs by testifying to "another dimension." Sacramental theology has often pursued its explorations on the assumption that human encounter with God takes place not at the level of signs but solely at a deeper, internal level. As Jones perceives, to treat sacraments as accommodations to human infirmity implies that embodiment is itself an infirmity; whereas Christian faith treats the body as a glory of a human being.[1]

Historically, this view of sacraments has been allied with the quasi-Marcionite idea that the transition from old to new in the history of salvation is a transition from a more sociological form of religion to a more spiritual one. This becomes more obvious and deviant in late medieval spiritualism, Renaissance humanism, and modern philosophy and sociology of religion when an explicit Marcionism entered an alliance with a renunciation of all sacraments,[2] but a moderate form of this alliance is formative not only of heresy but of orthodoxy.[3] As detailed below, these problems appear already in Augustine, and

---

1. David Jones, *Epoch and Artist: Selected Writings,* ed. Harman Grisewood (London: Faber and Faber, 1959), 165.

2. Henning Graf Reventlow, *The Authority of the Bible and the Rise of the Modern World,* trans. John Bowden (Philadelphia: Fortress, 1985).

3. Both at the Council at Florence (1439) and at Trent (1545–1563), the sacraments of the new law were sharply distinguished from those of the old. According to the *Decree for the Armenians* promulgated at Florence, the sacraments of the new law "differ greatly from the sacraments of the old law. For the latter did not cause grace, but only prefigured it as to be given through the Passion of Christ; but these our sacraments both contain grace and confer it upon those who receive them worthily" (quoted in Bernard Leeming, *Principles of Sacramental Theology* [London: Longmans, Green and Co., 1956], 27-28). See Calvin's criticism of this position in *Institutes of the Christian Religion,* ed. John T. McNeill (Philadelphia, PA: Westminster, 1960), 4.14.21-26.

thus helped shape Protestant as well as Catholic sacramental theology.

There are strands in Augustine's thought, however, that point to a very different formulation of sacramental theology. If one insists that humans, as creatures made in the image of the Word, live and move and have their being within an economy of linguistic and other signs, then there is no reason to deny that the divine-human encounter takes place at the level of signs. The physicality of the sacraments can then be taken not as an accommodation to a human defect or a temporary expedient but as the necessary form of any possible encounter with God. Not only does this imply a more satisfying account of the progress of redemptive history but also suggests broader conclusions about the nature of salvation, for one can argue that Christ instituted physical rites for his church because his redemptive activity aims at saving embodied persons and at erecting redeemed communities that, like all other communities, are constituted through signs. Against the view that the economy of salvation is internal and that the sacraments "point to" that economy, salvation itself embraces the social, public, visible, earthly, and historical, according to this alternative concept.

In this chapter, I will first examine some way stations along the way of traditional quasi-Marcionite sacramentology and then examine the "grammatical" and "pragmatic" account of signs in some of Augustine's letters and treatises.

Old and New and the Economy of Signs

In *de Magistro, de Doctrina Christiana,* and Book 15 of *de Trinitate,*[4] Augustine imports questionable notions into his definitions of *signum* that have the double effect, when applied to sacramental theology, of reducing the sign to a secondary and somewhat unfortunate necessity and, conversely, of interiorizing the "thing" or reality signified by the sacrament. After beginning *de Magistro* by leading Adeodatus toward the conclusion that we learn nothing apart from verbal or gestural signs (10.29-30), he immediately veers in another direction by claiming that knowledge is more valuable than signs, which (questionably) assumes that a thing can be cognitively grasped without the use of signs (10.31). He then states this dilemma: "When I am shown a sign, it cannot teach me anything if it finds me ignorant of the reality for which the sign stands; but if it finds me acquainted with the reality, what do I learn from the sign" (10.33; 11.36)? Knowledge of reality does

---

4. I have used the following translations: *On Christian Doctrine,* trans. D. W. Robertson (Indianapolis, IN: Bobbs-Merrill, 1958); *The Teacher; The Free Choice of the Will; Grace and Free Will,* Augustine, The Fathers of the Church: A New Translation, trans. Robert P. Russell (Washington, D.C.: Catholic University of America Press, 1968); and *The Trinity,* The Fathers of the Church, trans. Stephen McKenna (Washington: Catholic University of America Press, 1963).

not come through signs after all, but the reverse; one can know that a sign is a sign only when one knows the reality, so that knowledge is gained precisely by opening a gap between *signum* and *res* (10.33), which Augustine eventually bridges with the *deus ex machina* of the "Interior Teacher," Christ.[5] Adeodatus concludes that human teaching does not transmit knowledge and deploys *verba externa* to remind us that Christ dwells within.[6]

The semiotic theory of *de Magistro* is consistent with that of *de doctrina Christiana,* where Augustine's explanation of signs comes in the context of a distinction between things to be used and things to be enjoyed. As *peregrini* in this world, Christians must merely make use

---

5. A *distinction* of *signum* and *res* seems necessary to any sane involvement in the world. A *gap,* however, implies that one comes to know things only by leaving *signa* behind and raises the specter of skepticism. In fact, we simply move from one sign-encoded reality to another.

6. That this model of signs and knowledge is not part of a youthful neoplatonism is indicated, first, by the fact that in *Retractions,* Augustine does not revise his teaching and says that the whole purpose of *de Magistro* was to defend philosophically Jesus' statement that he alone was to be teacher. Second, Augustine's discussion of the "interior word" prior to all language in the later treatise *de Trinitate* (15.10.17–15.11.20) is a variation of the same type of theory. As Charles Taylor points out in a somewhat one-sided account, Augustine believed that the human problem is absorption in sensible and external things rather than in the higher reality that they manifest (Charles Taylor, *Sources of the Self: The Making of Modern Identity* [Cambridge: Cambridge University Press, 1989], 128).

of the things of this world, lest their enjoyment entangle them so that they never reach their destination. A *signum* is a certain kind of *res,* differing from other things in that it brings something to mind that goes beyond the impression it makes on the senses (2.1.1).[7] Since signs are things, we can ask whether signs are to be used or enjoyed, and Augustine's answer is clearly the former since, ultimately, only Father, Son, and Spirit are to be enjoyed.[8] Signs are, specifically, to be used as means to

---

7. Todorov is correct to point out that the distinction between *signum* and *res* dissolves somewhat, since a *res* that is properly used is transitive, leading the user to the enjoyment of God. Thus, every *res* is, for the pious mind, at least potentially, a *signum.* Without modifying the starting definition of *signum,* however, this cannot save Augustine's doctrine from the charge of subordinating signs to a dispensable role in humanity's relation to God. No matter how widely one applies the term, a sign remains, in Augustine's concept, a step on the ladder of ascent to an unmediated encounter (Tsvetan Todorov, *Theories of the Symbol,* trans. Catherine Porter [Oxford: Blackwell, 1982], 46–47).

8. In large measure, Augustine's distinction between *utile* and *fruendum* is a polemic against idolatry. He defines enjoyment as enjoyment of something *propter seipsum,* and thus by definition he is forced to say that only God is to be enjoyed. Moreover, he does indicate that things might be enjoyed, so long as they were enjoyed for the sake of union with God, and not *propter seipsum.* Still, Augustine's view–in addition to the ascetic implication that we love other humans without enjoyment–is not compatible with his creationist emphasis. Since existence itself is wholly a gift of God, and since I am maintained in existence only by his mercy, it is impossible to enjoy God without enjoying what he has given, for I who enjoy him *am* what he has given. Augustine's concept assumes that humans have a

move toward the realities that they "bring to mind." The whole concept, as R. A. Markus says, pictures language and signification as a stream running parallel to experience and reflecting it, rather than a stream running through the midst of existence.[9]

Applied in sacramental theology, Augustine's theory means that exterior sacraments point to something going on invisibly. Preaching before the celebration of the Eucharist, he distinguishes between what is seen in the sacrament and what is understood *(aliud videtur, aliud intelligitur)*, the former having to do with corporeal things and the latter with spiritual fruit *(Sermo 227; PL 38, 1099–1101)*.[10] In *de catechizandis rudibus,* he uses similar language to distinguish between the visible *signacula rerum divinarum* and the *res ipsas invisibiles,* and compares this to the difference between the sound of Scripture *(carnaliter)* and the *spirituale* significance (PL 40, 344-45). And in his second letter to Januarius, he de-

---

measure of independent or autonomous existence from God.

9. R. A. Markus, "St. Augustine on Signs," in *Augustine: A Collection of Critical Essays,* ed. R. A. Markus (Garden City, NY: Doubleday, 1972), 72.

10. Yet there is evidence of a different concept in this sermon, since the spiritual fruit to which the sensible sacrament refers is the unity of the ecclesial body, so that anyone who receives the sacrament without holding to the *vinculum pads* receives the mystery not *pro se* but as a *testimonia contra se.* See below for further development of this thematic in Augustine.

fines sacraments as celebrations that bring something to the understanding, and compares the sacramental use of material elements to the rhetorical use of "parables" from the whole of creation that "illustrate" religious truth.[11]

A remarkably similar structure, using some of the same vocabulary and imagery, emerges in *de doctrina Christiana* to describe the transition from Old to New Testament. Augustine is warning against taking the figurative as literal, which, he adds, was the error of the Jews, who adopted the "habit of taking signs for things" and thus fell into a "miserable servitude," in which they were not "able to raise the eye of the mind above things that are corporal and created to drink in eternal light" (3.5.9). Israel, to be sure, was more fortunate than the pagan world, since, by God's ordination, they were capable of serving him in their signs, while even if a pagan were to ascend from *signum* to *res,* he will not be profited, since the *res* itself is an idol. Christ has a twofold effect on the signs of the old world: Christianity liberated the Jews from useful signs, "elevating them to the things which the signs represented," while it destroyed pagan signs, not to lead them to "servitude under useful signs" but "rather to an exercise of the mind directed toward understanding them spiritually" (3.8.12). Just as there is a gap and a *transitus*

---

11. *Epistle* 55; PL 22, 205, 210–11; Augustine, *Letters,* 6 vols., trans. Sister Wilfrid Parsons (New York, NY: Fathers of the Church, 1951-56), 1.261–62, 271–72.

from sign to thing in the sacrament, so there is a *transitus* from useful signs of the old to the *vera res* of the new.[12] To be sure, even in this treatise, Augustine does not hold that Christianity wholly transcends signs.[13] Yet, the way Augustine uses "bondage of signs" suggests that signs inhibit rather than make possible fellowship with God; he is not merely warning against abuse of signs, for even religious expression through "useful signs" is "bondage" (3.6.10; 3.8.12; cf. 3.9.13). In any case, the proper use of signs requires the opening of a gap between *signum* and *res* that is bridged by the mind; for Augustine, the glory of New Testament signs is, in Derridean terms, the introduction of a radical form of logocentrism where even the voice is given a secondary status in relation to the true inner word.[14]

---

12. Augustine's use of *utiliter* in this section of book three apparently recalls the discussion of book one that distinguishes sharply between things that are to be enjoyed and those that are to be used.

13. The dualism of sign and reality is even more pronounced in Origen, who breaks the Pauline baptism in the Red Sea into a double transition. See Jean Laporte, "Models from Philo in Origen's Teaching on Original Sin," *Living Water, Sealing Spirit: Readings on Christian Initiation,* ed. Maxwell E. Johnson (Collegeville, MN.: Liturgical Press, 1995), 114.

14. Compare John Milbank, *The Word Made Strange: Theology, Language, Culture* (Oxford: Blackwell, 1997), 88–92, who argues that Augustine's notion of the "internal word," by construing thought linguistically, furnishes materials for a very different semiotic.

Augustine is the touchstone of Western sacramental theology, and the double *transitus* in his theory of signs is a continuing subtext of the later tradition. I will briefly examine two examples. First is the ninth-century "debate" between Paschasius Radbertus and Ratramnus, authors of the first treatises on the Supper.[15] It is simplistic to describe this as a debate between Paschasian realism and the "symbolic view" of Ratramnus, for on the question of *figura* and *veritas* they define their terms so differently that they are simply talking past each other, assuming they were intending to talk toward each other at all.[16] Both, moreover, assume the Augustinian view that signs draw us from the sensible to an invisible reality, and each operates with an essentially individualistic framework.[17]

---

15. For accounts of these treatises, see Gary Macy, *The Theologies of the Eucharist in the Early Scholastic Period: A Study of the Salvific Function of the Sacrament according to the Theologians, c. 1080–c. 1220* (Oxford: Clarendon, 1984), 27–31; Paul H. Jones, *Christ's Eucharistic Presence: A History of the Doctrine* (New York, NY: Peter Lang, 1994), 72–79. Portions of Paschasius's treatise and all of Ratramnus's are translated in George E. McCracken and Allen Cabaniss, trans, and ed., *Early Medieval Theology*, Library of Christian Classics, vol. 9 (London: SCM, 1957).

16. For Paschasius, *figura* and *veritas* are two aspects of a thing (roughly equivalent to appearance and reality), while for Ratramnus, they are two different ways in which something may be represented (roughly analogous to figurative and literal language). Both conclude that the Supper has both "truthful" and figural aspects.

17. Macy, *Theologies*, 30, argues that the two differ in their under-

A genuine difference is found in their evaluation of the Old Testament sacraments. Ratramnus follows Augustine in his insistence that Christ was offered and received by the saints of the Old Testament, though under a different form. Denying that Israel was truly baptized in the Red Sea contradicts Paul's statement in 1 Corinthians 10, he argues, and he goes so far as to say that the cloud and sea contained *(continebant)* the invisible operation of the Spirit for the sanctification of the people. Similarly, the manna and water given in the wilderness substantially administered the power of the Word to Israel.[18] The substance of the sacraments remains the same throughout salvation history, as also does the visible-invisible structure of their operation. Both old and new offer both sign and reality.

Paschasius seems more "realist" than Ratramnus largely because his anxiety to avoid identifying the sacraments of the old and new leads him to insist that the

---

standing of the place of the Eucharist in salvation. For Ratramnus, the Supper symbolizes the "spiritual union between the divine Christ with the soul of the believer achieved by faith," while Paschasius emphasizes that through the Eucharist the believer's nature is joined to the human nature of the incarnate Christ.

18. Cf. the strong statement of section 25: *Ipse namque qui nunc in Ecclesia omnipotenti virtute panem et vinum insui corporis carnem et proprii cruoris undam spiritualiter convertit ipse tunc quoque manna de coelo datum corpus suum, et aquam de petra profusam proprium sanguinem, invisibiliter operatus est* (PL 121,138–39).

sacraments of the new law contain something above and beyond those of the old. He is willing to grant that the Supper has a figural element so long as it is clear that "not every figure is shadow or falsehood" (4.46; *non enim omnis figura umbra vel falsitas*), and *umbra* is to be understood in the sense used in the epistle to the Hebrews (cf. 5.20-26; 15.77-87). He affirms that Israel ate the same food as the church but only in a qualified sense: By contrast to the Supper, the manna of Israel was spiritual and heavenly food and participated in the mystery of Christ only in type and figure, not in truth. Directly contradicting Augustine's insistence that the *res* of the sacraments was the same in both Testaments, Paschasius concludes that the sacraments of the old and new are the same *necdum in re* but only *in specie ac figura* (5.64-66),[19] For Paschasius, the old covenant was a covenant of "mere" signs, and if the Supper is to be understood within an economy of signs, it is still *umbra*. Something "extra" must therefore be attached to the sign in the new covenant. Paschasian realism turns out to be a reflection of his belief that

---

19. There is a textual problem in this line. McCracken and Cabaniss translate as "in appearance," assuming *in specie,* while the Corpus Christianorum text reads *in spe* and includes a note on variant texts. While the argument leading to this conclusion does emphasize a promise-fulfillment pattern and *veritas* is defined in terms of fulfillment, the denial that the sacraments of the Old were not the same *in re* shows that, whatever the proper reading, Paschasius was specifically challenging the Augustinian concept.

the old covenant signs were mere *figura,* while those of the new are *simul veritas et figura.* For Ratramnus, in both old and new, Christ was *vere* offered and received through different *figura.*[20]

Our second example is from Continental Protestant debates on infant baptism of the mid twentieth century, first touched off by Emil Brunner's brief comment that the current practice of infant baptism was "scandalous"[21] and given further impetus by Barth's impassioned lecture, delivered in 1943.[22] According to Barth, baptism is not a cause of redemption but is an auxiliary rite concerned with the *cognitio salutis.* Christ's word and work alone cause salvation, but this word and work seeks to be seen and publicly recognized and therefore takes on a sacramental *Gestalt.* Baptism thus answers to the believer's desire to "get sight" of his fellowship with Christ by giving him a picture of his death and resurrection with Christ. On the basis of this cognitive concept of baptism, which Barth

---

20. On the influence of Paschasian eucharistic theology into the twelfth century, see Macy, *Theologies,* 44–72. The cultural implications of the rupture of symbol and reality have often been commented on; for my purposes, it is highly significant that this rupture occurred in tandem with a rupture of Old and New.

21. Emil Brunner, *Truth as Encounter* (Philadelphia, PA: Westminster Press, 1964), 131.

22. For a summary of the subsequent debates, see Aidan Kavanagh, *The Shape of Baptism: The Rite of Christian Initiation* (Collegeville, MN: Liturgical Press, 1978), 86-97.

claims to derive from Calvin, he castigates infant baptism as a "wound in the body of the church," as a "hole" in baptismal practice, and as "arbitrary and despotic." Infant baptism turns what should be a free dialogue into an act of violence, imposing a religious identity on the baptized without his consent. If baptism answers the desire to "get sight" of one's fellowship with Christ, then the baptized must come to baptism rather than be brought to it.[23] Throughout, Barth's argument rests on the assumption that salvation as such is an essentially private and invisible reality that comes to sacramental expression at some logically and perhaps temporally subsequent stage. The saving encounter with Christ does not occur at the level of signs but at another, more inward level. Despite his opposition to traditional sacramentalism, Barth perpetuates one of its most basic features.

Barth takes note of the traditional Reformed analogy of circumcision and baptism but dismisses it with the comment that circumcision was a sign of natural birth into the lineage of Israel.[24] In the fragment on baptism in *Church Dogmatics* IV/4, Barth concedes that the connection between circumcision and baptism is "intrinsically correct and important" because it highlights the "unity of the old and new covenants in spite of their formal distinc-

---

23. Karl Barth, *The Teaching of the Church Regarding Baptism*, trans. Ernest A. Payner (London: SCM, 1948), 27–28, 40–42, 47.

24. Ibid., 43.

tion." Still, this does not imply that the "definitions and meaning of the two were interchangeable" because the church, in contrast to Israel, is "not a nation. It is a people freely and newly called and assembled out of Israel and all nations." It is recruited not by birth but through the new birth, so that "Christian baptism, as distinct from Israelite circumcision, cannot be on the basis of the physical descent of the candidate."[25]

All this simply evades the problem. Even if one concedes Barth's debatable point that circumcision had a purely "national" character, it cannot be denied that it was also a religious initiation, since the nation was religiously constituted. Belonging to Israel meant belonging to the people of Yahweh, which ipso facto meant belonging to Yahweh himself: "Your God shall be my God" entailed "your people shall be my people." This means, then, that Old Testament religion not only permitted but required the "violence" of a religious identity imposed upon its male infants; to fail in imposing this identity was to break the covenant. Barth's complaint about infant baptism thus is a complaint against the form of religion of the Old Testament, and it makes it difficult to believe he is completely serious about the unity of the covenants. Barth's protest suggests that the religion of the church is

---

25. Karl Barth, *Church Dogmatics IV/4: The Christian Life (Fragment): Baptism at the Foundation of the Christian Life,* trans. G.W. Bromiley (Edinburgh: T&T Clark, 1969), 177–78.

radically different from that of Israel: While religion in the Old Testament embraced the whole national life of a community, the New Testament church is a religious association, consisting of those who have made free and conscious decisions. Nowhere in his discussion of baptism and circumcision does Barth justify this profound ecclesiological shift.[26]

A remarkably similar set of assumptions concerning rites, symbols, and "true religion" is apparent, albeit more subtly, in certain turns of arguments in defense of infant baptism. Oscar Cullmann directly challenges Barth's "weak" discussion of the relation of circumcision and baptism. Circumcision, he insists, is not a sign of reception into a "natural racial succession" but rather is a "seal of faith" (Rom. 4:11), and this from the outset envisioned the inclusion of the nations. Even in the old covenant, Abraham is father of believers in a salvation-historical rather than a racial sense. Thus, rightly understood, circumcision is not merely an outward, national sign but has to do with the heart.[27] Significantly, Cullmann defends

---

26. What is implicit in Barth's treatment comes to extreme and explicit expression in the work of Paul K. Jewett. His entire argument against infant baptism turns on a distinction between old covenant and new covenant in terms of a contrast among earthly, temporal, and typical realities on the one hand and the heavenly and eternal realities on the other (Jewett, *Infant Baptism and the Covenant of Grace* [Grand Rapids, MI: Eerdmans, 1978], 90–91, 234).

27. Oscar Cullmann, *Baptism in the New Testament*, trans. J. K. S.

what might be called the genuinely religious character of circumcision by insisting that it has to do with inner and individual piety. What he does *not* say is that physical descent from Abraham, Isaac, and Jacob and citizenship in Israel, as such, were religiously significant.[28] Cullmann, like Barth, appears to assume that true religion is an internal reality and has a more positive evaluation of circumcision than Barth simply because he believes that circumcision was a "spiritual" as well as a "national" sign. In his evaluation of Israel-as-nation, Cullmann stands very close to Barth.

Symphony in Two Movements

Already in Augustine an alternative concept, both of religious signs and of the relation of the old and new, was available but largely untapped until this century.[29] Epis-

---

Reid (London: SCM, 1950), 58–59.

28. Physical descent never did provide any guarantees, but despite that, blood relation was not outside the concern of Israel's religion; and, to repeat, this is not theologically indifferent, since Israel's generations are the beginning of the redemption of human generations.

29. But cf. Thomas Aquinas, *Summa Theologiae* 3a.61.1. In this century, De Lubac's *Corpus Mysticum: L'eucharistie et l'église au moyen age,* 2nd ed. (Paris: Aubier, 1949) has inspired a rearticulation of the "sociological" model of the sacraments that I am advocating. Anthropological theories of ritual, despite theologically questionable assumptions, have also aided in the refurbishment of Augustine's insights.

tle 138 to Marcellinus provides a compact discussion of the way these issues are brought together. Marcellinus has been challenged to explain how there can be a change in rites without implying either that God had changed or that the old rites were evil, since a good thing rightly done ought not to be changed. Augustine responds first by pointing out that change is the story of life: Seasons change and humans grow through various stages, though behind this constant change is the immutable *divinae providentiae ratio*. His second response is to distinguish between the "fitting" (*aptum*) and "beautiful" (*pulchrum*). The second is unchanging, but whether or not a thing is apt depends on its connections with other things, so that as the total web of circumstances changes, what is *aptum* changes with it. The Old Testament sacraments were *aptum* for their time but are no longer so. There was no change, however, in God or in his plan, since the transformation of sacraments was in fact prophesied by the Old Testament.

Though Augustine refuses to elaborate the causes of the change in rites, he offers a brief but immensely fruitful metaphor as explanation. Just as verbal signs—the letters of a written verb or the sounds of a spoken verb—change according to the time that the verb indicates, so the rites of the church change to indicate a shift in tense from the time of anticipation to the time of fulfillment.[30] By this analogy, Augustine is able to secure a number of things. First, the analogy is consistent with his repeated insistence that the "substance," or, continuing Augustine's analogy, the "Verbal root," remains the same in both Testaments. Christ is the *res* offered and received in the sacraments of old and new; he is the Word conjugated throughout the course of redemptive history.[31] Equally importantly, the analogy gives Augustine ample room to agree that as times change, the tense of the church's worship changes with it. Yet, the change in tense does not imply that words give place to silence, that rites give place to pure interior worship, or that the New Testament opens a gap between rites and realities that was not apparent in the old. In both old and new, Augustine implies, the church

---

30. *Verumtamen breviter dici potest, quod homini acuto fortasse suffecerit, aliis sacramentis praenuntiari Christum cum venturus esset, aliis cum venisset annuntiari oportuisse; sicut modo no idipsum loquentes, diversitas verum compulit etiam verba mutare. Siquidem aliud est praenuntiari, aliud annuntiari; aliud cum venturus esset, aliud cum venisset* (PL 33, 528). He uses the same analogy in *Contra Faustum*, 19.16 (PL 42, 356–57).

31. Hence, in *Contra Faustum* 19.16, he gives the following as examples of changing verb tenses: *futurum et factum, passurus et passus, resurrecturus et resurrexit,* which implies that the story announced by the sacraments remains the same, though it differs as promise and fulfillment.

performs sacramental signs, and these are embedded in and are the very form of genuine worship.[32]

Though initially distinguished, *aptum* and *pulchrum* are harmonized later in Epistle 138 with a musical analogy. By variations in what is fitting, the sovereign God orchestrates history so that the beauty of the entire world (*universi saeculi pulchritudo*) swells to become a "mighty song of some unutterable musician" (*magnum carmen cujusdem ineffabilis modulatoris*), which raises worshipers to contemplation and adoration. Two points are suggested by this analogy. First, on Augustine's view, theology cannot dispense with the first movement of this two-part symphony without vitiating the beauty of the whole; the melody of the new lacks aesthetic power if unaccompanied by the (more darkly colored) harmonies of the old. Secondly, rites and sacraments are not a grudging concession to the weakness of the flesh. Instead, they are necessary in the new age for the full development of the motif of redemption in the music of universal history. The new is a surprising development and variation on the themes of the old, but it is neither Cagean silence nor a wholly new musical departure.[33]

---

32. Augustine also uses the analogy to highlight the distinction between the momentary performance of the rite, which he compares to the evanescence of spoken words, and their enduring *donum spirituale* (*Contra Faustum* 19.16).

33. In comparison with the Baroque polyphony of the old, the new

As the footnotes above indicate, much the same argument appears in *Contra Faustum*, with an important development. Faustus, a Manichean who combines a gnostic detestation of the "abominations" of the Jews (22.2) with an early form of New Testament source criticism (17.1-2; 18.3), charges Augustine and Catholics in general with hypocrisy: You attack us for dispensing with the structures of the old order, Faustus argues, but you Catholics do not offer sacrifice, keep the Sabbath, or refrain from unclean meats, so you as much as we are dispensing with the old (18.1; 19.4; 22.2). Augustine responds by referring to Jesus' words in Matthew 5:17, distinguishing two senses in which Jesus fulfills the law. With regard to the moral precepts of the law, Jesus enables Christians to fulfill the law by keeping the commandments. With regard to the typical ordinances of worship, the law and prophets foretell that these would cease with the coming of the Messiah, so Jesus' removal of the ordinances *is* the fulfillment. Christians do not circumcise because Jesus fulfilled the law (18.4; 19.8–9, 11, 14). Yet, the new order is not without its sacraments and rites, and, in fact, these also are part of the fulfillment of the old rites. Au-

---

is a kind of "minimalism." The sacraments of the new order are fewer, easier to perform, most sublime in implication, most "upright in observance" (*de doctrina Christiana* 3.9.13; *Contra Faustum* 19.12; PL 42, 355; *Epistle* 54; PL 33, 200). What is significant here, again, is that Augustine refuses to "spiritualize" the new. The rites are simplified, but they are still necessary to man's approach to God.

gustine treats the new less as a "spiritualization" of the old than as a "humanization," with the ancient rites and institutions fulfilled in practices and life of the body of Christ. Thus, the church does not continue to practice Levitical baptisms since Christ came to "bury us with Himself by baptism into death."[34] Christ fulfills the dietary laws by refusing to incorporate any who are like unclean animals into his body,[35] and there is no physical tabernacle because believers are the dwelling of God (19.10).

More theoretically, Augustine explains the continuing necessity for sacraments in the age of the Spirit by saying that no religious society can be united without some visible signs (19.11).[36] Similarly, in *de doctrina Christiana*, Augustine treats signs to an unprecedented extent within the context of a theory of communication, such that signs are means by which one passes on the motions of his soul to another. While this concept has an overly intellectualist cast, it moves in the direction of a sociological view of signs (which is at the same time a theological view)

---

34. *Venit enim consepelire nos sibi per Baptismum in mortem* (PL 42, 354).

35. *Non admittens ad corpus suum . . . quidquid per illa ammalia in moribus hominum significatum est* (PL 42, 354).

36. *In nullum autem nomen religionis, seu verum, seu falsum, coagulari homines possunt, nisi aliquo signaculorum vel sacramentorum visibilium consortio colligentur: quorum sacramentorum vis inenarrabiliter valet plurimum, et ideo contempta sacrilegos facit. Impie quippe contemnitur, sine qua non potest perfici pietas* (PL 42, 355).

by emphasizing their role in interpersonal relations. And this enters his explicit sacramental theology: Augustine insists that Christ is the *res* of the sacraments, but the Christ who is such is the *totus Christus* of Head and Body. In *Contra Faustum* 19.14, Augustine points out that the saints of the Old Testament were willing to give their lives for the sake of their sacraments, which were *rerum complendarum.* How much more then should Christians be willing to suffer *pro signo Christi,* since these are *indicia completarum,* evidence that the promised redemption has occurred. Augustine goes on to suggest that what was promised in the old and now fulfilled is eternal life, but, significantly, this life comes by union with the *corpus Christi.*[37] Signs are not conceived in these passages, as they were in *de Magistro* and certain portions of *de doctrina Christiana,* as external to experience but as enmeshed in the life of a community. A *signum* is not a *res*

---

37. See the comments in *de doctrina Christiana* 2.25.39, where he classifies clothing, weights and measures, differences of value among the *innumerabilia genera significationum sine quibus humana societas, aut non omnino, aut minus commode geritur.* Elsewhere, he writes that by the consecration of the Word, the bread and cup are the body and blood of Christ, and as the faithful receive these, they are joined together as the members of that body. As Augustine puts it to his congregation, *vos estis quod acceptistis (Sermo* 227; PL 38, 1099). Also, in *de civitate Dei* 10, Augustine makes it apparent that the binding of human to human is a form of humanity's binding to God, and therefore of the essence of Christian sacrifice.

that "bring other things to mind." *Signa* are the coinage of social and religious transactions.[38]

This more sociological concept is allied, as is the more intellectualist one, with a particular view of the transition from old to new. In *Contra Faustum,* Augustine argues that the old covenant order pointed to its fulfillment in Christ, but since Christ is not only head but body, the types of the old order point also to the church. And since no organized religious body can exist without signs and rites, the rites of the old covenant pointed to the sacraments of the new. This challenges any effort to locate the discontinuity between old and new as a discontinuity in the operation, importance, or function of signs. Since God has called a people in both old and new and since a people exists only through the circulation of signs and language, sacraments have the same communal function throughout redemptive history.

At a more theoretical level, this alternative concept throws into radical question the dualisms of traditional sacramental theology. First, the dualism of *signum* and *res.* If the *res* of the sacrament is the *totus Christus,* and if the goal of the sacrament is to unify the church in Christ, then contemplating the sacrament (assuming that con-

---

38. Similarly, Wittgenstein's opening gambit in the *Philosophical Investigations* places language in the pragmatic context of trade. See Fergus Kerr, *Theology after Wittgenstein,* 3rd ed. (London: SPCK, 1997), 57–59.

templation is what one is supposed to do with it) does *not* bring something *else* to mind. What is sensibly apparent in the Eucharist *is* what is brought to mind, and this, in turn, is what is accomplished—the unity of the body.[39]

Second is the dualism of outward sign and inward grace. Hugh of St. Victor's comparison of the external sacraments to a "container" of grace depends on his assumption that the human disease is located, primarily if not exclusively, within.[40] On this view, the specific form of the rite is comparatively indifferent, since what matters is the invisible medicine poured out through the ritual container; who cares if the bottle is green or blue, conical or cylindrical? If, however, the human sickness consists in strife, violence, and disruptions of community—in a refusal to sit at a common table in the presence of the one God—as well as in sins of the heart, and if salvation consists in the gathering of all nations into one body, then the form of the sacrament is simply indistinguishable from the grace. The answer to the question: "What

---

39. Of course, only the body and not the head of the *totus Christus* is visible in the rite, so there is in this sense an invisible *res* in the Eucharist. But what is invisible is, for Augustine, continuous with the visible body, profoundly united to its head.

40. Hugh of St. Victor, *On the Sacraments of the Christian Faith,* trans. Roy J. Deferrari (Cambridge, Mass.: Mediaeval Academy of America, 1951), 1.9.4.

are you trying to accomplish by gathering these people for this meal?" is, "To gather these people for this meal."

Conclusion

The sociological and pragmatic model of the sacraments, with its accompanying account of the relation of old and new, provided Augustine and his successors with the framework for examining the mechanisms of sacramental theology according to the pattern of the mechanisms of Old Testament rites. Sacramental theology, however, followed the more intellectualist concept of signs, and, at the same time, dug out an even deeper chasm between the sacraments of old and new than Augustine had done. As a result, when the scholastics took up technical questions of sacramental operations, their answers were structured by questionable dualisms, Old Testament ritual patterns were more or less ignored, and categories were borrowed from Aristotle rather than from Leviticus. Efforts to rehabilitate Augustine's sociological model of the sacraments thus need to be complemented with an effort to bring Old Testament conceptualities into play.

CHAPTER FOUR

MORE THAN A DAINTY SIP: OLD AND NEW IN AUGUSTINE'S CONTRA FAUSTUM

From the beginning, Augustine has been a strategic battleground in the warfare between Protestants and Catholics. Calvin boasted that Augustine *totus noster est*, and Catholics had a strong enough claim on Augustine for Diarmaid MacCulloch to draw the conclusion that the Reformation was a debate taking place in Augustine's head.[1] There is therefore no better topic for an Evangelical-Catholic colloquium than the work of Augustine, and I believe that attention to Augustine's treatise against Faustus the Manichean is especially relevant in today's setting.

Augustine's response to Faustus accents Christian *practice*, and thus provides a framework for correcting common misrepresentations of the battle lines of the Ref-

---

1. MacCulloch, *The Reformation: A History* (New York, NY: Viking, 2003), 108.

ormation. Evangelicals, and Catholics too, characterize the Reformation as a doctrinal conflict over justification by faith, taking for granted the oft-cited axiom of Princeton Presbyterian B. B. Warfield that the Reformation, inwardly considered, was the triumph of Augustine's doctrine of grace over Augustine's doctrine of the church.[2] Yet criticism of medieval liturgical theology and practice was equally central to the Reformers' program, and Augustine's writings provided much of the ammunition for their assault.[3] Statistics are inconclusive, but it is revealing that in the final edition of his *Institutes of the Christian Religion*, Calvin cites Augustine sixty-eight times on sacramental theology and fifty-four times on ecclesiology, compared with only thirty-four references in his treatment of free will and twenty-eight in his discussion of grace.[4] When Evangelical-Catholic discussions focus on

---

2. Warfield, *Calvin and Augustine* (Phillipsburg, NJ: P & R Publishing, 1980), 332.

3. Edward Muir has recently described the Reformation as a revolution in ritual theory and a ritual process. Muir, *Ritual in Early Modern Europe*, 2nd ed. (Cambridge: Cambridge University Press, 2005), chs. 5-6. For a similar assessment of the German Reformation, see Susan C. Karant-Nunn, *The Reformation of Ritual: An Interpretation of Early Modern Germany* (London: Routledge, 1997).

4. S. J. Han, "An Investigation into Calvin's Use of Augustine," *Acta Theologica Supplementum*, no. 10 (2008), 77. This is hardly surprising, since Calvin in fact disagreed with some basics of Augustinian soteriology, including his definition of *iustificare*.

justification, merit, and other soteriological issues to the exclusion of questions of ecclesiology and liturgical practice, the game is being played with half a deck.[5] A study of Augustine's arguments in *Contra Faustum* in the light of Reformation debates shows how, contrary to Warfield, the Reformers worked within an Augustinian sacramental theology as well as an Augustinian soteriology, and suggests the possibility that they considered his ecclesiology to be precisely a soteriology.

Contra Faustum is a massive rambling repetitive treatise, and in this chapter I focus on only one of its major themes. My title comes from Book 32. As usual in this treatise, Augustine begins the chapter with a long quotation from Faustus' *Capitula* before giving his reply, and in Book 32 he quotes Faustus' charge that while Catholics claim to receive the entire Scripture, Old and New Testaments, in practice they accept only prophecies and reject everything else—circumcision, sacrifices, Sabbath, unleavened bread, the whole gamut of Old Testament rites. The gospels themselves are shot through with Jewish nonsense, says Faustus, so even the gospels ought not be accepted wholesale by genuine Christians. Why do the

---

5. In this respect, Evangelical Protestantism has to take more account of the theological implications of recent social history of the Reformation than it has done. The literature is considerable, and growing fast. The classic studies are Keith Thomas, *Religion and the Decline of Magic*; Eamon Duffey, *The Stripping of the Altars*; and John Bossy, *Christianity and the West, 1400-1700*.

Catholics demand that Manicheans believe the Old Testament and the gospels, since, Faustus concludes with a flourish, "you . . . take so dainty a sip from the Old Testament, that you hardly, so to speak, wet your lips with it"?[6] These arguments over the Christian significance of Old Testament ceremony highlight a crucial, if sometimes submerged, topic of Reformation debates. As I will detail below, the Reformers viewed Catholics as Judaizers who failed to reckon with the radical differences between Old covenant and New, while Catholics returned the insult, though they sometimes appealed to Levitical practices in defense of Catholic liturgical traditions.

This chapter admittedly comes from the hand of a partisan and so is recognizably *Protestant*, but my intention—mostly implicit and undeveloped, given the limits of the paper—is to contribute to ecumenical theology. The subliminal message here is that the way forward for Protestant-Catholic, especially for Evangelical-Catholic, dialogue, is to put the lie to Faustus' charge by drink-

---

6. *Contra Faustum*, 32.7. This is the translation of the NPNF. The recent New City Press translation by Roland Teske renders this as "There is, then, no reason why you should think that I ought to believe all the things that the gospels contain, since you yourself . . . do not touch with the tips of your lips, as they say, the supreme liquor of the Old Testament." The Latin is: *Nihil ergo est iam cur me omnia credere existimes debere, quae continent Evangelia; cum tu, ut supra ostensum est, Testamenti Veteris supremum liquorem vix summis, ut aiunt, labris attingas.*

ing deep from the Old Testament and by drawing out the liturgical implications of Augustine's treatment of the sacraments of the Old Law. If both Catholics and Protestants were to take "more than a dainty sip," and if both sides were to learn from Augustine and the New Testament how to transpose from Old to New, we might be able to make significant progress in breaking down the barriers of centuries.

This chapter develops in several stages. First, I briefly examine how the charge of "judaizing" functioned in Reformation liturgical debates. Next I turn to Augustine's rebuttal to the "dainty sip" charge. We will see that Augustine's position cuts somewhat across Catholic/Reformation divisions, and from the treatise in conjunction with the Scriptures I draw some guidelines for liturgical theology and practice that I consider needful and relevant to both Catholics and Protestants. I close with reflections concerning the import of Augustine's treatise for specific liturgical clashes between Protestants and Catholics.[7]

---

7. In this chapter, I step into a half dozen academic fields for which I am inadequately prepared and in which I have been unable to find adequate guidance in secondary literature. There is at least an article, perhaps a book, to be written on each of the topics. I have found surprisingly little secondary literature on *Contra Faustum*. Far and away the most lucid recent discussion is found in Paula Fredriksen's *Augustine and the Jews: A Christian Defense of Jews and Judaism* (New York, NY: Doubleday, 2008), esp. 211-289. Jason David BeDuhn's multivolume *Augustine's Manichaean Dilemma* (Philadelphia, PA: University of Pennsylvania Press, 2010) will likely prove to be a stan-

I. Reformation "Judaizing"

With his quip about the dainty drinking habits of Catholics, Faustus hit on a sore spot in patristic orthodoxy. Though the church was undoubtedly right to honor the Old Testament as authoritative Scripture and simultaneously to refuse to observe its ceremonies, the resulting dance has not always been graceful. For many church fathers, heresy was nearly defined by failure to maintain the rhythm of this two-step. Some heretics, like Faustus and Marcion before him, renounced the Old Testament

---

dard account, but thus far he has not covered the treatise in any detail, though he does provide an illuminating summary of the life and thought of Faustus (ch. 4). Yet, I have found no concise comprehensiveness displayed in, for example, recent articles on *de Trinitate* from Rowan Williams, Lewis Ayres, Michel Rene Barnes, and others. We need a brief overview of the treatise, and it would not hurt to have a monograph on it. I have found nothing substantial on the Reformers' use of *Contra Faustum*, even though it plays a significant role in the work of many leading Reformers. (From the extensive but admittedly incomplete collection on the Alexander Street Press, "Digital Library of Classic Protestant Texts," Vermigli refers to the treatise fifty-five times, Chemnitz forty-two times, Bucer sixteen times, Calvin eleven. Johann Gerhard [1582-1637] makes one hundred and twelve references to *Contra Faustum*. In all, the collection lists over five hundred references to Augustine's treatise.) The most thorough study of "Judaizing" in the Reformation was published in 1925: Louis Israel Newman, *Jewish Influence on Christian Reform Movements* (New York, NY: Columbia University Press, 1925). For the intra-mural Protestant use of this rhetorical device, we now have G. Sujin Pak, *The Judaizing Calvin: Sixteenth-Century Debates over the Messianic Psalms* (Oxford: Oxford University Press, 2009).

entirely, but more commonly the fathers judged that heretics tipped in the other direction. "Arianism" has been called the "archetypal heresy," but Athanasius and others had a pre-existing label to attach to the Arians—that of Judaizer. Patristic genealogists of heresy nearly always start with Simon Magus or another Jewish figure from the New Testament.[8]

Today, such claims are viewed as boilerplate invective: Jews are vicious and bad, so calling heretics Jews creates a noxious cloud around Arians, Apollinarians, and even, strangely enough, Marcionites and Manicheans. Others today see patristic polemics against Judaizers as mechanisms for Christian self-definition or as part of a Christian struggle for market share.[9] I believe on the

---

8. Alison Salvesen finds a tilt toward "Hebraization" in Origen's and

Jerome's reliance on Jewish tools and Hebrew texts in their biblical work. See "A Convergence of the Ways? The Judaizing of Christian Scripture by Origen and Jerome," in Adam H. Becker and Annette Yoshiko Reeds, eds., *The Ways That Never Parted: Jews and Christians in Late Antiquity and the Early Middle Ages* (Minneapolis, MI: Fortress, 2007), 233-257.

9. See, e.g., Averil Cameron, "Jews and Heretics–A Category Error?" in Adam H. Becker and Annette Yoshiko Reed, eds., *The Ways that Never Parted*, 345-360; see Judith Lieu, *Neither Jew Nor Greek? Constructing Early Christianity* (Edinburgh: T &T Clark, 2005); Lieu, *Image and Reality: The Jews in the World of Christians in the Second Century* (Edinburgh: T & T Clark, 2003).

contrary that the church fathers had substantive doctrinal reasons for using this label.

Paul used the word ιουδαιζειν (Gal 2:14) to describe Gentiles who, under pressure from Jewish believers, adopt Jewish customs: Why, Paul asked in exasperation, do you who are free from the Torah force Gentiles to judaize? For Paul, "judaizing" violated the gospel because it practically undermined the church's confession concerning the finality of Jesus' death and resurrection. Following Paul's lead, patristic authors leveled the charge of "judaizer" against Christians who keep Old Testament food laws, attend Jewish feasts and fasts, frequent the synagogue, or literally become Jews by circumcision. But during the early centuries the term took on wider connotations. In some texts, a "judaizer" is a Christian who has done no more than give aid and comfort to Jews. More substantively, Arians were "judaizers" because they denied the divinity of the Son, as first-century Jews had done before them. On the assumption that the Jews interpreted Scripture literally, Christian literalism was denounced as "judaizing."[10]

---

10. See Shaye J. D. Cohen, *The Beginnings of Jewishness: Boundaries, Varieties, Uncertainties* (Berkeley, CA: University of California Press, 1999), 175-197; Robert L. Wilken, *John Chrysostom and the Jews: Rhetoric and Reality in the Late Fourth Century* (Berkeley, CA: University of California Press, 1983). On Cyril of Alexandria's attempt to keep the rhythm of the two-step, see Robert L. Wilken, *Judaism and the Early Christian Mind: A Study of Cyril of Alexandria's Exegesis and Theology* (Eugene, OR: Wipf & Stock, [1971] 2004), esp. chs.

How far this instinct to sniff out Galatianism in every heresy persisted through the Middle Ages is a topic that demands more attention. Jewish and judaizing influences are detectable in Catharism, among the Waldensians, and among the Passagii in twelfth-century Lombardy.[11] Jan Hus was denounced as a judaizer, and the early Reformers, influenced by the Humanist drive *ad fontes*, earned the moniker by studying Hebrew, Jewish commentaries, and the Kabbalah.

When the Reformers condemned their Roman Catholic opponents as judaizers, they added a new dimension to the term. In his treatise on "The Necessity of Reforming the Church," Calvin describes Catholicism as a *novus iudaismus* because, though Catholics rightly discontinued Jewish ceremonies "which God had distinctly abrogated," they did so only to replace them with "numerous puerile extravagances, collected from different

---

3-4. Wilken concludes that, in the end, Cyril leans to the side of discontinuity.

11. See Newman, *Jewish Influence*, Parts I-II. Intriguingly, Camilla Adang explores the "Judaizing" tendencies in medieval Islam in "Ibn Hazm's Criticism of some 'Judaizing' Tendencies among the Malikites," in Ronald Nettler, ed., *Medieval and Modern Perspectives on Muslim-Jewish Relations* (Oxford: Harwood Academic Publishers, 1995). See the paragraph on "Judaizing" heresies in medieval Spain in Norman Roth, ed., *Medieval Jewish Civilization: An Encyclopedia* (New York, NY: Taylor & Francis Books, 2003), 199. The author comments that "the subject deserves a complete investigation."

quarters." According to Calvin, there were many abuses in Catholic ceremonies, the first being that "an immense number of ceremonies, which God had by his authority abrogated, once for all, have been revived again." In the background is Augustine's repeated claim (in *Contra Faustum* and elsewhere) that the rites of the New Testament are fewer, simpler, and clearer than the rites of the Old, a thesis that leads Calvin to conclude that any proliferation of rites is, almost by definition, a reversion to the Old order. He cites Paul's claim in Galatians 4 that the elementary principles of the world were "weak and beggarly" and warns that the turn to "abstinences, vigils, and other things" shows a preference of "shadow" over the "substance," which is Christ. Alongside these complaints, Calvin also charges that the forms of worship in the Catholic church are treated perfunctorily, so that "they think they have fulfilled their duty as admirably as if these ceremonies included in them the whole essence of piety and divine worship." The dislodging of externals from the inner state of the soul is the "most deadly evil of all."[12]

---

12. Calvin, "Necessity of Reforming the Church." Calvin makes the same argument in his reply to Sadoleto. Catholics have "more than enough" ceremonies, but they are childish, superstition, and have little power to preserve and sustain the church. The Reformers aimed "to restore the native purity from which they had degenerated, and so enable them to resume their dignity." Many ceremonies have been abolished, but Calvin almost seems apologetic about the extent of the purge: "We were compelled to do so." Ceremonies had filled the

For the Reformers, the central instance of Catholic "judaizing" was the belief that the Mass was a sacrificial rite, repeating (so Protestants understood) the slaying of Christ in a manner resembling the repeated burnt offerings of Israelite worship. In his 1548 *Treatise on the Sacrament of the Body and Blood of Christ*, Miles Coverdale points out the difference between the Old Testament figural ceremonies and the sacrificial meal of the church: "By the institution of Christ we are not commanded to offer a sacrifice, but to take and eat the thing that is already offered and sacrificed." In Catholic theology, Coverdale argues, what was unique to the death of Christ has been transferred to the Mass, which Catholics offer believing that it will "satisfy God for our offences, and that we might be reconciled by it." The Reformed Supper, by contrast, is compatible with the new covenant because it

---

minds of the laity with superstition, and these "could not possibly remain without doing the greatest injury to the piety which it was their office to promote." But the purgation was also needed because the complexity of the Catholic church's liturgical life "had degenerated into a kind of Judaism." Calvin's assault was not on ceremonies per se, which he considered not only divinely instituted but also necessary to communal religious life, but for pastoral reasons, the Reformers believed they could retain only "those which seemed sufficient for the circumstances of the times." Calvin was not alone in these sorts of arguments. In his letter to Emperor Charles on the "*fidei ratio*," Zwingli condemns as "Judaism" "*variis unctionibus, ungentis, oblatiibus, victimis, ac epulis.*"

brings "no new sacrifice" but is "the application of that only sacrifice whereof I have spoken."

Thomas Becon's condemnation of the Mass as a Judaizing rite is more sharply worded. After pointing out that bloody sacrifices have ended with Jesus' death, he addresses Catholics directly: "Ye, whose desire always is to come as near unto Christ, or unto his holy ordinance, as the hare covet to come nigh unto a tabret, refuse Christ's order, and despise the table, spitefully calling it an oysterboard; and, like heathenish and Jewish priests, ye build altars, and upon them ye offer your vile and stinking sacrifice, not unto God, but unto the devil, and unto antichrist."[13] For Becon, it is not just the repeated sacrifice of the Mass that hearkens back to the Old Testament rites, but all the superfluous accoutrements of the Mass as well. Where do Catholic priests get "your game-players' garments"? he wonders. If from pagans, then Christians should have "nothing to do" with them. If from the Jews, then "that law is abrogated by Christ's

---

13. *The Displaying of the Popish Mass* (1559). A few lines later, Becon added that "All bloody sacrifices for sin cease now in the new testament, for the which altars served: therefore Christ ministered unto his disciples the sacrament of his body and blood not at an altar, but at a table. But you, although all bloody sacrifices for sin were not yet gone, have still your altars, and offer sacrifice upon them, as the heathenish and Jewish priests did. They killed and sacrificed brute beasts upon their altars; and you take upon you to sacrifice the Son of God, and to make him meat, when it pleaseth you."

coming, of whose virtues the garments of the priests were figures and signs."[14]

In an extended dialogue between Protestant John Rainolds and Catholic John Hart,[15] Rainolds broadens the point to emphasize the relocation of the sacred following the death and resurrection of Christ. Christians have no altars, no bloody sacrifices, no holy or unholy land: "Every coast is Jewry, and every town Jerusalem, and every house Zion, and every faithful company, yea, every faithful body a temple." Priests of Israel burned incense in the temple, while Christians pray without incense everywhere. Rainolds expects that his Catholic opponent will not grasp his point, since "your Popish worship is so like the Jewish." Citing 2 Corinthians 3, Rainolds asserts that Popery amounts to a "vail" that has "brought in a Jewish

---

14. Becon tells the story of a Jew who refused to convert to Christianity because he found Christian worship too frivolous and merry, and complained that it was idolatry to fall down and worship a piece of bread and a silver cup." Specifically, the Jew abhorred the fact that the priest "that stood at the altar in the gay coat, did both eat and drink all alone, giving you no part with him," a practice that to the Jew reflected a lack of charity. Intriguingly, Becon appeals to Jewish rituals to support his claim that Christians should sit, rather than kneel "as the papists do" at the table.

15. *The Sum of the Conference Between John Rainolds and John Hart* (1598).

kind of worship" that hides the truth of Christ from the eyes of Catholics.[16]

Catholics did not take the charge lightly, and answered strenuously. Hart objects to Rainolds' characterization of Catholic practice, quoting Innocent III's insistence that "the sacrament of unction (or anointing) doth figure and work an other thing in the new testament then it did in the old" and Innocent's sharp conclusion that therefore "they lie who charge the church with Judaizing . . . in that it celebrateth the sacrament of unction." Some Catholics acknowledged the continuity of Jewish and Catholic worship, but simultaneously denied they were reverting to the old covenant. In his *Rejoinder to M. Jewels Reply Against the Sacrifice of the Mass* (1567), Catholic Thomas Harding claimed that the Sabbath, Pascha, Pentecost, Sacerdos, Altare, Sacrificium all admit of two uses, old and new, legal and evangelical. He agrees that Old Jewish observances expired with Christ, because Christ Himself died with the *Consummatum est* on his lips. Still, "faithful Christians now keep, use, and cele-

---

16. Coverdale agreed: "Since that Christ appeared in the flesh, look, by how much more the doctrine is lightened, so much are the figures diminished. Seeing therefore we have the body, we must leave the shadows. For if we will replenish the abolished ceremonies, we shall patch again that veil that Christ brake in sunder by his death; and so shall we obscure and darken the light of the gospel. Thus do we perceive, that this multitude of ceremonies which is seen in the mass, is the form of the Jewish law, utterly contrary to the Christian religion."

brate their Sabboth, that is to say, their restingtide, their Parasceve, or preparingtide, commonly called Goodfriday, their Pascha, or Easter, their Pentecost, or Whitsontide, their Priesthod, their Aulter, their Sacrifice, in suche manner, order, sense, and meaning, as the new state and condition of the Church succeding the Jewish Synagoge, requireth: that is, not according to the figure, shadow, letter, or signification, but according to the truth, the body, the spirite, and the very things." As we will see below, Hart's paradigm for dealing with the old and new is quite close to Augustine's views as expressed in *Contra Faustum*.

Catholic William Rainolds, brother of the Protestant John Rainolds mentioned earlier, turns the tables and accuses the Reformers of judaizing. In *A Treatise Containing the True Catholic and Apostolic Faith of the Holy Sacrifice and Sacrament* (1593), Rainolds assesses the Calvinist doctrine of the Supper in light of the standard scholastic distinction between the sacraments of the Old Law that represent grace and the sacraments of the New Law that cause and confer grace: "The Calvinian communion is particularly conferred with a like ceremony used of old among the Jews: and against Calvin and Beza it is by plaine demonstration out of their owne doctrine and writings proved, that their supper is nothing better then a mere graceless Jewish supper or ceremony." Indeed, "the Sacrament after Calvin's doctrine is much inferior to the like Sacrament (either the Paschal supper, and especially

Manna) of the Jews." Thus, "both their Sacraments (baptisme and the supper) . . . appertaine rather to the law of Moses, than to the gospel of Christ." Calvin appealed to 1 Corinthians 10 in his rejection of the scholastic view that there is a "great difference between the sacraments of the old and new law, as though they figured only the grace of God, and these gave it presently," but Rainolds dismisses the argument. Calvinists who follow Calvin are in the way of eternal damnation "for this particular blasphemous heresy of matching the base Jewish ceremonies with Christ's most heavenly and divine Sacraments."

Reformers shortly turned on each other, and when they did charges of judaizing flew back and forth intramurally. For the Lutheran Aegidius Hunnius, Calvin's "literal," non-Messianic treatment of the Psalms smacked of judaizing.[17] Not to be outdone, Catholics charged one another with judaizing too. Ambrosius Catharinus Politi accused Cajetan of judaizing when the latter denied that Elohim refers to the Trinity.[18]

The charge of "judaizing" complicates our understanding of the Reformation in various ways. It suggests

---

17. See Pak, *Judaizing Calvin.*

18. See Magna Saebo, *Hebrew Bible/Old Testament: The History of Its Interpretation* (Göttingen, Germany: Candenhoeck & Ruprecht, 2008), 623; Donald McKim, *Dictionary of Major Biblical Interpreters* (Downers Grove, IL: InterVarsity Press, 2007), 286. Thanks to my colleague Ben Merkle for this reference.

the possibility that the visceral Protestant responses to Catholic "abominations" were overlayered with an equally visceral anti-Semitism. It also indicates that the Reformation was a battle over Christian practice as much as it was over formulations concerning grace, works, and justification. For most Christians of the sixteenth century, the most evident effect of the Reformation was liturgical, and the Reformers aimed to convince their congregations that the changes represented an evangelical purgation of judaizing corruptions.

Augustine's treatise was directly implicated in these debates. Calvin draws on *Contra Faustum* at a number of key points in his discussion of sacrments. From Augustine he takes the notion that a sacrament is a sort of visible word (*Contra Faustum*, 19),[19] and his discussion of the differences between the sacraments of the Old and New employs material from Augustine's treatise as well (from books 6, 9, 12). More generally, Calvin cited the anti-Manichean writings of Augustine more than twice as often as his anti-Donatist writings (ninety-six to forty-six), and he used *Contra Faustum* especially "a course de

---

19. It seems that for the most part the Reformers used Augustine's *visibilia verba* in a sense different from Augustine himself. As noted below, Augustine introduces the phrase in a discussion of the changing rites from Old to New Covenant, comparing the change of rites to the conjugation of a verb. The Reformers emphasized the parallel between the sacrament and Word, and highlighted the visibility of sacraments.

la question de l'eucharistie."[20] Other Reformers also cited the treatise regularly, and, on the other hand, a search of a database of Catholic Reformation texts produced over a thousand occurrences. And so we come to Augustine.

II. Contra Faustum[21]

As is well known from *Confessions*, Faustus played a crucial role in Augustine's formation. As a young Manichean Auditor and devotee of astrology, Augustine puzzled over philosophical and quasi-scientific conundrums that he wanted to pose to a Manichean master. When Bishop Faustus visited Carthage, Augustine found him affable, humble, charming, but unable or unwilling to give an opinion on speculative or dogmatic questions. Faustus' combination of Manicheanism and Academic skepticism, the latter learned from his reading of Cicero, gave his mind a decidedly practical orientation that allowed him to answer Augustine's questions with a cheerful, nonplussed "I don't know."[22] Faustus was not the kind of

---

20. Luchesius Smits, *Saint Augustine dans l'oeuvre de Jean Calvin* (Assen: Van Gorcum, 1956), 155-156, 181.

21. I rely throughout on the translation by Roland Teske, *Answer to Faustus, A Manichean*, The Works of Saint Augustine: a Translation for the 21st Century (Hyde Park: New City Press, 2007). I have consulted the Latin edition available at http://www.augustinus.it/latino/contro_fausto.

22. BeDuhn (*Augustine's Manichaean Dilemma*, 112-113, 125-126) emphasizes the philosophical "subtext" of Faustus' tolerant liberal

guide Augustine was looking for. He maintained contact with Faustus perhaps until he left Carthage for Rome, but he eventually abandoned the Manichees and found a more intellectually satisfying mentor in Ambrose.[23]

Faustus' version of Manicheanism was indebted to the earlier work of Adimantus or Adda, who adapted the Manichee system to Western categories, employed skeptical arguments to deflate dogmatic certainty, and appropriated "Marcionite Christian critiques of the Old Testament."[24] The last aspect of Faustus' thought is at the center of Augustine's concern. Faustus' *Capitula*, to which Augustine responds, was a series of apologetic "talking points" for Manicheans to use against Catholics. Each chapter begins with a question posed by Catholics to Manicheans, followed by Faustus' response. Displaying the rhetoric skill and wit for which Augustine admired him, Faustus goes about his business cleverly; he cites no Manichean texts and skirts specific Manichean beliefs and gives attention exclusively to Catholic Scriptures. When Augustine points to New Testament evidence that contradicts Faustus—Paul's claim that Jesus was born a

---

Manicheanism.

23. BeDuhn carefully reviews the mostly implicit evidence of a deeper relationship with Faustus (*Augustine's Manichaean Dilemma*, 131-134).

24. BeDuhn, *Augustine's Manichaean Dilemma*, 111.

son of David according to the flesh, or the genealogy that begins Matthew's gospel—Faustus seeks refuge in text criticism: Matthew the disciple did not write the first gospel, and therefore his testimony is not authoritative, and since Paul elsewhere claims that Jesus was from God, and since Paul cannot contradict himself, Romans 1:4 must be from someone other than Paul.

Nearly half of the sections of Faustus' treatise deal with the question of the relation of Old and New Testaments. For Faustus, Israel's prophets never spoke of Christ, the God of the Jews is a demon, and the fact that the Jews used Moses to condemn Jesus shows that Moses and Jesus are radically at odds. Insofar as the Old Testament is concerned with flesh, it reflects not a predecessor to the Christian faith but a rival: "the *Capitula* called into question the very concept of orthodoxy's double canon."[25]

Faustus' critique of the Catholic endorsement of the Old Testament hit home with particular power because, as Paula Fredriksen has brilliantly detailed, the *contra Iudaeos* tradition in the church shared an uncomfortable degree of common group with Manicheans and Marcionites. Faustus condemns the literalism of the Jews; so do Catholic writers. Faustus abhors animal sacrifice; Catholic writers regularly express the same repugnance, and some interpreted the destruction of Jerusalem's tem-

---

25. Fredriksen, *Augustine and the Jews*, 214.

ple in AD 70 as a demonstration that God never wanted the Jews to perform sacrifice in the first place.[26] Faustus' attacks are directed not only at the Old Testament but also at Catholic Christians, whom he considers lukewarm judaizers—judaizers because they continue to affirm the authority of the Old Testament and return to the weak and beggarly elemental things from which Christ sets us free (Book 8), lukewarm because they refuse to practice the rites that the Old Testament requires. Catholics are mixed vessels, adding vinegar to the honey, water to the wine, fish sauce to the vinegar (*melli fel, et aquam vino, et aceto garos*, Book 15). Vessels should be filled with a single uniform substance, and Faustus calls Catholics to abandon their adulterated faith (Book 15).[27] Better to give up the Old Testament entirely, Faustus insists. Old Testament promises, after all, are offered to the circumcised, and since the church no longer practices circumcision, they are not heirs to those promises. No follower of Jesus cares to inherit Jewish promises anyway, since they are "miserable and bodily" (*misera . . . et corporalis*) and distant from the soul (*longe ab animae commodis*; *Contra Faustum*, 4). Not only the inheritance of the Jews, but their practices are shameful and needless (*supervacua*), if not idolatrous. Manicheans laugh at Jewish festivals, their

---

26. Fredriksen, *Augustine and the Jews*, 223-234.

27. Given his line of argument, it is ironic that Faustus implicitly invokes biblical prohibitions on forbidden mixtures.

forbidden mixtures, their absurd rules against shaving. So do Catholics, and the only difference is that Catholics "choose to lie and to act like a slave by praising in words what you hate in your mind" (Book 6).

Behind this assault is Faustus' conviction that practice rather than belief or profession is the heart of religious life.[28] "You ask if I believe the Old Testament," he writes. "Of course not, for I do not keep its precepts" (*Contra Faustum*, 6.1). Do I believe the gospel? he asks in another place, and answers "You ask me if I believe it, though my obedience to its commands shows that I do." He turns the question back to the Catholic interlocutor: "I should rather ask you if you believe it, since you give no proof of your belief" (*Contra Faustum*, 5.1). Catholics counter by citing Jesus' statement that he came to fulfill, not abolish the Law. Faustus acknowledges that Jesus spoke the words of Matthew 5, but questions which law he meant. There are three laws: the law of sin and death, the law of the Gentiles, and the law of truth. Likewise, there are three types of prophets: Jews had prophets, but there were prophets among the Gentiles and there were

---

28. Though Manicheanism is often characterized as an intellectualist form of Gnosticism, BeDuhn has argued persuasively that participation in bodily disciplines and rituals are what make a Manichean a Manichean. See BeDuhn, *The Manichaean Body: In Discipline and Ritual* (Baltimore, MD: Johns Hopkins, 2000). BeDuhn emphasizes the practical orientation of Faustus in particular throughout his chapter in *Augustine's Manichaean Dilemma* (ch. 4).

also prophets of the truth, who preceded the Jews. When Jesus defended the law, he was not speaking of the Jewish law, but the older law. Jesus' commandments fulfill *that* law. As for Jewish law, it is eradicated, and Faustus cannot resist finishing this line of argument with a repetition of his favorite *tu quoque*: By their actions, Catholics show that they too believe Jesus abolished Jewish law (Book 19). In practice, which is the only thing that matters, there is no difference between "fulfill" and "destroy."

Though Augustine had the arsenal of the *contra Iudaeos* tradition at hand, he had become dissatisfied with it. After his debate with Fortunatus the Manichean, Augustine embarked on a deep study of Paul and Genesis and came to recognize the weaknesses of this tradition, whose arguments were neither faithful to the biblical text nor convincing responses to heretics. We can see the difficulty in his initial rebuttal to Faustus' attack on the Old Testament. In Book 4, Augustine responds by drawing a distinction between the Old Testament promises, which concern temporal things (*temporalium . . . rerum promissiones*) and the promises of the New, which have to do with eternal life in the kingdom of heaven (*aeternae vitae promissio regnumque coelorum*). This initial "spiritualizing" hermeneutic plays into the Manichean hands: If Catholics are seeking spiritual religion, why cling to the fleshly Old Testament canon? Why not become purely spiritual and join the Manichees?

Augustine's distinction of temporal and eternal promises is somewhat stronger than this, since it is homologous with his distinction of time and eternity. Though the promises of the Old were temporal and the New eternal, the temporal promises were figures of the future eternal promises (*in illis temporalibus figuras fuisse futurorum, quae implerentur in nobis*), a point Augustine supports by appeal to Paul's claim in 1 Corinthians 10:11 that the exodus account was written "for our instruction, on whom the ends of the ages have come." Christians do not seek to understand the Old Testament in order to acquire what the Old Testament promises, but rather study the temporal figures in order to understand what the New Testament grants. Citing Jesus' appearance to the two disciples on the road to Emmaus, who recognized the Lord only in Word and in the breaking of bread, Augustine points out that carnal senses can be deceived and their dullness needs to be enlivened by the witness of Israel's Scriptures. By introducing the category of "testimony," Augustine underscores the continuing usefulness of the Old Testament. It is not an antiquated figure but a witness to the church in the *present*.[29]

---

29. See Kari Kloos, "History as Witness: Augustine's Interpretation of the History of Israel in *Contra Faustum* and *De trinitate*," in Christopher T. Daly, et. al, eds., *Augustine and History* (Lanham, MD: Lexington Books, 2008), 31-51.

As the treatise progresses, Augustine's responses become more penetrating. After Old Testament promises, he takes up the question of Old Testament commandments. All authority is practical authority, Faustus assumes, and he asks, How can Catholics affirm the authority of the texts but refuse to practice Jewish rites? Augustine's response relies on a Christological hermeneutical framework. Scripture as a whole speaks of Christ, a point he elaborates with a thrilling florilegium of types and shadows (Book 12). That Christocentric principle applies as much to the commands of the Old Testament as to the promises and narratives. Israel receives the Law to enact a living parable of the coming Messiah.[30]

In developing this point, Augustine introduces a new distinction between precepts that regulate life and precepts that signify life (*inter praecepta vitae agendae, et praecepta vitae significandae*). "Do not covet" regulates life, "circumcise on the eighth day" symbolizes life. Along with circumcision, the Sabbath, sacrificial rites, and prohibitions of unclean meats also symbolize life. Though Christians no longer observe these rites, they were suitable in their time *as commands* (*quae utique illi*

---

30. In this first foray into this question, Augustine ends by turning the Judaizing charge back on Faustus. He does not understand because he does not believe, and he does not believe because he refuses to learn from the church. Clinging only to the promises of the New, without recognizing that they are fulfillments of the figurative promises of the Old, leaves him still in the Old.

tempori congruebant, *Contra Faustum*, 6).[31] This distinction overlaps the earlier distinction between earthly, temporal figures and later, eternal realities. Commandments
that symbolize life are figural shadows of the future (*um-
bram futuroum*), but the commands that regulate life are
permanent.

Yet the symbolic regulations do not simply pass
away. Instead, they give way to the realities of Christian
experience. Christians no longer circumcise, but through
the power of Jesus' resurrection, Christians strip off the
flesh of passion and thus experience the circumcision of
the heart figured by Jewish circumcision. Christians do
not keep Sabbath, but they have a present hope of eternal
rest, and so reading about and understanding the figural
Sabbath enables Christians to grasp the significance of the
rest they even now enjoy in Christ. Though now useless to
observe literally, the Sabbath rules are "not useless to read
about or understand." Israel's sacrifices were not, as Faustus contends, idolatrous, but foreshadowed the church's
memorial celebration of the one sacrifice symbolized by
the multiple and varied sacrifices of the temple (*quia et
ipsa figurae nostrae fuerunt, et omnia talia multis et variis
modis unum sacrificium, cuius nunc memoriam celebramus,*

---

31. Circumcision of the foreskin was doubly appropriate, since the
sign of regeneration is rightly placed on the organ of generation and
because concupiscence is concentrated in sexual organs.

significaverunt). All of these remain "in the authority of their meaning," even if the practices ceased. In all these examples, Augustine's argument moves from practice in the old to understanding in the new, from Israel's practice to the church's meaning, from doing to reading. And this is a movement from body to spirit: Christians are not to observe *corporaliter*, but to understand and do *spiritualiter* (6.9.1).

Christian study of the symbolic laws does not involve Judaizing, but is instead a witness to Christian freedom. While Jews and literal Judaizers read about circumcision in a "superstitious" way, Christians read, understand, and practice them in a "religious" manner (Book 8). Without acknowledging its roots in Israel's life, Christian freedom lacks definition and specificity. We need to know the contours of Jewish "bondage" before we can understand the trajectory of Christian freedom.

When he turns to the typology of unclean foods, Augustine introduces a linguistic analogy that lays a foundation for the later arguments. Paul's claim that all things are clean (1 Tim 4:4) does not contradict the Old Testament, since Paul is talking about the nature of things and not about what they signified in the old economy. Unclean meats, like Sabbath and circumcision, provided "certain prophetic signs suited to that time." What was unclean was not the animal itself, but the thing signified by the animal—not the pig but porcine human behavior. In speech, Augustine points out, the words "fool" and "sage" are both "clean" with regard to their "nature"—the sound is not polluted, nor the visual signifier on the page. What the words signify, however, is different. "Fool" is "unclean" because of the unclean person that it signifies. Similarly, the words "pig" and "lamb" are both clean in nature, but signify an unclean and a clean animal respectively. In the case of unclean meats, signification is doubled. The *word* "pig" refers to an animal, but that animal is in turn a *signum* of a human *res*. With the doubling of signification, the uncleanness is put off to a second remove. Not just the word "pig" but the animal itself is "naturally" pure and good, being a creation of the Holy God. In its prophetic significance, however, the animal is a quasi-linguistic signifier of a certain kind of human.

Relying on Leviticus 11, Augustine notes the specific features of the pig that make it an unclean animal: It divides the hoof but it does not ruminate. These features of piggishness are not defects in a pig, since it is in the nature of pigs to divide the hoof but not ruminate. The absence of rumination signifies a human defect. Some hear the words of God, but store them away and never bring them up again "from the stomach of thought" so they can ruminate on them *spiritualiter*. The prohibition of pork thus served a useful purpose, and learning about this prohibition remains useful, insofar as it warns us "to avoid such a defect" and encourages us to ruminate again and again on the nourishing word of God.[32] If one is looking for a *res* corresponding to the *signum*, one need look no further than Faustus: Manicheans are among the pigs, for they do not ruminate on Scripture and they do not "divide the hoof" by acknowledging two testaments (Book 16).

From this complex analogy, it becomes clear that for Augustine "spiritual" observance is not simply mental or incorporeal observance, not *merely* a matter of reading and understanding. The rules of unclean meats inculcate forms of responsiveness proper to the word of God. Augustine extends the same pattern of reflection to other institutions of the Old order. Unleavened bread was a shadow of the future, and Christians are no longer bound to expunge leaven for a week after Passover. Since the final Passover has been sacrificed, however, we are to continuously expel the leaven of malice and wickedness. It is no longer a sin to refrain from participating in the feast of tabernacles, as once it was, but it *is* a sin not to be part of the tabernacle of God, *quod est Ecclesia*. It is no longer a sin to wear clothing of mixed fabric, but it *is* sinful to "live in a disordered way and to want to con-

---

32. The realities of Christian living had to be foretold in action as well as word. Once the reality is revealed, the burden of observance is lifted, but the authority of the prophetic meaning is commended to the church (*onera observationum non sunt imposita, prophetiae tamen auctoritas commendata*; Book 6).

fuse distinct vocations in life."[33] We can plow with an ox and an ass yoked together if we like; it makes for uneven furrows, but there is no sin. But we are prohibited from mixing folly and wisdom. Christian study of Old Testament practices nurtures New Testament practice. In fact, Christians not only study and understand but *practice* even the symbolic regulations of the law, though not in the same form as Israel did.

Augustine perfects earlier responses to gnostic Marcionism in another way as well. He shifts from a purely spiritualizing hermeneutic to a "typological" approach in which the gap between promise and fulfillment is temporal, not ontological. This implies that Israel's form of life foreshadows the church's. At least some of the Jews understood that their corporal actions and rites were prophetic of something better, but, even more importantly, Augustine suggests that even those who failed to grasp the ultimate intention of the rites were engaged in prophetic performance. Israel as a whole was prophetic, and became so precisely by taking the Law literally and performing it as God's commandment. In contrast to earlier Catholic writers, Augustine gives limited approval to Jewish literalism: God was not dissembling when He ordered sacrifice, instituted food laws, or delivered rules of purity from Si-

---

33. He illustrates with the examples of a nun who wears jewels and a married woman who dresses like a virgin (Book 6).

nai. He intended Israel to understand these laws *secundum litteram* and to obey them *secundum carnem*, with the goal that their bodily ritual performance would make Israel a *figura* of the good things to come. Israel plays its proper figural role only by being stubbornly literal.

We are beginning to see how Augustine can address Faustus' fundamental charge regarding the inconsistency of Christian practice. Augustine further clarifies his position in Book 19, the most-cited portion of *Contra Faustum* in the Reformation era and probably the most important section of the treatise throughout the church's history. The chapter deals with Jesus' claim that he has come to fulfill, not abolish, the law and the prophets. Augustine rightly sees that Faustus' conclusion that Jesus is not referring to Jewish law is special pleading that makes no contextual sense. But then the question is, What *does* it mean for Jesus to fulfill the law?

Jesus fulfills the law in two senses, which match the two sorts of precepts he identified earlier. With regard to the permanent precepts governing conduct, Jesus fulfills the law by giving us grace to do what the law demands. He fulfills the law *in us*, who constitute the body of the *totus Christus*. With regard to the symbolic regulations, Jesus fulfills the law by bringing in the reality that those observances figured. It is precisely *because* Jesus fulfilled the symbolic regulations that Christian do *not* practice them. Were Christians to observe these prophetic *signa futurorum,* they would betray in practice the fulfillment they announce in proclamation. The sheer non-practice of circumcision is a witness that the fulfillment of these regulations has occurred. Fulfillment does not rob these symbol laws of their continuing use, and in Book 19 Augustine emphasizes their *practical* use. Circumcision as practice does not dissolve into text, nor does Augustine moralize or spiritualize the symbolic regulations of the Old Covenant. Circumcision is fulfilled not only in the spiritual reality of heart circumcision but in a rite better than circumcision, a rite that announces the fulfillment of what circumcision figured in a shadowy way. Jesus' resurrection intervenes between Jewish circumcision and Christian initiation, and through his resurrection he enlivens the better sacrament of baptism. More generally, the Old figural and prophetic sacraments are fulfilled in new sacraments, *virtute maiora, utilitate meliora, actu faciliora, numero pauciora* (19.13). The church cannot exist without rites, any more than any society. For there is no religious society, Augustine insists, whether true or false, that does not need to be "coagulated" into a community by sacraments and signs.

A linguistic analogy again fills out the point. Augustine describes the sacraments as *visibilia verba,* but, against the Reformers' use of the phrase, his point is *not* to emphasize the visibility of the sacrament nor to draw an analogy between preaching and sacraments. Augustine introduces the phrase while comparing temporal and changeable sacred rites to the changing tenses of a verb. Two verb forms can refer to the same event. If the verb points to a future event, the verb is future: Baylor will make the Sweet Sixteen. If the event has happened, the verb is past: Baylor made the Sweet Sixteen. The reality is the same, but the form of the sign differs with the times. Just so, the event once promised by the linguistic signs *nasciturus, passurus, resurrecturus* is now announced as completed and fulfilled by the signifiers *natus sit, passus sit, resurrexerit*. Rites are verbal in *this* sense. Both Old and New sacraments refer to Christ in His atoning death and conquering resurrection, but they refer to Him differently—first as coming, now as come. Circumcision is a future-tense sign that promises a Christ to come; baptism, the present-tense rite of initiation, announces that He has come. Animal sacrifice figures a future Christ; Eucharist memorializes a final sacrifice. Rites are words because they morph to remain congruent with the times, as time moves from the time of promise to the time of fulfillment. Rites conjugate.[34]

To sum up: Faustus claimed that the Catholics belie their profession by their practice: They say the Old Tes-

---

34. I have developed this analogy at more length in "Conjugating the Rites: Old and New in Augustine's Theory of Signs," *Calvin Theological Journal* 34:1 (1999), 136-147 [published in this book as Chapter Three].

tament is Scripture, but do not practice it. Augustine's final answer is that Christians announce the fulfillment of the symbolic ordinances of the Old Covenant precisely by their non-observance of rites once commanded, and that Christian sacraments *are* the rites of the old law in fulfilled form. What unites these two responses is the conviction that, in Christ and His Body, Israel's future-tense is conjugated into the joyous perfect tense of the gospel.

IV. Rites of the Present Tense

We can see why both Catholic and Protestant might find aspects of Augustine congenial. Protestants frequently cited Augustine's formula about "fewer" and "easier" sacraments to build up their Judaizing charge against Catholics. By multiplying rites, the medieval church inverted the conjugation, flattening the times and implicitly reverting to a promissory liturgical future tense instead of practicing the rites of the declaratory present or perfect tense. On the other side, Catholics pounced on the spiritualizing drift of Protestantism, the tendency to minimize the importance of sacramental rites and signs or abolish them altogether. Instead of recognizing that the church practices physical sacraments more powerful than the sacraments of the old, as Augustine teaches, Protestants seemed to treat the sacraments as empty signs of spiritual realities that are present in some inaccessibly a-semiotic zone. Protestants were not conjugating rites, but changing the language of religious practice altogeth-er.[35] Insofar as Protestants leveled out the efficacy of Old and New, moreover, Catholics claimed that they were guilty of a form of Judaizing, attributing only a "Jewish" degree of efficacy to the rites of the church whose *virtus maior* should be celebrated.[36]

Who has the better of the argument? Who can truly say of Augustine *totus noster est*? In Augustine's terms, the trick is to conjugate the rite rightly. To do this, we have to go beyond Augustine, above Augustine, to the New Testament. The question is, What is the grammar of rit-ual conjugation? Why, for instance, is baptism a suitable present tense of a verb whose future tense was circumci-sion? How does the Eucharist announce the fulfillment of what the Old Covenant sacrifices promised? To answer these questions in detail would require a large book or a

---

35. This tendency is most prominent in Zwingli and the Anabap-tist movements influenced by him. See Carlos Eire, *War Against the Idols: The Reformation of Worship from Erasmus to Calvin* (Cambridge: Cambridge University Press, 1989). In this regard, Luther was vigor-ously opposed to Zwingli as any Catholic. See Jaroslav Pelikan, *Spirit versus Structure: Luther and the Institutions of the Church* (London: Collins, 1968).

36. Thomas's liturgical theology was in profound continuity with Augustine's. See Matthew Levering, *Christ's Fulfillment of Torah and Temple: Salvation According to Thomas Aquinas* (Notre Dame, IN: University of Notre Dame Press, 2002), ch. 5.

library of books, but I can sketch some general contours of this grammar.

Israel's rites were rites of exclusion. All the rituals of Torah revealed at Sinai were connected to the construction of the tabernacle and the presence of Israel's Holy God in the holy place in their midst. Given the rift between the Holy God and the unholy people, the house had to be hedged in by multiple protections. Purity rules kept unclean Hebrews at a safe distance, and required ablutions for them to approach. No matter how clean she became, Israel could come only so close. Even the priests were normally excluded from Yahweh's throne room, the Most Holy Place. Israel maintained contact with her God, but only through the mediation of animals transformed to smoke. As Michel Detienne has pointed out regarding Greek sacrifice, sacrifice was both a rite of communication and a reminder of the distance still to be traversed between the worshiper and his God. With the coming of Christ, that system of exclusion was dismantled. Jesus' death tore the veil, and instead of a temple that keeps people at a distance, we have in the New Testament a human temple made up of human temples in each of which God dwells by the sanctifying glory of His Spirit. The grammar that guides the conjugation of rites thus moves from exclusion promising future entry to present welcome, from a closed to an open door.

Though the Reformers never quite put their liturgical complaints against the Roman church in these terms, this captures the logic of Protestant protest, which, as we have seen, often took the form of accusations of "Judaizing." What was at stake was not merely the multiplication of rites but the ungrammatical Catholic conjugation of the future-tense rites into the present-tense sacraments. I will briefly highlight three areas where I think the Reformers accurately caught more than a whiff of Judaizing, or, at least, recognized the bad grammar of Catholic practice.

First, the sacred. Charles Taylor has recently expounded on the place of the Reformation in the formation of our secular age, and concentrates much of his attention on the Reformation denial of the sacred.[37] Taylor, I think, misstates the Reformation's aims and its effects in this regard.[38] The Reformers did not reject the category of "sacred" any more than they rejected the notion of "sacrament" or the practice of rites. Rather, they revised the ordering of the sacred that they discovered in medieval Catholicism and medieval culture generally. Holiness,

---

37. *A Secular Age* (Cambridge, MA: Belknap, 2007), 77-80. Taylor speaks of Reformation "disenchantment."

38. I agree with Ulinka Rublack, who argues that Protestants did not draw "clear and tight boundaries between 'religion' and 'magic,'" but instead "redefined the meaning of these terms, just as they redefined what was 'proper' ritual, rather than doing away with it" (*Reformation Europe* [Cambridge: Cambridge University Press, 2005], 156).

they insisted, no longer resides in objects or places. To treat the sacred in this way amounted to a reversion to an Old order of exclusion. Holiness is located in persons, and, most importantly, not merely in the ordained but in every member of the body of Christ. We are all "clerics"—that was Luther's original battle cry, as foundational to the Reformation as the *solas*. The Protestant mobs that removed the rood screens, enacted carnivalesque parodies of Catholic ceremonies, and destroyed or decapitated images were not energized by fine distinctions about the ground of justification. They learned that the church had for centuries excluded them from what was rightly theirs, and they were agitated by a new vision for the configuration of Christian community, a configuration that recognized the sanctity, the sainthood, of all.[39] What is a

---

39. On the destruction of images, see Lee Palmer Wandel, *Voracious Idols & Violent Hands: Iconoclasm in Reformation Zurich, Strasbourg, and Basel* (Cambridge: Cambridge University Press, 1994). On Protestant use of ritual parody, see the essays collected in R. W. Scribner, *Popular Culture and Popular Movements in Reformation Germany* (London: The Hambledon Press, 1987), esp. ch. 5. "Priesthood of the faithful" is of course a Catholic teaching, but, given Catholic views of ordination, this eventually deflates the lay priesthood to a "metaphorical" or "symbolic" or "interior" priesthood. Despite his ringing affirmations of the single Priesthood of Christ and the "whole community's" share in that priesthood, the late Herbert McCabe eventually de-sacramentalizes the priesthood of the laity, arguing that it is defined instead by a "personal element" (*The New Creation* [1964; repr. London: Continuum, 2010], 140-146). Matthew Levering's summary of Thomas's teaching on baptismal character is sim-

medieval Catholic layman to think when he watches the priest disappear behind the screen? If he knows Exodus and Leviticus, he may well conclude that he is still in the age of exclusion.

Second, multiplication of ceremonies. As noted at the outset, this was central to Calvin's repeated charge that the Catholic church had instituted a "new Judaism." Calvin did not attack ceremonies as such, but complained (appealing to an Augustinian formula) that there were too many and that they were too complicated. It seems a petty complaint, but I believe it gets to the heart of Calvin's reforming program. Calvin's liturgical reform was governed by a biblical regulatory principle. Catholic rites are not based on "what God has commanded" but instead reflect a proud "licence of devising modes of worship." God determines how He is to be approached, and Calvin says He "rejects, condemns, abominates all fictitious worship," that is to say, all worship manufactured by human ingenuity. It is clear elsewhere in Calvin that this charge does not reflect a rigidly legalistic view of worship, but is rooted in the promises of God. By devoting themselves to rites and ceremonies that have not been established by God, the Catholic faithful, with the encouragement of the clergy, seek God in places He has not promised to be. In his satiric "Inventory of Relics," Calvin shoos the

ilar: "The universal priesthood of believers . . . represents a passive or receptive power" (*Christ's Fulfillment of Torah and Temple*, 198n80).

pious away from what he considers man-made rites and signs and directs them to the divinely instituted water, bread, wine, and word that God Himself has established as vehicles of His presence to His people. Here again, the Reformation is not a denial of the sacred but a relocation. Holiness is in the events of preaching, baptism, and Eucharist.

Finally, the exclusion of the laity from the cup. I am tempted to speak of the exclusion of the laity from the Eucharist. Medieval lay people received Eucharistic bread, and were required to do so at least annually, but most Masses performed during the high Middle Ages had nothing to do with the laity. I am aware of the arguments put forward by Eamon Duffey, John Bossy, and others, to the effect that the medieval laity experienced the Mass as a momentous event of profound mystery. I do not doubt it, but that is quite beside the point. It is beside the point, first, because whatever their experience, the laity were not experiencing the sacrament Jesus instituted—a sacramental *meal*. It is beside the point, second, because if the grammar of conjugating rites moves from exclusion to inclusion, then the medieval Mass was ungrammatical. Jesus opened the table to His disciples, *all* of them. Communion in both kinds, full participation in the Eucharistic meal, is now more common in the Catholic church, and for that I am heartened. Yet, the claim of the Catholic catechism that "for pastoral reasons" communion in bread alone "has been legitimately established as the most common form in the Latin rite" jars the ear like a mismatched subject and verb. The Catholic Mass remains in this important respect a future-tense ritual. At best, a Eucharist in one kind is a half-present sacrament: Unlike the priests of old, the Catholic priest drinks wine in God's presence, but the Mass replicates Israel's worship because priests and no others have this privilege.

These reflections are ecumenical perhaps only in the fact that I have a pox to toss toward Evangelicals as well as Catholics. If Catholics drift toward Judaizing, Evangelicals drift toward Manicheanism, and as a result much Evangelical worship is ungrammatical as well. According to Augustine, the rites of the Old system are transposed by Christ into *rites* of the New system. According to the New Testament, old rituals of exclusion are not resolved into non-ritual spirituality, but into rites of inclusion and welcome. Insofar as Evangelicalism minimizes sacraments in its liturgical life, insofar as it minimizes the ordered liturgical rites instituted by Christ, it has more in common with Faustus than with Augustine.[40] Evangelicals are rediscovering liturgical worship these days, and that heart-

---

40. According to Jason David BeDuhn, some early Protestant readers of *Contra Faustum* resonated with the Manichean's attacks on Catholic ritual (*Augustine's Manichean Dilemma,* 112). He refers to Albert Emil Bruckner's *Faustus von Mileve: Ein Beitrag Zur Geschichte Des Abendlandischen Manichaismus* (1901), but unfortunately does not cite any specific writers or texts.

ens me as well, but I trust I am not being a Puddleglum to wonder whether Evangelicals have learned the grammar of Augustinian and biblical ritual conjugation.

IV. Conclusion

The implicit message of this analysis has been that one of the keys for progress in ecumenical dialogue is fresh attention to the Old Testament roots of Christian practice. For instance: A Christian hears from Leviticus that Israel's priests were forbidden to drink wine in Yahweh's presence, but knows that he now is invited to drink Eucharistic wine at church. That double witness is proof that the old is gone, the new has come. If, as Faustus prefers, the Christian is ignorant of the earlier prohibition, his enjoyment of the present fulfillment would be impoverished. Without the witness of the Old, believers do know not what we do. Similarly, knowing that the church is a baptized community is not sufficient. Only by recognizing that the baptized church fulfills what was once circumcised Israel can we know and become the sort of religious society we are called to be. Without the ballast of the old rites, the liturgical life of the church threatens to drift away on the boundless seas of spiritualism. We cannot know what is new in the new without knowing the old. Without careful attention to the *difference* in tense between old and new, the church is in danger of reverting to structures of exclusion that betray the gospel. To put it in terms that will delight medievalists and scholastics, the key is to re-envigorate what was once known as the "Treatise on the Sacraments of the Old Law."

CHAPTER FIVE

OLD COVENANT AND NEW IN SACRAMENTAL THEOLOGY NEW AND OLD

"The beginning of the gospel of Jesus Christ, the Son of God.… John the Baptist appeared in the wilderness preaching a baptism of repentance for the forgiveness of sins" (Mark 1:1, 4). So, curiously, begins the Gospel of Mark. We expect John, the forerunner, announcing the imminent appearance of the King. An eschatological kerygma that begins with *baptism*, though, is peculiar.

But to whom?

Apparently not those to whom John preached, for they responded with sufficient enthusiasm to alarm King Herod and win John an undisputed reference in Josephus. What did they think they were doing? Why was a man baptizing in the wilderness "good news"?

In the quotation from Isaiah (vv. 2–3), Mark hints at the answer. Though Isaiah's prophecy of Israel's "new Exodus" from Babylon had been fulfilled, by the first century the Jews had relapsed into a kind of exile and impatiently awaited another deliverance. And now, here is John, clearing the pathway of return. That he appears with water could only heighten expectations:

> The afflicted and needy are seeking water,
>> but there is none.
>> And their tongue is parched with thirst;
> I, the Lord, will answer them Myself,
>> As the God of Israel I will not forsake them.
> I will open rivers on the bare heights,
>> And springs in the midst of the valleys;
> I will make the wilderness a pool of water,
>> And the dry land fountains of water.
> I will put the cedar in the wilderness,
>> The acacia, and the myrtle, and the olive tree;
> I will place the juniper in the desert,
>> Together with the box tree and cypress....
> For I will pour out water on the thirsty land
>> And streams on the dry ground;
> I will pour out My Spirit on your offspring,
>> And My blessing on your descendants;
> And they will spring up among the grass
>> Like poplars by streams of water.
> (Isa. 41:17–19; 44:3–4; cf. Ezek. 36:24–27, 30)

When John's water falls on the scorched clay of Israel, it can only be a matter of time before she again crosses the sea, before Eden is restored.

In this wider perspective, Mark's opening verses reflect assumptions about the Gospel shared by the entire New Testament. A gospel that begins in baptism is a *Jewish* gospel, arising within the particular history of Yahweh's dealings with Israel. Since it deals with the fortunes of a historical people, a gospel that begins in baptism refuses to be tucked safely into the mystical interstices of human life. It is a *material* gospel, public truth. A voice that proclaims baptism must reverberate with political overtones.[1] Such a gospel thus stakes a claim in the field of history and culture, but this is ground that modern secularism has claimed as its exclusive possession. A boundary dispute is inevitable.

Mark's opening verses can serve as a touchstone for competing accounts of Christianity. To avoid this touchstone, which is for many thinkers a scandal, a stone of stumbling, secularism has attempted, with great success and considerable cooperation from Christians, to evict

---

1. Current Jesus scholarship has emphasized the "political" dimensions of Jesus' ministry and preaching, e.g., N. T. Wright, *Jesus and the Victory of God*, Christian Origins and the Question of God, no. 2 (London: SPCK, 1996). Pauline specialists have also recently accentuated his Jewish setting and therefore the ecclesial dimensions of his theology. The foundational text here is Krister Stendahl, "The Apostle Paul and the Introspective Conscience of the West," *HTR* 5 (1963).

the gospel to different ground. Against Mark, modern philosophy, sociology, and theology imagine that Christianity is "internal" and "spiritual." Thus, for Nietzsche, Jesus' teaching was a flight from the real world of culture to the inner kingdom[2] while for Kant true piety was rational moralism.[3] The evolutionary schema for religious development posited by Comtean sociology of religion cannot encompass a gospel that begins with baptism, nor can much modern, especially Protestant theology. Heralding baptism is fundamentally different from heralding Schleiermacher's religion of feeling or an evangelical gospel that combines an affirmation of disputed doctrines with the inner experience of the new birth.

Also against Mark, many modern accounts of Christianity, including theological ones, accept some form of Marcion's sundering of Old and New. Modern Marcionism, like its ancient counterpart, conspires with a gnostic ambivalence to physical creation and sees Christianity as removing the husks of materialism in religion. Christianity is not merely a different religion but a different *kind* of religion from that of Israel.[4]

---

2. Friedrich Nietzsche, *The Antichrist*, trans. H.L. Mencken (Costa Mesa, CA: Noontide Press, 1988), 29.

3. Immanuel Kant, *Religion within the Limits of Reason Alone*, 2nd ed.; trans. Theodore M. Greene and Hoyt H. Hudson (LaSalle, IL: Open Court, 1960), *passim.*

4. See my "Marcionism, Postliberalism, and Social Christianity," *Pro*

Treacherously, each stumbling stone serves as foundation for the other: the Marcionite account of history supports the reading of Christianity as private inwardness, and the interpretation of Christianity as fundamentally concerned with inward piety sets it off from the materialism and socio-political concerns of Hebrew sensibility.

Among the "husks" of Old Testament religion supposedly discarded in the emergence of the spiritual "kernel," ritual has first place. Hebrew religion is to Christianity as empty ritualism is to heartfelt piety, as Baroque Catholicism is to Puritan liturgical minimalism. Modern Marcionism thus has, at its heretical margins, completely repudiated sacraments. Far from proclaiming a gospel that begins in baptism, Marcionism preaches a gospel that ends baptism altogether.

Here, however, the problem is historically more intricate and challenging, for modern theology is not alone in combining an uneasiness toward rites and signs with ambiguity toward the Old Testament. A spiritualizing semiotic theory and a semi-Marcionite account of redemptive history form sizeable and mutually reinforcing eddies in the mainstream of the tradition.[5] By a "spiritualizing

---

Ecclesia 8:1 (Winter 1999), published in this book as Chapter Six.

5. I have dealt with Augustine in this regard in "Conjugating the Rites: Old and New in Augustine's Theology of Signs," *Calvin Theological Journal*, no. 34 (1999), published in this book as Chapter Three.

semiotic theory," I refer to the belief that signs and rites function as more or less dispensable aids to invisible spiritual transactions, or the similar notion that signs aim primarily at channeling grace to the soul. As David Jones puts it in his much-cited essay, "Art and Sacrament," defenders and opponents of a sacramental economy of grace share the assumption that interior grace is "what matters," disputing only the usefulness of external signs for achieving this internal state.[6] Both, in my terminology, share a "spiritualizing semiotic." By "semi-Marcionite," I mean a structuring theological narrative that, while remaining within orthodox parameters, betrays reservations about Old Testament materialism or legalism, or minimizes the grace offered to Israel. I shall call the intertwining of these themes "Marcionite sacramental theology" or some variation of that label.

Marcionite sacramental theology can lead in an arealist or a mystical direction. Realists construe the Old as a covenant of "mere signs," while the sacraments of the New are "effective signs," "signs that contain or confer realities," or signs that veil some underlying "substance." For mystics, the rites and signs of Hebrew religion are bound up with the material and outward form of the Old Covenant, whereas Christianity begins an ascent to spirit, a descent into the heart, or both at once. From

---

6. David Jones, *Epoch and Artist: Selected Writings*, ed. Harman Grisewood (London: Faber and Faber, 1959), esp. 165–166.

the perspective developed here, realism and mysticism are variations within a Marcionite framework, since both dig a chasm between Old and New and both aspire to a divine-human encounter beyond signs. Because of the influence of semi-Marcionite sacramental theology, the church has not preached a gospel of baptism, or supplied an evangelical theology that apprehends how baptism and the gospel arise together.

Even theologians who do not embrace Marcionite assumptions often implicitly rely on them. Scholastic theology detached technical or mechanical questions of sacramental operation from patristic and early medieval typological mystagogy, so that, for example, Thomas construed sacramental "causality" in the categories of Aristotle rather than according to biblical patterns of flood, Exodus, or the ablutions of Leviticus. Answers to scholastic questions (*quaestiones*) were thus sought outside the typological reading of Scripture (*lectio*).[7] Marcionite sacramentology thus shapes method as well as content.

For many, the assumption that Christian sacraments operate on a completely different level from those of the Old Testament is so fundamental that it is never mentioned or argued for; the Old Testament is simply

---

7. M.-D. Chenu, *Nature, Man, and Society in the Twelfth Century: Essays on New Theological Perspectives in the Latin West*, trans. Jerome Taylor and Lester K. Little (Chicago: University of Chicago Press, 1968), 127.

more or less ignored. In a recent introductory study of sacramental theology, John Macquarrie begins with an affirmation of a basic dualism in reality, and describes the sacraments as doorways between these two worlds.[8] The thing (*res*) of the Christian sacraments thus is "what takes place in the soul," the "inward" transformation that the outward sacrament symbolizes, and thus the "inward reality" of baptism is "entrance into the Christian life." Macquarrie gives only the slightest attention to the Old Testament, and says that answering the question of whether or not the Last Supper was a Passover is irrelevant to its meaning.[9]

De Lubac likewise manifests the ambiguities inherent in the tradition. On the one hand, few modern theologians have taught so strongly as he that the sacraments are sacraments of unity celebrated by the society of the church, that Eucharist and church are correlates. Yet, quoting de Maistre, de Lubac also defines sacraments as "the sensible bond between two worlds," and says that since the sacraments are signs of something else they must be "passed through, and this not in part but wholly," since a sign, like a word, is useless if it does not "dissolve before the face of what it manifests." Significantly, this characterization of the sacraments as passageways or win-

8. John Macquarrie, *A Guide to the Sacraments* (London: SCM, 1997), 1–6.

9. *Ibid.,* 47, 55–57, 67, 101–102, 110, 113.

dows through which one passes to insignificant realities is followed by de Lubac's positioning of the church's present situation between the Old Law of "figures pure and simple" and the eschatological order of full possession of "truth." Refuting the neo-joachimism of Lessing, de Lubac employs the traditional formula that, in contrast to the Old Law of pure signs, "Today we have reality in our signs."[10] So the transition between Old and New is a difference in the functioning, the "mechanism," of signs.

In the following pages, I first examine several classic statements of Western sacramental theology to explore more fully the problematics of Old and New, and to suggest that semi-Marcionite sacramental theology is fairly pervasive in the tradition. Then I examine two twentieth-century sacramental theologies to indicate that the same problematics have persisted, in spite of efforts to overcome them. Finally, in conclusion, I offer a few thoughts regarding the future progress of sacramental theology.

Old and New and the Economy of Signs

Though he employs *sacramentum* in the expansive patristic sense, Hugh of St. Victor's *De sacramentis* includes elaborate consideration of sacraments more narrowly conceived. To his credit, Hugh continually takes note of

---

10. Henri de Lubac, *The Splendour of the Church*, trans. Michael Mason (London; Sheed and Ward, 1956), 147, 150.

the physical and material character of the sacraments and of their specific symbolisms,[11] but the dualistic structure of his theology ultimately leads, as Macy says, to a "mystical" sacramentology.[12] Sacraments are a medicinal remedy for sin, conferring an invisible antidote (*invisibilium antidotum*) through the visible rite. Metaphors of sacramental "medication" are patristic, but Hugh conflates them with a vague form/matter distinction, so that the

---

11. Throughout I have used the translation of Roy J. Deferrari, *On the Sacraments of the Christian Faith*, trans. Roy J. Deferrari (Cambridge, MA: Mediaeval Academy of America, 1951), while Latin citations are from Migne's *Patrologia Latina*. As explained briefly below, Hugh's claim that sacraments are given for *humilitatio* and *exercitatio* is an important move, despite the dualistic form it eventually takes (1.9.3). He notes, further, the appropriateness of circumcision, which causes physical pain, as a sign of a covenant of law, while the painless ablution of baptism is appropriate for a covenant of charity (1.11.8).

12. The following examples are drawn from many: The firmament created on the second day of the creation week represents reason as the boundary between the sensual nature (*sensualis natura hominis*) and the heavenly purity of intelligence (*puritas intelligentiae*; 1.1.19; PL 176, 200D). Though in a sense there are *vestigia Trinitatis* of power, wisdom, and love in the visible creation, these are "mere signs" (*signa tantum*) while interior things are the very *image* (1.3.28; PL 176, 230C). In fact, bodily natures are not capable of bearing a similitude to Divinity (*corporea natura similitudinem capere non potuit Divinitatis*; 1.6.2; PL 176, 264D). He affirms that embodiedness was part of Adam's original good nature, but sin caused something like a "fall into language": prior to the fall, God instructed Adam *intus* but afterward *foris* through the *species rerum temporalium et visibilium* (1.7.33; PL 176, 302D).

sacramental rite becomes the "container" of the medicine of grace. It is only an analogy, but Hugh is willing to press the analogy: "vases do not cure the sick but medicine does."[13] "What matters," to borrow Jones's phrase, is what is inside the bottle.[14]

Containers themselves (i.e., the external sacrament) are "medicine" only in a subtly inverted sense. According to Hugh, attachment to visible things corrupted Adam, a belief that, as with Augustine, blends Christian polemics against idolatry with anxiety about physical creation. Outward and visible as they are, sacraments in themselves serve only to exacerbate sinners' unhealthy infatuation with the visible. Yet, God instituted these paradoxical remedies to show that he alone promotes health (1.9.5; PL 176, 325–326). External rites thus become

---

13. 1.9.4; PL 176, 323. Thomas uses the medicinal analogy in denying that there were sacraments in paradise (*ST* 3a.62.2).

14. A similar spiritualizing move is implicit in Peter the Lombard's general definitions of sacraments, drawn from Augustine and the *Summa sententiarum:* "sacred sign, visible form of an invisible grace" (*sacra signa, invisibilis gratiae visibilis forma*; PL 192, 839). The *Summa sententiarum* adds, in baptism an interior washing is figured in an external and visible way (*in sacramento baptismatis figurabatur ablutio interior per illam exteriorem et visibilem;* PL 176, 117). If grace is invisible, and if sacraments are grace-causing signs, then by definition sacraments have as their "target" an internal transformation (cf. Gary Macy, *The Theologies of the Eucharist in the Early Scholastic Period: A Study of the Salvific Function of the Sacrament According to the Theologians, c. 1080–c. 1220* [Oxford: Clarendon, 1984], 122–124).

remedial when we learn that external rites cannot possibly be remedial, and so are forced to look beyond visible things for healing. Sacraments also contribute to saving humility by subjecting the proud to insensible and visible things over which they were created to rule (1.9.3; PL 176, 319–320).[15]

Hugh's sacramental theology is set in a historical narrative progressing from the shadow (*umbra*) of natural law, through the image or figure of truth (*imago vel figura veritatis*) associated with the written law, to the body of truth (*corpus veritatis*) of the time of grace, which looks to the truth of the spirit (*veritas spiritus*) of the consummation (1.11). In part, this is no more than an unveiling: As history moves toward the sunrise of the Incarnation, spiritual realities are increasingly illumined.[16] Expiation and justification were hidden in the tithes and oblations of the natural law, became more openly evident in circumcision, and were manifestly declared (*manifeste declaratur*) in baptism. History's trajectory *also* runs, however, from outside (*foris*) to inside (*intus*): oblations "cut off" part of a man's wealth, circumcision "cut" a superfluous body part, but baptism wounds more deeply, declaring "the perfect cleansing of man and the interior lustre of the

---

15. See Peter the Lombard, *Sententiae* 4.1.3 (PL 192, 839–40).

16. Heinz Robert Schlette, "Die Eucharistielehre Hugos von St Viktor," *ZKT* 81 (1959), 163.

soul."[17] Eschatologically, humanity follows the same trajectory, eventually resuming its prelapsarian communion
with God, which, like the angels, was wholly internal,
wholly outside a symbolic and linguistic medium.

In their structure and operation, the sacraments
duplicate the mystical, inward trajectory of redemptive
history. Old sacraments were "visible and signs of the visible" (*visibilia, et signum visibilium*), but the New, though
"in truth visible," are "signs and sacraments of invisible
grace" (*invisibilis gratiae signa et sacramenta*; 1.11.2; PL
176, 343). Like Ratramnus, Hugh contends that the Mosaic sacraments were effective, deriving sanctification as
pure signs (*signa tantum*) of Christian sacraments (1.11.1,
5; PL 176, 343, 345).[18] Sacraments of the church, however, contain "their own" sanctification (1.11.2; PL 176,
343). Thus, though "sign" and "figura" (*signum et figura*)
adequately describe the Old rites, the New are, strictly,
sacramenta, since they contain "by sanctification some
invisible and spiritual grace" (1.9.2; PL 176, 317–319).
Though Hugh does not draw the conclusion of some later

---

17. The Latin is: *quod perfectam hominis emundationem et interiorem
animae candorem* (1.11.8; PL 176, 348).

18. Martin Chemnitz saw Hugh's theory as the first departure from
the more straightforward patristic consensus, still affirmed by Bede,
that the sacraments of the Law conferred eternal life through the
power of Christ (*Examination of the Council of Trent, Part II*, trans.
Fred Kramer [St. Louis, IL: Concordia, 1978], 46–47).

writers that the Old Law had no sacraments, the sacraments of the two covenants have different structures and operate according to different logics.[19]

Methodologically, Hugh's formulations imply that one cannot conduct an inquiry into the "How?" or even the "What?" of Christian sacraments by examining the "How?" of Old Testament rituals. Dualist anthropology, which reflects an ontological dualism, trumps typology. Thomas implies the same methodological conclusion when he denies that the sacraments of the Old Law contained or caused grace and defines them, in very "Protes-

---

19. Consistent with his definition of *sacramentum,* Lombard hesitates to apply the term to the Old Covenant rites and signs, since, as Hebrews says, they were incapable of making a man just (*Sententiae* 4.1.2; PL 192, 839). Despite Thomas' appreciation for the embodied form of Christian practice, Victorine static disturbs his arguments for the necessity of sacraments. He first roots signs anthropologically: Humans know spiritual realities through the senses, which, it seems, is an unexceptionable condition of created life. Contradictorily, Thomas also explains the physical character of the sacraments as an accommodation to sin and borrows Hugh's idea that sacraments are physical to foster humility (*ST* 3a.61.1). A similar ambivalence toward signs is evident in Thomas' denial that sacraments were necessary in Eden. Before the fall, there was a proper hierarchy: with Adam's body subject to his soul, it therefore would have been *contra ordinem* if he had needed anything *corporale* to achieve perfection (3a.61.2). The New Law is, further, "intermediate" between the *figura* of the Old and the *nude et perfecte* eschatological manifestation of truth (3a.61.4). The church thus walks a pathway that leads out of the thicket of signs into the clean and open field of naked spiritual encounter.

tant" fashion, as certain professions of faith (*quaedam illi-us fidei protestationes*) that did nothing more than (*solum*) signify faith in the Passion of Christ (*ST* 3a.62.6). Thus, he explains the causality of the New Covenant sacraments by the distinction of principal and instrumental causality (3a.62.1) and does not refer at all to the rites of the Law. While scholastics used Old Testament ceremonies typologically and examined the fittingness of Old Testament ritual law, these considerations were not germane to their explanations of the "mechanics" of Christian sacraments.

Implicit in Hugh, semi-Marcionite sacramentology became more formalized in the later Middle Ages in the distinction between *opus operatum* and *opus operans*.[20] Though often employed to underscore the Augustinian view that the moral state of a minister is irrelevant to the validity of a sacrament, this distinction also formed the

---

20. Without using this technical terminology, the *Decretum pro Armenis* of the Council of Florence (1439) claimed that sacraments of the Old Law prefigured the passion of Christ but were not causes of grace, while those of the New contain and confer grace (*continent gratiam, et ipsam digne suscipientibus conferunt;* Henricus Denzinger, Henricus, ed., *Enchiridion Symbolorum: Definitionum et Declarationum de Rebus Fidei et Morum,* 33rd ed. [Freiburg: Herder, 1965], 333). Trent followed Florence (Session VII, Canon 6), buttressing its claims with the technical term *ex opere operato* (Canon 8). On the development of *opus operatum/opus operans* and its relation to the Old/New distinction, see Bernard Leeming, *Principles of Sacramental Theology* (London: Longmans, Green, and Company, 1956), 7–12; Artur Landgraf, "Die Gnadenökonomie des Alten Bundes nach der Lehre der Frühscholastik," *ZKT* 57 (1933), 241–242.

boundary between the sacraments of Old and New. Jewish sacraments were not efficacious by virtue of the thing done (*opus operatum*) but by virtue of the recipient's faith (*opus operans*); in the church, by contrast, sacraments are effective simply by being rightly performed on a subject who places no obstacle in the way of grace. Behind Reformation polemics against Catholic *ex opere operato*, then, were differences concerning the relation of Old and New, and Luther, Calvin, and Chemnitz attacked Catholics on the latter point as well as the former.[21]

In practice, however, Protestant theology continued to play a semi-Marcionite tune. Immediately after affirm-

---

21. Luther claims that the argument put forward by medieval theologians in favor of the notion of "effective signs" is the Paschasian one: If the sacraments of the New Testament are "mere signs," there is no difference between Old and New (Luther, "The Babylonian Captivity of the Church," in Helmut T. Lehmann, gen. ed., *Luther's Works*, 55 vols., trans. A.T.W. Steinhäuser [Philadelphia, PA: Muhlenberg Press, 1959] vol. 36, 64–66). Chemnitz asserts that "the man-made opinion of the *opus operatum*" was invented by scholastics following Hugh and Peter the Lombard in order to make a "distinction between the sacraments of the two Testaments" (Chemnitz, *Examination*, 47). "We must," Calvin agrees, "utterly reject that Scholastic dogma… which notes such a great difference between the sacraments of the Old and New Law, as if the former only foreshadowed God's grace, but the latter give it as a present reality." Israel received in their sacraments the same thing Christians do, "Christ with his spiritual riches" (*Institutes* 4.14.23; the translation is that of Ford Lewis Battles, *Institutes of the Christian Religion*, 2 vols.; LCC #20–21; ed. John T.McNeill [Philadelphia, PA: Westminster Press, 1960], 1299).

ing that the sacraments of the Old and New are equally effective, Luther explains that the sacraments of the New Law are like those of the patriarchs, while both differ "vastly" from Mosaic "legal symbols," which did not have any promise attached to them. Reversing the scholastic *operatum/operans* distinction, he claims that the sacraments of the Mosaic order were not sacraments of justification but "only sacraments of works. Their whole nature and power consisted in works, not in faith. Whoever performed them fulfilled them, even if he did it without faith." Efficacy in Christian sacraments, by contrast, wholly "consists in faith itself" so that one may fulfill them even without enacting the rite.[22] In spite of his vigorous affirmation of continuity both of substance and operation between Old and New Covenants, Calvin's theology of baptism begins with the New Testament, and, apart from a brief typological meditation on the Exodus and an extended polemic for infant baptism from its analogy with circumcision, the Old Testament plays comparatively little role in his fundamental theology of baptism (*Institutes*, 4.15–16). Theoretically, Calvin overcomes scholastic Marcionism; in practice, he perpetuates it.[23]

---

22. Luther, "Babylonian Captivity," 64–66.

23. With its doctrine of the covenant and its emphasis on continuity between Old and New, later Reformed theology mitigated Marcionite tendencies to some extent. Yet it persisted in drawing the (very traditional but confusing) distinction between a "material"

The Inward-Outward Conundrum

Some major liturgical works of the last century, particularly studies of the Eucharist, have sought to expound Christian liturgy by explicit reference to Old Testament or later Jewish rites and institutions. Yet, semi-Marcionite sacramental theology remains widespread. To demonstrate this, I tell several stories of twentieth-century sacramental theology.

Influenced by Odo Casel's "mystery" view of Christian worship, recent liturgists have interpreted the Eucharistic *anamnesis* ("Do this in remembrance of me") "dynamically" as "the making effective in the present of an event in the past."[24] For Casel, this means not only that "Christ himself is present and acts through the church," but also that the God who exists outside time permits the church in the liturgy to "enter into the divine present and

---

Old and a "spiritual" New Covenant (cf. Calvin, *Institutes* 2.11–12), which was sometimes allied, as with Zwingli, with an—at best—ambivalent affirmation of the necessity and efficacy of sacraments; see especially Carlos M. N. Eire, *War Against the Idols: The Reformation of Worship from Erasmus to Calvin* (Cambridge: Cambridge University Press, 1986).

24. Quoted from the Windsor statement of the Anglican/Roman Catholic International Commission by Geoffrey Wainwright, *Doxology: The Praise of God in Worship, Doctrine, and Life: A Systematic Theology* (New York, NY: Oxford University Press, 1980).

everlasting Today" so that at worship "there is neither past nor future, only present."[25]

In several respects, Casel's work is important and fruitful: he broke with both cognitive and expressivist models of Christianity, attacked individualism in eucharistic theology, and his insistence that the encounter with mystery must be embodied in signs, rites, and gestures prepared for the "interpersonal" emphasis of Schillebeeckx and P. Schoonenberg (see below).[26] Yet, Casel explicitly grounds his theory in supposed analogies between Christianity and Greco-Roman cults, whose mysteries were closer to Christian worship than anything in the worship of Israel. Casel argues that Passover was a memorial event but not a mystery, since it was "related first of all to human events, and human deliverance." Because of their legalism and their belief that God was "a powerful, terrible ruler, separated from mankind by an unbridgeable gap," the Jews developed no liturgical sense of "close relationship" with God, and Christ's Pasch has "no expression in the old covenant." Fortunately, outside Israel, God was preparing "certain religious forms" that "could offer words and forms to express this new, unheard-of" personal relationship. Thus, "the Hellenes

---

25. Odo Casel, *The Mystery of Christian Worship and Other Writings*, ed. Burkhard Neunheuser (Westminster, MD: Newman Press, 1962), 141–142.

26. For some of these themes, see Casel, *Mystery*, 9–13, 21–23, 30.

sometimes found it easier to grasp and to grasp more deeply the truth of the gospel than did the Jews with their purely Semitic, imageless, legal thinking. The Christianity of the ancient world appears to us as the fulfillment and glorification of what Greco-Roman antiquity was."[27] Liturgical expressions of the Old Covenant are now used in a "higher sense concerning the purely spiritual facts of the new," so that New Covenant worship reaches toward "a new and higher kind of reality."[28]

Casel's Marcionism colludes with a semiotic theory surprisingly close to Zwingli. Baptismal water, he claims, "can only be the exterior and visible expression of the inward, real birth from *pneuma*." Though in itself the water has "only symbolic value," this symbolism is "absolutely necessary," since "without this exterior act we could not recognize God's act."[29] Signs as "mere signs" have no po-

---

27. Casel, *Mystery*, 31–37

28. Casel, *Mystery*, 40. Louis Bouyer, rather mildly, finds it "somewhat disconcerting" that Casel, with many liturgical scholars, seeks antecedents of the Eucharist "outside of Judaism." Casel "looks for neither origin, nor explanation anywhere except in the pagan mysteries" (*Eucharist: Theology and Spirituality of the Eucharistic Prayer*, trans. Charles Underhill Quinn [Notre Dame, IN: University of Notre Dame Press, 1968], 16–17).

29. Casel, *Mystery*, 41.

tency but only express invisible realities; "what matters" is what takes place behind the veil of symbols.[30]

The contributions of Schillebeeckx and Schoonenberg are welcome developments in sacramental theology.[31] Employing a phenomenology of "personal presence," they emphatically reject any local or quasi-physical presence of Christ in the eucharistic elements. At least in part,

---

30. A rarity in modern theology, but this story has a happy ending. Having examined the Old Testament background of the *anamnesis,* Max Thurian and Joachim Jeremias discovered that it has very little to do with Casel's time-bending speculations or "dynamic representation." Biblical memorials instead present a material or enacted "reminder" to God. For Thurian, the church joins the heavenly intercession of Christ through its sacramental action, imploring the Father "to recall and not to forget, to have respect unto the covenant, to arise and plead" (*The Eucharistic Memorial,* 2 vols. in 1; trans. J. G. Davies, Ecumenical Studies in Worship no. 7–8 [London: Lutterworth Press, 1960–1961], vol. 2: 35, 40–41). For Jeremias, the Eucharist "represents the initiated salvation work before God" so that the Father will remember the Messiah and bring in the fullness of the kingdom (*The Eucharistic Words of Jesus,* New Testament Library, 3rd ed., trans. Norman Perrin [London: SCM Press, 1966], 252–254). Both present a thoroughly anti-Marcionite account of *anamnesis* allied with a "pragmatic" semiotic in which rites and signs are, in their materiality and bodiliness, "instruments" in the church's liturgical transactions with God and in the realization of His redemptive purposes.

31. See the careful discussion in P. J. FitzPatrick, *In Breaking of Bread: The Eucharistic Ritual* (Cambridge: Cambridge University Press, 1993), 49–107, which presents the historical background. Also Paul H. Jones, *Christ's Eucharistic Presence: A History of the Doctrine,* American University Series, *Theology and Religion,* no. 157 (New York, NY: Peter Lang, 1994), 197–237.

they locate the change that takes place in the Eucharist at a "sacramental" level, highlight the corporate dimensions of the rite, and eschew "substance" and "causation" in favor of phenomenological categories that emphasize person, gift, and embodiment. A number of these moves provide a setting in which the traditional anxiety about signs might be overcome.

But the program is not followed through, for reasons that grow directly out of some of the basic premises of this "interpersonal-encounter model." According to Fitz-Patrick's account, Schillebeeckx's views are guided by two principles, which he labels the "Givenness of Reality" and the "Humanness of Perception." Since reality is God's creation and revelation, it has mysterious depths that human beings reach for but never grasp entirely. What we know therefore "points towards the mystery that ever escapes and is ahead of us," and this means that "all our explicit contents of consciousness do no more than point towards the mystery; we know reality only in signs."[32] This is so not only in the sense that the contents of my thoughts "point towards" the reality of the thing about which I am thinking (my thought of a chair is a sign of the chair), but, more than that, the content of my thoughts points toward what is "really real," the "mystery" of the God who reveals himself in apparent reality. The phenomena that

---

32. E. Schillebeeckx, *The Eucharist*, trans. N. D. Smith (London: Sheed and Ward, 1968), 129.

provide the material for my thoughts are also "signs." De-fining phenomena to include not only "what pertains to the senses" but also "everything in reality that is *expressed* there, or specifically appears to us," Schillebeeckx denies that reality "lies behind" the phenomena and insists that "it is reality itself that appears to us."[33] Yet he also states that "there is a certain distinction between phenomena and reality" such that "what appears—the phenomenal—is a *sign* of reality; it signifies reality." One should not pic-ture this distinction of phenomena and reality as a kind of "veneer" of accidents covering an underlying substance. The distinction arises instead because of the "complex way in which we approach reality," or rather because of the "inadequacy of our knowledge of reality."[34]

Throughout, Schillebeeckx sets his eucharistic views in a worryingly epistemological and individualist frame-work. For why is the Eucharist an epistemological issue? He appears to be operating with a picture of a solitary man confronted by the data of the world, with no explicit recognition of epistemological mediation of social tradi-tion, language and culture. But it is especially the final line quoted above that alarms. Why is knowledge through

---

33. It is not uncharitable, I hope, to quote FitzPatrick's comment on this insistence: "Theologians may be better behaved, but when phi-losophers give such reassurances we know that they mean to do more or less the opposite of what they say" (*In Breaking*, 93).

34. Schillebeeckx, *Eucharist*, 147–148.

signs "inadequate" knowledge? Inadequate for what purpose? Is limited knowledge, knowledge that grasps at but never encompasses, "inadequate"? It is only so if one's ideal of knowledge is that it be comprehensive and transparent, but Schillebeeckx has already insisted that this kind of knowledge is simply unavailable to us. The passing description of the inadequacy of knowledge embedded in signs suggests that Schillebeeckx is still yearning for a contact unmediated by signs. Schillebeeckx appears to be disturbed by the fact that he is a creature.

I have similar reservations about some of Schillebeeckx's discussion of the body. The body is a "sign" that both reveals and veils the interior man. Thus, "the inward man manifests itself as a reality that is in this world through the body. It is in his body and through his body that man is open to the 'outside,' and that he make himself present to his fellow man."[35] But surely this is, at best, terribly over-simplified. First, the body is not merely a manifestation of what is inward, but also reacts to what is outward. Curly flinches when Mo tries to poke his eye, but the flinch cannot be reasonably read as a "sign" that "reveals and veils" Curly's inner state of fear. The self, not just the body, is embedded in the world. Second, Schillebeeckx's model operates in one direction, from inner man to outward manifestation. Yet, in many

---

35. *Christ, the Sacrament of Encounter with God*, trans. Paul Barrett and N. D. Smith (London: Sheed and Ward, 1963), 15.

cases it is just as reasonable to say that the inner man is a "sign" of the outer as to say the opposite. The pimpled teen's poor "inner" self-image (image!) is a product of a bodily state not a cause of it, or, better, the two are so intricately connected, and connected with so many other factors, that matching a single input to a single output is a hopelessly inadequate description of the reality. Only if Schillebeeckx's unidirectional inner/outer model is renounced can a truly adequate sacramental theology be constructed.[36]

Given this philosophical background, it is not surprising that, despite certain contrary statements, a traditional dualism of sign and thing permeates Schillebeeckx's account of the sacraments. On the one hand, he wishes "to arrive eventually at the insight that the sacraments are the properly human mode of encounter with God," and he insists that the church is not merely a means of salvation, but is itself salvation in visible, earthly manifesta-

---

36. The body "is no more than a sign of the inner life of man's spirit, though belonging to it as a part of his 'sign-making' activity; it can be no more because it veils and alienates that life even while providing it with the means of expression. For indeed it is only in an element borrowed from the world that the human spirit can express itself" (*Ibid.*, 76). The juxtaposition of the last two sentences indicates that the bodily expressions of the human spirit are necessarily alienated from the life of the spirit, and this suggests again that bodiliness and sign-making are a somewhat unfortunate obstacle to expression and communion. Again it appears that Schillebeeckx is actually complaining against a fundamental condition of creaturely life.

tion.[37] On the other hand, he also writes of the "inward grace" that comes to visible expression in religious rites and practices and of the church as the "visible presence" of salvation and grace in history that is, like Christ himself, an "invisible communion" with God "manifested in visible human form," the "inward invisible communion" become visible. In Christ, the divine power to save "appears to us in visible form." The "grace of redemption becomes visible in the church" through the hierarchical office and the charism of the laity. The church is a "mystery," that is, "a sign bearing within itself the reality of inward union with God in Christ."[38]

Though these expressions may seem benign, the whisperings of a butterfly's wings can stir up storms at large distances. Schillebeeckx's language consistently implies that salvation and grace as they appear in history are the "presence" or "manifestation" of something more fundamental that is not available empirically. In a revealing footnote to his comment that Christ "sacramentalizes" his heavenly intercession in the church, Schillebeeckx explains "sacramentalizes" as the activity of Christ by which he gives "visible shape to his invisible saving activity or gift of grace."[39] Similarly, in describing Christ as the "sac-

---

37. *Ibid.*, 4, 6, 9, 56.

38. *Ibid.*, 10, 13, 15, 55, 61.

39. *Ibid.*, 53–54.

rament" of God, he explains that "a sacrament is a divine bestowal of salvation in an outwardly perceptible form which makes the bestowal manifest; a bestowal of salvation in historical visibility,"[40] which surely implies that salvation as such is not "outwardly perceptible." When he writes of the sacramental character of Christ and of the church, then, he assumes a definition of "sacrament" that, despite the phenomenological pyrotechnics, remains bound by the traditional definition of sacraments as "visible signs of invisible grace."

This is also implicit in the way he justifies the continued use of signs in the church as a replacement for Christ's bodily presence, now that he is no longer visible on earth.[41] The entire discussion hinges on the problematic of relating visible and invisible.[42] Though somewhat more sophisticated than earlier conceptions, in the end this is another way of saying that sacraments are an accommodation to some defect in God's relation to man (in this case, Christ's invisibility), rather than the necessary form of any conceivable divine-human encounter.

---

40. *Ibid.*, 15.

41. *Ibid.*, 49–50.

42. Though elsewhere Schillebeeckx gives welcome attention to Pentecost, here he lapses into the traditional effort to make the sacraments, rather than the Spirit, bridge the gap between heaven and earth. In my view, this mistake is the source of much confusion in traditional sacramental theology.

On this conception, the church cannot simply *be* Christ's saving activity, though this is apparently what Schillebeeckx at other moments wants to affirm. Even with his insistence that the sign effects what it signifies, his conception is inadequate, for so long as what is "signified" is understood as "invisible grace," the saving encounter is not genuinely taking place at the level of signs, and that is to say that the encounter is not actually located in history, and that is to say that salvation remains unrealized in the creation. Schillebeeckx says that introducing any dualism between the "inward communion" with God in Christ and the "juridical" church is "evil,"[43] but it is precisely this evil of which Schillebeeckx is guilty, and it is precisely because he continues to characterize that "communion" with God in Christ as "inward."

Naturally enough, Schillebeeckx is dissatisfied with an account of the eucharistic elements limited to transsignification, since this lacks, in his judgment, sufficient "metaphysical density." It is not enough that the bread and wine be body and blood in the sense of being "signs," even if "sign" here is taken in the robust sense as a gift that communicates a personal presence, even if the gift is a gift of self. In part, as FitzPatrick notes, this dissatisfaction derives from Schillebeeckx's principle of the "Givenness of Reality," which requires that reality be traced back to

---

43. *Christ the Sacrament.* 56.

"God's creative gift." Just as important, however, is Schillebeeckx's finding that Trent requires transubstantiation: "The church's sense of the faith has urged in the strict sense the *reality* of what is eucharistically present." But the philosophical baggage comes through: here at the Lord's Table especially "the distinction obtrudes itself between reality and this reality as it appears (the phenomenal)."[44] The presence of the gifts of Christ and the presence of Christ by the Spirit in the community are not sufficient; above and beyond the exchange of signs, the Giver, gift and reception, there must be a substantial presence. If sign-embedded knowledge is "inadequate," can the intercourse with God that takes place through eucharistic signs and actions be any less "inadequate"—and, indeed, inadequate precisely because it is an exchange of signs?[45]

Transsignification is, sometimes self-consciously, offered as a "Hebraic" account of the eucharistic presence. Given the linkage between Christianity's historical ambiguity about signs and its ambiguity about Old Testament religion, a renewal of the former should involve a more adequate approach to the latter issue. Schillebeeckx describes Israel's history and institutions in terms of the

---

44. *Eucharist,* 147–150.

45. Behind this ambiguity concerning signs is not only ambiguity concerning the body but concerning difference. Schoonenberg sees it as a frustrating limitation that "the whole body never enters that of another" (quoted by FitzPatrick, *In Breaking,* 135).

history of God's covenant, and insightfully suggests that Israel's participation in the mystery of Christ is based on the fact that, in Israel, the "Christ-event" was already beginning. The Old Testament, therefore, did not bestow the fullness of grace but only the grace of an "open readiness" to receive the Messiah. Schillebeeckx claims that this is the meaning of the Council of Florence's statement that the Jewish sacraments did not "confer" grace.[46] From what we have seen above, this historical interpretation of Florence seems questionable, but it is undeniable that Schillebeeckx's brief comments on the sacraments of the Old Law are moving in a fruitful direction. For there is no implication here that the weakness of the Old Law consisted in an inherent weakness in sign or ritual; the weakness instead is explained in terms of a progress in redemptive history, but this is not described in terms of a progress that leads beyond signification.

Despite this, the advocates of the personal encounter model are, in practice, at one with the tradition we have been examining. Unless one argues for a transubstantiation of the manna in the wilderness, then any doctrine of transubstantiation inevitably entails a discontinuity between the feasts of the Old and New that is of ontological dimensions. One might inquire of Schillebeeckx whether "transsignification" is an adequate description of

---

46. *Christ the Sacrament*, 11–12.

Old Covenant sacramentality, and I would expect a positive answer, but a transformation of signification is not sufficient to account for the New Covenant.

De Baciocchi, something of a pioneer in the revision of Catholic eucharistic theology, illustrates the persistence of semi-Marcionite sacramental theology among theologians trying to reform the Western tradition. In a 1955 article exploring biblical perspectives on the Eucharist, he strongly emphasizes its continuity with the Passover. Yet, there is "a new thing" in the Eucharist, which had no analogue in the Jewish Passover. This is, of course, perfectly true, but the question is what is this "new thing"? De Baciocchi moves immediately into a discussion of transubstantiation, which occupies the remainder of his article. Thus, the Jewish Passover is adequately accounted for as union with the believing community, which is on the way toward the promised salvation. As such, the Passover "re-immerses" the community in the historical current of the covenant and "reconnects" the past with the future redemption. While an adequate definition of the sacraments of Israel, this is a necessary but not sufficient description of the New Covenant sacraments. The church has moved beyond the mere sign, and therefore the meal is no longer a meal in the way Israel's meals were.[47]

---

47. J. de Baciocchi, "Le Mystere eucharistique dans les perspectives de la Bible," *Nouvelle revue theologique*, no. 6 (1955), 561–580: Passover effects a "union avec la communaute croyant en marche vers

Conclusion

Whither sacramental theology, then? First, sacramental theology must renounce the temptation to ascend beyond signs. Though it is of course true that the personal and covenantal exchanges that take place in Baptism and the Supper are with an invisible God and have invisible features (as do inter-human relationships), that does not mean that the visible sign is merely a stepladder to "what matters" that can be safely kicked away once we have arrived at our destination, any more than the gestures we employ in our inter-human relationships are merely "means" toward a gestureless and wordless fusion of souls. We pour out our souls to one another in gesture and word. Nor is God's communication through signs some sort of "second best" form of fellowship, an "accommodation" to some defect in human nature. It is instead the necessary form of any communication from God to embodied creatures. Seen from this angle, it is apparent that this temptation is of the essence of original sin, since it is a temptation to attempt to transcend our creatureliness, and to be as God.

Second, this temptation is interwoven with many of the traditional readings of redemptive history, which is seen as an ascent beyond signs just to the extent that it is seen as an ascent beyond creaturehood. Christian faith

---

le salut promis," which "se replonge dans le courant historique de l'Alliance, reliant le grand evenement passe a la redemption future."

is not merely a repetition of Judaism, but neither is it a repudiation of the political, public, embodied, verbalized, and ritualized form of faith found in the Old Testament. In this, as in many other ways, Christian theology and practice must learn to embrace its Hebraic roots without being Galatians. Especially, Christian sacramental theology must attempt to find what resources it can in the ritual texts of the Old Testament, for New Testament sacramental theology was surely forged in a religious context centered on temple, sacrifice, circumcision, and ritual bath.

Finally, the methodological upshot of all this is that sacramental theology would do well to operate within the typological framework characteristic of patristic theology. Typological readings (*lectio*) should provide not only the context for grasping the symbolic significance of water, bread, and wine, but also the context for exploring the technical aspects of sacrament—how they "work." Preachers, catechists, and mystagogues have always indulged in luxuriant meditation on sacramental types, but theologians have frequently looked outside biblical typology for answers to their questions. It is essential that sacramental theology revive, as a prolegomenon to understanding Christian sacraments, the venerable but under-appreciated and under-developed scholastic treatise on the "sacraments of the old law" (*sacramenta veteris legis*).

CHAPTER SIX

MARCIONISM, POSTLIBERALISM, AND SOCIAL CHRISTIANITY

Two of the key ingredients of theological liberalism were adherence to what Stephen Sykes has called the "inwardness tradition" and a sharp, quasi-Marcionite separation of Christianity and the religion of the Old Testament. Adolf von Harnack is illustrative of both tendencies. In his third lecture on the *Essence of Christianity,* delivered at the turn of the century, Harnack offers this description of the kingdom of God:

> Anyone who wants to know what the kingdom of God and the coming of this kingdom mean in Jesus' preaching must read and meditate on the parables. There he will learn what the kingdom is all about. The kingdom of God comes by coming to *individuals,* making entrance into their *souls,* and being grasped by them.... Everything externally dramatic, all public historical meaning van-

ishes here; all external hope for the future fades also.... It is not a matter of angels and devils, nor of principalities and powers, but of God and the soul, of the soul and its God.[1]

As Harnack continues, the Marcionite basis for this description of the kingdom becomes clear. Jesus "severed the connection existing in his day between ethics and external forms of religious worship and technical observance" and traced moral issues to their "root, that is, to the disposition and intention."[2] Continuing this work, Paul "delivered the Christian religion from Judaism," by virtue of his insight that "religion in its new phase pertains to the individual" and by introducing the dichotomies of spirit/flesh, inner/outer, life/death.[3] Harnack recognizes that the gospel has a bearing on the problems of law, society, culture and work,[4] and justifies the formation of churches by noting that religion cannot remain "bodiless." But these "externals" are not constitutive of Christianity *per se,* and Harnack argues that these necessary forms took on a life of their own, transforming Christianity into Cathol-

---

1. Adolf von Harnack, *What Is Christianity?*, 5th ed., trans. Thomas Bailey Saunders (London: Ernest Benn, 1958), 49-50.

2. Harnack, 60.

3. Harnack, 130.

4. Harnack, 65–94.

icism. In the West, the church came to be seen as a necessary institution and, in Eastern Christianity, worship turned from "a worship of God in spirit and in truth into a worship of God in signs, formulas, and idols."[5] In his work on Marcion, Harnack was explicit in his endorsement of a modernized Marcionite program.[6] Thus, the "inward" form of Christianity is defined by opposition to the "external" form of religion found in Judaism and the Old Testament. Marcion is brought forward in defense of pure inward piety.

Already at the beginning of the nineteenth century, Schleiermacher set modern Protestant theology off on a similar course. For all his opposition to the Enlightenment's rationalistic view of religion, he shares its view of the Old Testament. In what Brunner calls the "decisive sentence of his dogmatics,"[7] Schleiermacher argues that the connection of Christianity with "Mosaic institutions" is purely historical, while "as far as concerns its historical existence and its aim, [Christianity's] relations to Judaism and Heathenism are the same." The Old Testament itself, Schleiermacher claims, "ascribed to the New Covenant

---

5. Harnack, 153–154, 169.

6. Adolf von Harnack, *Marcion: The Gospel of the Alien God*, trans. John E. Steely and Lyle D Bierma (1924; repr., Durham, NC: Labyrinth, 1990), 133-142.

7. Emil Brunner, *Truth as Encounter* (Philadelphia, PA: Westminster Press, 1964), 245.

a different character from the Old," even an "antithesis" between them. This view of the transition from Old to New means, theologically, that the Old Testament may be safely ignored by the dogmatician, indeed that it is to be "utterly discard[ed]," since it is merely the "husk or wrapping" and since "whatever is most definitely Jewish has least value." The "most definitely Jewish" elements are "a legalistic style of thought or a slavish worship of the letter," which improperly enters the church when the Old Testament is used for the expression of Christian piety. The early church's example of preaching and teaching from the Old Testament furnishes no warrant for continuing this practice; in the apostolic age, the connection was "historical," and the connecting threads have rightly frayed with the passage of time.[8]

Most importantly for Schleiermacher, the form of Christianity's piety and of its religious consciousness is wholly different from that of Judaism.[9] The members of

---

8. Friedrich Schleiermacher, *The Christian Faith*, 2nd. ed, trans. H.R. MacIntosh and J. S. Stewart (Edinburgh: T&T Clark, 1928), 60-62, 608–611.

9. In *On Religion,* Schleiermacher claims that the leading idea of Judaism was its belief in "universal immediate retribution," that God disciplines individual sins. By contrast, Christianity's leading idea is that God overcomes all obstacles and resistance of finite being to unity with the Whole (Friedrich Schleiermacher, *On Religion: Speeches to its Cultured Despisers,* trans. John Oman [New York, NY: Harper Torchbooks, 1958], 239–241). It should be noted that Schleiermach-

what Schleiermacher calls the "true church," as opposed to the institutional clingers-on, have no need of text or letter, as was necessary under the Old system. Consistent with this is Schleiermacher's effort to define an irreducible "essence" of religion and religions. Such a program falters before the religion of Israel, in which the covenant with Yahweh, embodied in texts, rites, feasts, sanctuary, and religious hierarchy, embraces the whole of the nation's life; the externals in Israel's religion are not a dispensable husk protecting an internal seed but much more an onion. Schleiermacher's definition of religion as a "modification of feeling" or a "taste for the Infinite," however brilliantly qualified to accommodate the social aspects of religion and to explicate the connection of feeling with acting and knowing, simply cannot embrace the religion of the Old Testament. Schleiermacher does not follow Kant in denying that Judaism is a religion,[10] but he treats the forms of

---

er was not personally anti-Semitic; he took the unpopular stance of defending the extension of full civil rights to Prussian Jews (Richard Crouter, "Introduction" to Friedrich Schleiermacher, *On Religion: Speeches to its Cultured Despisers* [Cambridge: Cambridge University Press, 1988], 15).

10. According to Kant, "The *Jewish faith* was, in its original form, a collection of mere statutory laws upon which was established a political organization; for whatever moral additions were then or later *appended* to it in no way whatever belong to Judaism as such. Judaism is not really a religion at all but merely a union of a number of people who, since they belonged to a particular stock, formed themselves into a commonwealth under purely political laws, and not into

Old Testament religion as so much rubble that must be removed to find the religious treasure buried beneath. In short, some variation of Marcionism is essential to Schleiermacher's definition of religion and therefore at the heart of his entire system, as Harnack realized.[11]

---

a church; nay, it was *intended* to be merely an earthly state so that, were it possible to be dismembered through adverse circumstances, there would still remain to it (as part of its very essence) the political faith in its eventual reestablishment (with the advent of a Messiah)." Christianity "completely" forsook Judaism and was "grounded upon a wholly new principle" that required "a thoroughgoing revolution in doctrines of faith," though this was a revolution for which Judaism somehow prepared. Typological and allegorical efforts to connect Judaism and Christianity are not theologically substantive but only provide evidence of the sensitivity of Christians to the prejudices of the first-century; early Christianity sought to introduce a "purely moral religion in place of the old worship, to which the people were all too well habituated, without directly offending the people's prejudices" (Immanuel Kant, *Religion Within the Limits of Reason Alone*, 2nd ed., trans. Theodore M. Greene and Hoyt H. Hudson [LaSalle, IL: Open Court, 1960], 116–118). For the medieval and early modern roots to Kant's enlightened faith, see Henning Graf Reventlow, *The Authority of the Bible and the Rise of the Modern World*, trans. John Bowden (Philadelphia, PA: Fortress Press, 1985). For Kant's influence on Schleiermacher, see Crouter, "Introduction," *On Religion*, 23–28.

11. According to Harnack, critical philosophy, as developed by Schleiermacher and Hegel, implies that the Old Testament cannot have any authority in Christianity and he commended Schleiermacher for recognizing this and giving Marcion his due (Harnack, *Marcion*, 137). Otto Bachli traces a line from Marcion, through Morgan and Semler, to Hegel, Schleiermacher, and Harnack, all under the heading, "Das Alte Testament als Document einer Fremdreligion"

A sharp renunciation of the "inwardness tradition" has been one of the notable developments of recent theology, often taking the form of an assault on the Cartesian and Kantian assumptions underlying modern theology.[12] The issues at stake here are not, however, narrowly theological or philosophical. Recent theological critiques of the Cartesian and Kantian elements of modern theology have been enlisted in a theological attack on secularism, and this is ultimately in the service of formulating a social account of Christianity. According to John Milbank's brilliant account,[13] modern philosophy (and, in its wake, the social sciences) have in various ways "confined" religion to the inner recesses of the heart or shoved it to the sublime margins of human life. Accepting this marginalization, theologians become the "useful idiots" of secular

(Otto Bachli, *Das Alte Testament in der Kirchlichen Dogmatik von Karl Barth* [Neukirchener, 1987], 22–23).

12. See Stanley Hauerwas, *The Peaceable Kingdom: A Primer in Christian Ethics* (Notre Dame: University of Notre Dame Press, 1983); George Lindbeck, *The Nature of Doctrine: Religion and Theology in a Postliberal Age* (London: SPCK, 1984); George Lindbeck, "The Gospel's Uniqueness: Election and Untranslatability," *Modern Theology*, 13:4 (1997); Fergus Kerr, *Theology after Wittgenstein* (Oxford: Blackwell, 1986); Nicholas Lash, *Easter in Ordinary: Reflections on Human Experience and the Knowledge of God* (London: SCM, 1988); John Milbank, *Theology and Social Theory: Beyond Secular Reason* (Oxford: Blackwell, 1990).

13. Milbank, *Theology and Social Theory*, 1990.

order: by providing theological support for privatized religion, they leave politics and culture to the amoral rule of mechanistic and impersonal forces. Schleiermacher may serve to illustrate. Religion, he insists in his *Speeches,* is necessarily "positive," and he rejects the idea that natural religion is somehow more pure. Nonetheless, the church does not constitute a political community in any sense. On the contrary, part of his refutation of the charge that positive religion breeds civil strife is to say that dragging religion "from the depths of the heart into the civil world" is a perversion.[14]

At this point, again, we see Marcionism raising its head: whatever "positive religion" means for Schleiermacher, so long as it excludes a strong public and even civil presence for religion, it does *not* describe Israel. A genuinely social Christianity, and a forceful theological attack on secularism, thus demand an equally forceful attack on Marcionism. Yet, the Marcionite ingredient of modern theology and philosophy has not been so carefully analyzed as the Cartesian/Kantian element.[15] This is not, in my judgment, because it is less fundamental: The Marcionite bias is historically prior to Descartes and Kant, and I see no reason to believe that a theologian's epistemological assumptions are more "basic" than his

---

14. Schleiermacher, *On Religion,* 215–216.

15. But cf. Lindbeck, "Gospel's Uniqueness"; Milbank, *Theology and Social Theory,* 92–98; Reventlow, *Authority of the Bible, passim.*

stance toward the Old Testament—indeed, I suspect that
something like the opposite is true. In the following pages, I want to suggest that the comparative weakness of
the critique of modern Marcionism arises from the fact
that even anti-liberal accounts of Christianity (including
pre-liberal accounts) contain traces of Marcionism that
forge an alliance with traces of the "inwardness tradition."
This alliance with the enemy weakens the refutation of
liberalism and secularism and makes a positive social theology more difficult to construct.

To illustrate, I will examine Henri de Lubac's largely
successful and always enlightening effort to delineate a
"social Christianity." This will show that even today, even
in some of the best of theologians, the ghost of Marcion
haunts theology. I shall end the paper on a more constructive note. Some of the most promising tools for a
consistently anti-Marcionite public Christianity appear
in recent New Testament scholarship that emphasizes the
political and ecclesiological dimensions of early Christianity. As a small first step toward a thorough social Christianity and a thoroughly postliberal theology, I will end
the chapter by briefly reviewing some of this literature.
I will suggest that, even with a consistent purge of Cartesian assumptions, so long as theology operates within
a practical Marcionism, it has not arrived at a truly social Christianity or a truly postliberal stance. Refuting
Descartes and Kant bruises liberalism's heel; exposing,

renouncing, and correcting liberalism's implicit or open Marcionism comes nearer to crushing the head.

Marcionism and Social Christianity

In his now-classic work, *Catholicism*, de Lubac rehabilitates the classical view that salvation is "essentially social" in the "heart of its mystery, the essence of its dogma," to such an extent that social Catholicism should be considered a pleonasm.[16] Redemption means restoration of the primordial unity not only between God and mankind but also among men, a unity that the church completes and in a sense is.[17] Even in the eschaton, there is community, for *consortium* is "part of the beatitude."[18] Elsewhere, de Lubac insists that all Christian living, including that of the most isolated hermit, serves the goal of building up the community of believers, and he polemicizes against a "pure inwardness" that would seek to escape from the church and thereby leave the field of public social life to the rough play of purely secular forces.[19]

---

16. Henri de Lubac, *Catholicism: A Study of Dogma in Relation to the Corporate Destiny of Mankind* (London: Burns, Oates, and Washbourne, 1950), x.

17. De Lubac, *Catholicism*, 8, 17.

18. De Lubac, *Catholicism*, 51, 60.

19. Henri de Lubac, *The Splendour of the Church* (trans. Michael Mason; London: Sheed and Ward, 1966), 130-132.

Intimately linked with the social character of salvation is its historical form. The stages of history are the "stages of an essentially collective salvation,"[20] and de Lubac brilliantly shows that a social and historical understanding of salvation was implicit in patristic typological exegesis. "If salvation is social in its essence," he writes, "it follows that history is the necessary interpreter between God and man."[21] Patristic exegesis was thus not mainly an allegorical effort to divine metaphysical principles but a way better to understand history.[22] Here and now, moreover, true spirituality depends on the "historical fact" of Christ and church, an insight that de Lubac illustrates by pointing to how the fathers applied tabernacle, house, and city imagery both to individual and church.[23]

At the same time, de Lubac makes a firmly anti-Marcionite move in emphasizing the continuity between the Old Testament and the New Testament. Christianity receives its social form from Judaism: Paul "pours Christian teaching" into the Jewish "mold," so that Christianity is "a transfiguration rather than fresh creation." Like the old, the new Israel is "still a nation" though it embraces

---

20. De Lubac, *Catholicism*, 69, 73.

21. De Lubac, *Catholicism*, 83.

22. De Lubac, *Catholicism*, 83, 86.

23. De Lubac, *Catholicism*, 100-1.

all nations.[24] Christianity's appreciation of the historical nature of salvation also derives from Judaism.[25] Again, patristic exegesis of the Old Testament provides important evidence of the fathers' endorsement of the Jewish view of the historical and social character of salvation. For the fathers, "to rend [Scripture] by rejecting the Jewish books" is as much a "sacrilege" as rending the body of Christ.[26] Old Testament history provides a key to history in general because the preparatory education of mankind for the coming of Christ takes place "especially among the Jews."[27]

In several respects, however, de Lubac fails to carry his insights through consistently and remains entrenched in traditional, but ultimately unsatisfactory, terminology and categories.[28] Patristic exegesis assumed that redemptive history had moved, de Lubac suggests, from literal to spiritual, so that the division of Scripture into Old and New Testaments is something like body and soul in

---

24. De Lubac, *Catholicism*, 21–22.

25. De Lubac, *Catholicism*, 76.

26. De Lubac, *Catholicism*, 85, 89.

27. De Lubac, *Catholicism*, 130.

28. That he sounds most like a modern Marcionite when he is being perfectly traditional suggests that the problem I am addressing is deeply rooted in the tradition.

man.[29] Traditional though this language is, it must be fundamentally assailed, and de Lubac has in fact provided most of the necessary ammunition. If the Old Testament types were types of the church, and if the church is, as de Lubac insists, a historical and visible as well as an eschatological community, then the transition from Old Testament types to New Testament realities is not adequately described as a transition from letter to spirit or from body to soul. A salvation that is social and historical is necessarily a bodily salvation, and requires the intervention of texts and letters, of words and signs.

Similar problems are apparent in de Lubac's contrast of the written law of the Old Testament to the "evangelical perfection" of the New. Citing the patristic defense for the delay of the incarnation, he writes that man's idolatry made it necessary that God raise him up gradually to salvation, protecting and guiding him through the institutions of the Law: "It was because the wine of the natural law had run out as a consequence of the guests' extravagance that they were reduced to the water of written law." The written law is "in itself" inferior to the natural, a "deterioration" from the pre-Mosaic order, which is transcended by the "wine of the law of grace."[30] De Lubac is, as always, quoting the fathers. Venerable as it is, this formulation is

---

29. De Lubac, *Catholicism*, 89.

30. De Lubac, *Catholicism*, 130.

theologically untenable. In the Old Testament, the written is never subordinated to the natural and unwritten but on the contrary the written Torah is celebrated as the perfecting, life-giving, illuminating Word of Yahweh (cf. Pss. 19, 119). Recent Pauline research, further, has challenged the idea that the letter/spirit contrast in Paul means what de Lubac suggests it means. Scott Hafemann argues rather that "letter" signifies for Paul the law in the absence of the Spirit, while "Spirit" is shorthand for one who possesses the Spirit and is therefore made conformable to the written law.[31] The New Testament does not promise a passage to a law beyond written texts; Paul is much more the grammatologist than de Lubac realizes.

Nor is the transition of Old to New captured by a contrast of exterior to interior, as de Lubac claims: "Christ, like a good teacher, arouses in man the train of thought which turns him from exterior to interior things and raises him up from the sensual to the spiritual."[32] In the same context, de Lubac says that many of the rites of Moses originated in "grossness of Gentiles," citing the example of the purity rules that focused on clean bodies in order to lead men to the "conception of purity of mind."[33] At one

---

31. Scott J. Hafemann, *Paul, Moses, and the History of Israel: The Letter/Spirit Contrast and the Argument from Scripture in 2 Corinthians 3* (Peabody, Massachusetts: Hendrickson Publishers Inc., 1995).

32. De Lubac, *Catholicism*, 131.

33. De Lubac, *Catholicism*, 131.

level, this can be taken as an important protocol against idolatry; we are to worship and serve the invisible Creator rather than the (visible or invisible) creature. Yet, at another level, de Lubac's statements seem to imply a retreat from or elevation above creation in the New Covenant. It is not at all obvious that the New Testament anywhere privileges "purity of mind" over against purity of body, or interior over against exterior purity (cf. Rom. 12:1–2; 1 Cor. 6:12–20). In both Old and New, purity in act and purity of heart were demanded for those who would approach Yahweh's holy hill (cf. Pss. 15, 24:3–4). Purity is, to be sure, defined differently in the New Testament in that it is maintained without ceremonial regulations of the Law but this difference is not a movement from a concern with "bodily" purity to a concern with "mental" purity. Rather than picturing the transition as a movement up a spiritual hierarchy, a musical analogy would be preferable: the New Testament is a modulation of Old Testament motifs into a new key. This picture is more complex than a simple transition from "sensual to spiritual" and is meant to emphasize that the sensual remains completely intact in the New order.

The same contrast of Old and New emerges in de Lubac's discussion of church-state relations in *The Splendour of the Church*. In contrast to all ancient societies, including Israel, he writes, the gospel introduces a hitherto unknown dualism between "temporal and spiritual." De

Lubac's point is mainly the good one that Christianity's establishment of a public community serves as a counterweight to the state's claims to omnicompetent jurisdiction, and he exquisitely makes the related point that a spiritual, non-ecclesiastical religion is easily coopted by tyranny. But his claims go beyond this, for ultimately he roots the social division of temporal and spiritual in man's twofold nature, "animal and spirit," which is the basis for man's destiny, natural and transnatural.[34]

---

34. De Lubac, *Splendour of the Church*, 115-116, 118. Underlying many of my criticisms of de Lubac's program is my suspicion of and opposition to the nature/supernature framework with which de Lubac was so concerned. Several general criticisms may be offered here: 1) Nature/supernature frameworks are incompatible with a vigorous doctrine of creation. In *The Mystery of the Supernatural*, de Lubac cites, with apparent approval, Marechal's denial that created things "exist in themselves" and his claim that they display an "ontological poverty" and a "need of a principle of being" (Henri de Lubac, *The Mystery of the Supernatural*, trans. Rosemary Sheed (London: Geoffrey Chapman, 1967], 42n65). But to say that created things do not exist in themselves is tautologous. Perhaps compared to God one might say that creation displays an "ontological poverty," but this hardly counts as a defect, unless being created is itself a defect; but this would involve a gnostic identification of creation with fall. See also de Lubac's claim that by fact of creation man is "companion in slavery" with nature (de Lubac, *Mystery of the Supernatural*, 148). 2) Anthropologically, nature/supernature doctrines tend to suggest that "humanness" is a state that needs to be "transcended." After stating that man insofar as he is "natural" is in slavery, de Lubac adds that insofar as man is *imago Dei* he is capable of beatific vision; but this suggests a division between something in man that is not image and something that is, whereas I would submit that man is the image of

There is a basic confusion in this. De Lubac quotes Rousseau's complaint that Christianity destroyed the unity and simplicity of ancient community by introducing new laws, a new master, a new motherland, so that a Christian's loyalties are always divided between Fatherland and Mother Church.[35] Apart from the lament, Rousseau is exactly right, but this shows how inadequate it is to suggest that Christianity introduced a division of "temporal" and "spiritual." What Christianity introduced was not a "spiritual" counterweight to the polis, but an alternative, non-political *civitas Dei* within the city of man.

God. Even if man is made "after" the image of God, in the image of the image that is the Son, there is still no reason to suggest that there is anything in man that is not image. There is, de Lubac claims, a distinction between the gift of creation and the "wholly distinct" call to deification (1967: 98), and the gratuity of adoption "transcends" the gift of creation (de Lubac, *Mystery of the Supernatural*, 114–115). But Adam was created a son, so adoption and creation coincide, and the call to deification, to Godlikeness, is simply the eternally renewed call to be authentically and wholly human (i.e., wholly a son), not a transcendence of humanness. 3) Nature/ supernature doctrines tend to occlude culture as a religiously significant factor by shunting it off to the "natural" destiny of man that must be "transcended." It is possible, of course, to argue that man's supernatural destiny embraces and absorbs into itself humanity's cultural achievements, but it appears that culture plays no ultimate role in humanity's incorporation into the life of the Trinity. Poesis, though perhaps not secularized, is also not given the high profile that Milbank suggests it should have in Trinitarian theology (John Milbank, *The Word Made Strange: Theology, Language, Culture* [Oxford: Blackwell, 1997], chs. 5, 7).

35. De Lubac, *Splendour of the Church*, 116.

De Lubac's formulation of this suggests that Christianity inaugurates the process that ends with modern secularism but this is to adopt the Marcionite "liberal Protestant metanarrative"[36] that underwrites an individualistic account of Christianity.

Thus, de Lubac's insistence on the irreducibly social nature of salvation and of Catholicism is undermined by claims that imply that Christian salvation is, even if social, in the end interior and invisible. "The highly developed exterior organization that wins our admiration," he writes in a discussion of the church as sacrament and continuation of Christ, "is but an expression, in accordance with the needs of the present life, of the interior unity of a living entity, so that the Catholic is not only subject to a power but is a member of a body as well." The Catholic not only obeys the orders of the church but "shares in a life, to enjoy a spiritual union."[37] De Lubac thereby reduces "organization," which is a necessary aspect of any social grouping, to an "expression" of some more fundamental ecclesial reality.[38] In both the Old and

---

36. Milbank, *Theology and Social Theory*, 93–98.

37. De Lubac, *Catholicism*, 29.

38. Again, the picture needs to be changed, and the New Testament image of the body is pertinent. Outward unity of a body is not an "expression" of a real unity within; the outward unity *is* the body's unity. Or, one could follow Buber's suggestion that man's relationship with God is best understood on analogy with interpersonal human

New Testaments, however, "organization" is a "spiritual" concern; as a covenant people, Israel was to be governed by elders (Exod. 18:13-27), Solomon requested wisdom from God to lead and guide Israel (1 Kings 3:1-15), and Paul lists "leadership" among the gifts conferred by the Spirit of the enthroned Christ (Rom. 12:8). In passing, we can note that de Lubac's distinction of "organization" and "power," on the one hand, and "interior unity," on the other, implicitly endorses the privatization and secularism that is his main target.

These accommodations to the "inwardness tradition" that weaken the sociality and historicism of de Lubac's theology arise, it must be emphasized, in the context of discussions of the relation of Old and New, contrasted as exterior/interior, body/soul, letter/spirit. A quasi-Marcionite account of redemptive history leaves de Lubac far too close to the individualism, secularism, and liberalism he wishes to reject.

---

relations, for the union of two persons simply cannot be a purely inward one, or even an inward unity with outward "expressions." Instead, the outward gestures and exchanges are as essential to the relationship as inner sympathy. Thus, if de Lubac is right that salvation is inherently social, then the visible and exterior is as primordial as the interior, and it is impossible to say finally which is the "expression" of which. As de Lubac taught us, the "Eucharist makes the church," which means that the invisible/visible unity is an "expression" of the outward celebration of the rite (Henri de Lubac, *Corpus Mysticum: L'eucharistie et l'eglize au moyen age: Etude historique*, 2nd ed. [Paris: Aubier, 1949]).

Renouncing Marcion

The discussion of de Lubac indicates the ease with which the most robust orthodoxy slips into a quasi-Marcionism, and shows that purging Marcion involves a wide-ranging refinement of orthodox teaching and language. Ironically enough, New Testament scholars, whose discipline in its modern form has been constituted by its embrace of a Marcionite history,[39] have begun to provide the tools for

---

39. J. C. O'Neill comments that in New Testament studies "Marcion the historian had his greatest success in the nineteenth century" (J. C. O'Neill, "The Study of the New Testament" in *Nineteenth Century Religious Thought in the West*, 3 vols., eds. Ninian Smart, John Clayton, Steven Katz, and Patrick Sherry [Cambridge, 1985], vol. 2, 171). The revolutionary reassessment of the New Testament by the members of the Tubingen school was based on F. C. Baur's reconstruction of a conflict between Pauline and Judaizing apostles in the early church (Horton Harris, *The Tubingen School* [Oxford: Clarendon, 1975], 181–184; O'Neill, "Study of the New Testament"; N. T. Wright, *The New Testament and the People of God* [London, SPCK, 1993], 20-30). Though Baur repudiated Marcion's idea of two gods, the opposition between Paul's genuine spiritual gospel and the Judaizing, Catholicizing gospel of his opponents has a Marcionite provenance (O'Neill, "Study of the New Testament," 2.146; cf. Reventlow, *Authority of the Bible*, 379, 403). Bultmann remained largely at one with the previous century on this matter, and thus was one of many who bequeathed to modern New Testament scholarship a negative view of Old Testament religion. Specific details of the Old Testament are, for Bultmann, irrelevant to Christian life and theology: "insofar as they are cultic and ritual in character [they] are either bound to a primitive stage of man's social life, economics, government, and so on, or to the history of a particular people." Old Testament history

exorcizing the remaining traces of Marcion's ghost and giving exegetical grounding to a thoroughly public and social Christianity. By placing the ministry of Jesus and the apostles in their Jewish setting, New Testament scholars have stressed the continuity between the religion of Israel and the religion of the church. Jesus and the apostles did not preach interiorization but a gospel that proposed new directions, including new political directions, for the nation of Israel. Here, I will briefly examine some of the Pauline work of James D. G. Dunn and recent works on Jesus by N. T. Wright and Marcus Borg.

Dunn has emphasized the need to move away from individualist assumptions in discussions of Paul's relation to the law toward an examination of the "social function of the law." Drawing on the work of Mary Douglas, Dunn suggests that food laws and circumcision were markers of communal identity, important because they "focused Israel's distinctiveness" and functioned as "badges" of Jewish superiority. Paul's phrase "the works of the law" was his "way of describing in particular the identity and boundary markers which Paul's Jewish (Christian) opponents

---

is not "our history," and the events of the history of Israel are no more relevant to the church than the history of Sparta or the life of Socrates. In short, the Old Testament is not directly God's word to Christians, as the church has made it (Rudolf Bultmann, "The Significance of the Old Testament for the Christian Faith," in *The Old Testament and Christian Faith: A Theological Discussion*, ed. Bernhard W. Anderson [New York, NY: Herder and Herder, 1964], 8-30).

thought, and rightly thought, were put under threat by Paul's understanding of the gospel." Paul's attack on justification by the "works of the law" was not, then, about works-righteousness in the Reformation sense, nor an attack on ritual *per se,* nor a rejection of other uses of the law, but focused upon the particular use of the law as a barrier to Gentile inclusion in the covenant community. The contest of Paul with Judaizers was not first of all about how sinners are saved (by the law or by grace) but about how one marks out the boundaries of the covenant people—that is, an ecclesiological contest.[40] Dunn's view entails a covenantal understanding of justification, conceived not only in terms of individual forgiveness but also socially and publicly as "God's recognition of Israel as his people, his verdict in favour of Israel on grounds of his covenant with Israel."[41] Dunn thus provides exegetical support for the best of de Lubac's efforts to trace the contours of a "social Christianity."

Recent work on the Gospels has undermined the liberal contrast between Jesus and Paul by emphasizing that Jesus as much as Paul was concerned with the community of Israel and her historical destiny. Marcus Borg has argued that Jesus' ministry centered on the "political" question of renewing Israel both as to her internal

---

40. James D. G. Dunn, *Jesus, Paul and the Law* (London: SPCK, 1990), 214-231.

41. Dunn, *Jesus,* 190.

organization and her proper course vis-a-vis Rome; like the Jews of his day, he was concerned with the question, "What does it mean to be Israel in these historical circumstances?" Jesus and the leaders of Judaism answered this question with the same word, "holiness," but there was fundamental conflict about the meaning and implications of holiness. First-century Judaism, according to Borg, was dominated by a paradigm that equated holiness with separation which, at its political limit, implied that the defiling Roman occupiers had to be driven from the holy land. Within Israel, holiness as separation created breaches between adherents of strict holiness codes (whether Pharisee or Essene) and all others who were ostracized as "sinners." In contrast to holiness as separation, Jesus taught a way of holiness as mercy and love, and this implied a particular stance toward the Roman occupation as well as a compassionate outreach to the oppressed of Israel. Jesus' challenge to the reigning paradigm of holiness was manifested in the provocative and politically charged fellowship meals he held with "sinners," his Sabbath teaching and practice, and his attitude toward the temple.

According to Borg, Jesus' "apocalyptic" preaching should be understood as an extension of his program for Israel. He did not foretell the end of the physical cosmos, but predicted a temporal, political catastrophe if Israel continued to pursue the politics of holiness, and this prophetic preaching was dramatized, as E. P. Sanders also highlights in a different way, in Jesus' temple action. Historically, this provocative challenge to Israel and her leadership is a key historical reason for his death.[42]

In *Jesus and the Victory of God*,[43] N. T. Wright examines Jesus in the light of the framework he first developed in *The New Testament and the People of God*. Wright characterizes first-century Israel's situation as one of continuing exile; Jesus was born into an Israel expecting Yahweh to vindicate himself and Israel by keeping his promises to deliver her from her enemies, to return to his temple, and to reestablish Israel's glory and that of David's house among the nations. Following Schweitzer, Wright argues that Jesus' praxis and teaching were those of an eschatological prophet announcing in words and acts an imminent fulfillment of these promises, summoning Israel to be Israel in a new way, and warning of judgment if Israel refused to follow him. Contrary to Schweitzer, and more in keeping with Borg, Wright contends that Jesus promised a fulfillment not in a "transcendent" realm beyond history but in the establishment of a new historical order,

---

42. Marcus Borg, *Conflict, Holiness, and Politics in the Teaching of Jesus*, Studies in Bible and early Christianity, no. 5 (Lewiston: Edwin Mellen, 1984); Marcus Borg, *Jesus: A New Vision* (London: SPCK, 1993); E. P. Sanders, *Jesus and Judaism* (Philadelphia, PA: Fortress Press, 1985).

43. N. T. Wright, *Jesus and the Victory of God* (London: SPCK, 1996).

and that the end Jesus announced was not the "end of the physical cosmos" but the end of Israel as a semi-independent Roman province. Those who followed Jesus would be delivered from the catastrophe, and they would constitute the new, vindicated Israel, their liberation being the coming of the kingdom and the establishment of the new order.

By his teaching and practice Jesus demonstrated that the kingdom of Jewish expectation was going to come in an unexpected manner, and that Israel's real enemy was not Rome but an evil far more profound; his was a revolutionary way of being revolutionary. Jesus' announcement of "repentance" had a specific focus: Israel was to give up her violent dreams of revolution and pursue the way of peace. This required an inner transformation, but Wright refuses to set internal and external in opposition, arguing that instead Jesus called for a transition from a state of inner and outer evil to a state of inner and outer renewal. Like Borg, he sees the challenge to Israel's conventional wisdom embodied in Jesus' attacks on distinctive Jewish institutions and symbols, such as the Sabbath, food laws, and temple. At the same time, beyond Borg, Wright insists that in Jesus' acts and words the God of Israel was actually doing something climactic, bringing the kingdom into reality. For Wright, Jesus intended his death to be the climactic act of the coming of the kingdom, and he expected resurrection to follow.[44]

My point here is not to endorse all the specific historical proposals of these scholars, much less their theological assumptions and implications. Dunn, for example, downplays the relevance of Reformation concerns, which do play a part in Paul's contest with Judaism. Borg may be criticized for trying to fit Jesus into cross-cultural "religious personality types," while refusing to accept the designation "Messiah,"[45] and he is more than a little anachronistic in his effort to present Jesus as a leader of a first-century peace movement. Borg also describes the contrast between the religion of Jesus and Judaism (as well as forms of Christianity) as a difference between a religion that "depended upon" external observance and one that focuses on internal transformation, and suggests that Jesus "spiritualized" religion. Along similar lines, his claim that Jesus called his disciples to die to the world of "culture" hints at a pervasive dualism of "spirit" and "culture," though the whole thrust of Borg's work suggests that Jesus intended to inaugurate, through the Spirit, a new cultural form of life.[46] To be sure, Borg makes it im-

---

44. Cf. also N. T. Wright, *Who was Jesus?* (London, SPCK, 1992).

45. Wright, *Jesus and the Victory of God*, 77.

46. Marcus Borg, *Jesus: A New Vision* (London: SPCK, 1993), 109–110, 113, 139–141.

possible to see the "Jesus movement" as in any simple way a "spiritualization" of Israel, but when he concludes that the kingdom means "the end of the world of ordinary experience, as well as the end of the world as one's center and security,"[47] he vitiates the historicism of his thesis and returns, by a circuitous route, to Bultmann.[48]

Though I am more completely favorable to Wright, there are a number of details to which I take exception. By characterizing Israel as being still in exile in the first century, he tends to underplay the significance of the restoration from Babylon as a real, albeit provisional, fulfillment of the promises of Jeremiah and Ezekiel. And, if Jesus' account of the kingdom was so "revolutionary," it is difficult to make sense of Jesus' charges that the Pharisees failed to believe in him because they had failed to understand the Scriptures. Jesus, it seems, expected people to see him as the embodiment of the Anointed One prophesied in the Old Testament.[49]

---

47. Borg, *Conflict, Holiness, and Politics*, 255.

48. Cf. Wright, *Jesus and the Victory of God*, 77.

49. Elsewhere, to be sure, Wright offers statements that balance his perspective. He argues, for example, that Jesus' personality and career fit perfectly with Old Testament descriptions of Yahweh's character and works (*Who was Jesus?*, 51–52).

Conclusion

Whatever the warrant of the specific historical and theological proposals, however, my general point stands, namely, that these scholars are offering an account of the nature and early history of Christianity that, by placing Jesus and Paul firmly in their historical context, overcomes modern Marcionism. Moreover, by emphasizing the political and communal dimensions of their teaching, they have provided a firm exegetical basis for a more consistent social theology than de Lubac offers. For the same reason, they open a door to a truly postliberal theology and to a thoroughgoing critique of the liberal secularism that liberal theology helped to produce. If the stakes are as high as I have suggested, we should hope that this is a door no one can shut.

CHAPTER SEVEN

SEMIOSIS AND SOCIAL SALVATION (MOSTLY) IN DE DOCTRINA CHRISTIANA

Augustine's theory of signs has been used in all sorts of ways in the past century. Wittgenstein begins the *Philosophical Investigations* with a tendentious and critical summary of Augustine's theory of language.[1] While denying that Augustine invented semiotics, Tzvetan Todorov suggests that Augustine was the first to meet the conditions for the construction of a genuine semiotic theory.[2] Umberto Eco claims that Augustine's discussion of the particle *ex* in *de Magistro* hinted that linguistic signs are "sets of instructions," an insight unrecognized and un-

---

1. Peter King defends Augustine against Wittgenstein in "Augustine on the Impossibility of Teaching," *Metaphilosophy* 29:3 (1998), 179-195.

2. *Theories of the Symbol*, trans. Catherine Porter (Ithaca, NY: Cornell University Press, 1982), 15.

developed until the twentieth century,[3] and many others have put Augustine's theory into conversation with post-structuralist grammatology, semiotics, and deconstruction.[4] R. A. Markus's articles have explicated Augustine's theory against the background of ancient sign-theory, and a number of other historians of late antiquity have jumped in to confirm and correct Markus.[5]

Much recent scholarship has emphasized Augustine's theological context, categories, and purposes. Clifford Ando goes so far as to say that Augustine has no theory of signs at all, no theory of language either, but only deals with signs, language, time, and other philosophical issues *ad hoc*, as they arise in the midst of religious instruction

---

3. Eco, "The Theory of Signs and the Role of the Reader," *Bulletin of the Midwest Modern Language Association* 14:1 (1981), 35-45.

4. Brenda Deen Schildgen, "Augustine's Answer to Derrida in the De Doctrina Christiana," *New Literary History* 25:2 (1994), 383-97; Jeffrey Ringer, "Faith and Language: Walter Hilton, Augustine, and Poststructural Semiotics," *Christianity and Literature* 53:1 (2003), 3-18; James K. A. Smith, "Between Predication and Silence: Augustine on How (Not) to Speak of God," *Heythrop Journal* 41 (2000), 66-86.

5. Markus's key works on the subject are collected in *Signs and Meanings: World and Text in Ancient Christianity* (Liverpool: Liverpool University Press, 1996). See also B. Darrell Jackson, "The Theory of Signs in St. Augustine's *De doctrina christiana*," *Revue etudes augustiniennes* 15 (1969), 9-49; Giuovanni Manetti, *Theories of the Sign in Classical Antiquity*, trans. Christine Richardson (Bloomington, IN: Indiana University Press, 1993).

or controversy. Insofar as he has one, his theory of signs is a *theology* of signs, intersecting with his Trinitarian theology, Christology, doctrine of creation, his eschatological, as well as his biblical hermeneutics and homiletics.[6]

Augustine gave most direct and sustained attention to signs in *de doctrina Christiana*. Given the intense and thoughtful scrutiny this treatise has received in the past few decades, I cannot hope to say much of anything original about its contents. I hope to explain Augustine's views accurately, but my real aim is to deploy Augustine's theory in ways that Augustine might not quite have recognized. In short, I aim to *use* Augustine. Now that, Augustine would have approved. He famously begins *de doctrina*

---

6. Ando, "Signs, Idols and the Incarnation in Augustinian Metaphysics," *Representations* 73 (2001), 24. Ando points out later in the article that many modern readers skim off the Christology to get to the atheological substance, but that for Augustine the Christology was the whole point (38). Other essays highlighting the theological interests of Augustine's theory include Rowan Williams, "Language, Reality and Desire in Augustine's *De doctrina*," *Literature and Theology* 3 (1989), 138-50; Oliver O'Donovan, "*Usus* and *fruitio* in Augustine, *De doctrina Christiana* I," *Journal of Theological Studies* n. s. 33 (1982), 361-97; Smith, "Between Predication and Silence"; Mark D. Jordan, "Words and Word: Incarnation and Signification in Augustine's *De Doctrina Christiana*," *Augustinian Studies* 11 (1980), 177-96; Luke Ferretter, "The Trace of the Trinity: Christ and Difference in Augustine's Theory of Language," *Literature and Theology* 12:3 (1998), 256-267. As the titles indicate, several of these articles combine theological interest with interest in confronting poststructuralist theory.

Christiana by distinguishing between *res uti* and *res frui*, things to be used and things to be enjoyed. Throughout, though, he remains certain that there is only one truly enjoyable thing, the Triune God. This is to say, Augustine would have *wanted* himself to be used. I trust that I have done what Augustine would have hoped—using him in love, using him in God.

Let me be more specific about the way I want to use Augustine. In one of the boldest and most-discussed theological works of the past few decades, John Milbank argues that modern social theory is either heretical or pagan, and thus confronts Christianity as an alternative theology and an alternative church. A self-professed "postmodern Augustinian," Milbank draws heavily on Augustine to unveil the social and political vision embedded within Christianity, concluding that with a theological sociology of its own, the church need borrow little from secular social theory.[7]

Augustine of course presents Christian social and political theory on a grand scale in *de civitate Dei*, but there are countervailing tendencies in Augustine's theol-

---

7. *Theology and Social Theory* (Oxford: Blackwell, 1991). The *nouvelle theologie* Catholicism of Henri de Lubac lurks in the background of Milbank's proposal. See de Lubac, *Catholicism: Christ and the Common Destiny of Man*, trans. Lacelot Sheppard and Sister Elizabeth Englund (San Francisco, CA: Ignatius, 1988) and Milbank, *The Suspended Middle: Henri de Lubac and the Debate Concerning the Supernatural* (Grand Rapids, MI: Eerdmans, 2005).

ogy that seem inimical to Milbank's claims. These difficulties come to a particular focus in Augustine's discussions of signs, scattered over his works from *de Magistro* (389) to *de Trinitate* (414). Augustine commonly disparages, or seems to disparage, the materiality of signs, often pointing to the fading breath of a spoken word to illustrate the frailty of human existence. Allied to this is what appears to be obsessive fear of falling prey to the seductive beauty of the world. Given these Plotinian tendencies, Milbank's notion that Augustine provides materials for a theology that is simultaneously a social science seems strained.

The purpose of this chapter is to examine the contribution Augustine's theory of signs might make to Christian social and cultural theology. The argument moves forward in quasi-Thomist fashion: First, I show how Augustine's theological conception of signification opens out into a theological sociology and cultural theory. Then (*videtur quod*), I examine how Augustine's theology of *peregrinatio* seems to undermine its own sociological thrust. Finally (*sed contra*), I show how he recovers the social and cultural dimension of his theory of signs within the category of *caritas*, and this (*responsio*) helps to vindicate Milbank's use of Augustine. I close with a series of lingering questions.

Signs and Things

Augustine claims that *doctrina* (teaching) is teaching of signs or things, and that knowledge of the former lead to the knowledge of the latter. The difference between *signum* and *res*, however, is not absolute. All signs are things, and some things signify: "the log that Moses threw into the bitter waters or the stone that Jacob used or the sheep that Abraham sacrificed for his son" are "things, but they are at the same time signs of other things" (1.4).[8] *Signa* and *res* are not two classes of things so much as two states in which things may stand.[9]

---

8. I am using the translation of R. P. H. Green in the Oxford World's Classics (Oxford: Oxford University Press, 1997). Citations are from that edition, using book number and the marginal paragraph numbering. The Latin reads, *Omnis doctrina vel rerum est vel signorum, sed res per signa discuntur. Proprie autem nunc res appellavi, quae non ad significandum aliquid adhibentur, sicuti est lignum, lapis, pecus atque huiusmodi cetera; sed non illud lignum quod in aquas amaras Moysen misisse legimus, ut amaritudine carerent neque ille lapis quem Iacob sibi ad caput posuerat neque illud pecus quod pro filio immolavit Abraham* (Latin texts available at: http://www.augustinus.it/latino/dottrina_cristiana/index2.htm.

9. William S. Babcock, "*Caritas* and Signification," in Duane W. H. Arnold and Pamela Bright, eds., *De doctrina Christiana: A Classic of Western Culture* (Notre Dame, IN: University of Notre Dame Press, 1995), 146. What Augustine does not say is that all things are in some sense signs, since they are all created to evoke the glory and character of God. This may suggest that Augustine appears to be operating with a conception of an inert "nature" as fundamentally insignificant, but his later distinction of things used and enjoyed makes it clear that even things of this world that are not specially designated as

What sort of *res* is a *signum*? In *de doctrina*, Augustine gives two answers.[10] A *signum* differs from a *res* properly speaking because the latter "is not employed to signify something," while "signs" are "things employed to signify something" (1.4; *signa, res . . . quae ad significandum aliquid adhibentur*). He gives a second definition in 2.1: "a sign is a thing which of itself makes some other thing come to mind, besides the impression that it presents to the senses" (*Signum est enim res praeter speciem, quam ingerit sensibus, aliud aliquid ex se faciens in cogitationem venire*). As Darrell Jackson points out, these definitions share two features: First, that *signa* constitute a subclass of *res*, and, second, that a *signum* is a kind of thing that bears a certain relation (a "signifying" one) with *aliquid*, something else. A *res* is a thing considered in itself, while a sign is a thing standing in some specified relation with another thing.

Beyond these similarities, the two definitions run in quite different directions. The first seems like a simple sign-referent description of signification, but the examples Augustine gives hardly fit that description. The log Moses threw into the bitter waters is a *res*-become-*signum*, and presumably the cross is the thing to which this sign

---

signs are to be used for the sake of knowing God, and thus function as "signs" in some sense.

10. I am particularly reliant on the careful discussion in Jackson, "Theory of Signs," 11-13.

points. But the cross is hardly a straightforward referent for the piece of wood. But put those complications aside. I wish to focus on the second definition, which, instead of defining the sign by reference to the sign-user or the sign-referent relation, defines the sign in terms of the effect on the sign-recipient. The first definition looks like a referential definition of sign (though it is more complicated); the latter is a pragmatic, perlocutionary, definition.

Having introduced this second definition, Augustine classifies signs in two categories, *signa naturalia* and *signa data*, a distinction that has to do with will. *Signa naturalia* lead to a *res* by means of inference: "we see a footprint and think that the animal whose footprint it is has passed by" (2.1). But footprints do not will to communicate. Given signs, however, are products of will:

> Given signs are those which living things give to each other, in order to show, to the best of their ability, the motions of their minds, or anything that they have felt or learnt. There is no reason for us to signify something (that is, to give a sign) except to express and transmit to another's mind what is in the mind of the person who gives the sign (2.3).[11]

---

11. *Data vero signa sunt quae sibi quaeque viventia invicem dant ad demonstrandos quantum possunt motus animi sui, vel sensa aut intellecta quaelibet. Nec ulla causa est nobis significandi, id est signi dandi,*

This is broad enough to include animal communication, for "a cockerel on finding food gives a vocal sign to its hen to come quickly, and a dove calls to, or is called by, its mate by cooing" (2.4), but Augustine of course has human signifying mainly in view. His stress on the will makes it clear that we are to take the *data* of *signa data* literally.[12] Variations on *dare—dant, dandi, dat*—bubble through the passage. And Augustine not only piles up the vocabulary of gift, but, in a rhyming formulation, defines signification as a kind of giving: *significandi, id est signi dandi.* To signify is to externalize what is within, to give public expression to the *motus animi.* To signify is also to give.[13] A sign is a thing, a thing gifted that gives the soul in its giving.

---

nisi ad depromendum et traiciendum in alterius animum id quod animo gerit is qui signum dat. Horum igitur signorum genus, quantum ad homines attinet, considerare atque tractare statuimus, quia et signa divinitus data quae in Scripturis sanctis continentur, per homines nobis indicata sunt qui ea conscripserunt.

12. As argued by J. Engels, "La doctrine du signe chez saint Augustin," *Studia Patristica* 6 (1962), 366-73.

13. Elsewhere, Augustine uses other phrases to describe what in the mind or soul is transmitted through signs. In *de Trinitate*, he describes the origin of signification as *id quod animo gerit*, "what is going on in the soul," and he calls this motion an internal word: *verbum quod mente gerimus.* He employs an incarnational model of linguistic signification in the first book of *de Trinitate*: "When we speak, the word which we hold in our mind becomes a sound in order that what we have in our mind may pass through ears of flesh into the listener's

Under his second definition, Augustine posits two poles of signification. The inner pole is the *motus animi*, while the external pole is the *signum* itself. In the following two sections, I examine these two poles in turn, beginning with the external *signum*.

Semiosis, Society, and Culture

Even when talking about *signa naturalia* Augustine has an expansive conception of sign. *Signa naturalia* includes the "expression of an angry or depressed person signifies an emotional state even if there is no such wish on the part of the person who is angry or depressed, and likewise any other emotion is revealed by the evidence of the face even if we are not seeking to reveal it" (2.2).[14] His category of *signa data* covers an even wider range of phenomena. Gestures are signs, both in common life and on the stage: "When we nod, we give a sign just to the eyes of the person whom we want, by means of that sign, to make aware of our wishes. Particular movements of the hands signify a great deal. By the movement of all their limbs,

---

mind: this is called speech. Our thought, however, is not converted into the same sound, but remains intact in its own home, suffering no diminution from its change as it takes on the form of a word in order to make its way into the ears. In the same way the word of God became flesh in order to live in us but was unchanged."

14. *Et vultus irati seu tristis affectionem animi significat, etiam nulla eius voluntate qui aut iratus aut tristis est; aut si quis alius motus animi vultu indice proditur, etiam nobis non id agentibus ut prodatur (2.1.2).*

actors give certain signs to the cognoscenti and converse with the spectators' eyes, as it were; and it is through the eyes that flags and standards convey the wishes of military commanders. All these things are, to coin a phrase, visible words" (2.5).[15] Visibility is not necessary. Any sense will do, and Augustine gives examples of significant sounds and smells.[16] Culture as a whole is a semiotic process, or a collection of semiotic processes: "such things as the conventional differences in dress and in bodily ornament, designed to distinguish sex or rank, and countless kinds of coded meanings (*innumerabilia genera significationum*) without which society would function less smoothly or not at all, and everything in the realm of weights and measures, coinage, currency, which are peculiar to individual states and peoples and so on" (2.100).[17]

---

15. *Nam cum innuimus, non damus signum nisi oculis eius quem volumus per hoc signum voluntatis nostrae participem facere. Et quidam motu manuum pleraque significant, et histriones omnium membrorum motibus dant signa quaedam scientibus et cum oculis eorum quasi fabulantur, et vexilla draconesque militares per oculos insinuant voluntatem ducum. Et sunt haec omnia quasi quaedam verba visibilia (2.3.4).*

16. "Our Lord gave a sign through the smell of the ointment by which his feet were anointed, and...in the sacrament of his body and blood he signified his wishes through the sense of taste, and...the healing of the woman who touched the border of his garment has its significance" (2.6-7).

17. *Commoda vero et necessaria hominum cum hominibus instituta sunt, quaecumque in habitu et cultu corporis ad sexus vel honores discernendos differentia placuit, et innumerabilia genera significationum*

Signa data, especially the *signa data* of language, unite human beings to one another. In the preface to *de doctrina*, Augustine ponders why God teaches through human instruments rather than directly through the Spirit. One answer is to teach humility. Students must humble themselves to learn from a frail human teacher, and teachers, too, should humbly communicate what they have learned. It is an "arrogant and dangerous temptation" to pursue knowledge of the Scriptures without dependence on anyone (Preface, 12).[18] Scriptural interpretation takes place within the church, and this leads to the second rationale for human mediation of the knowledge of God, love: "there would be no way for love, which ties people together in bonds of unity, to make souls overflow and as it were intermingle (*non haberet aditum refundendorum et quasi miscendorum sibimet animorum*) with each other, if human beings learned nothing from other human beings" (Preface, 13).[19] Scripture elicits love not merely

---

sine quibus humana societas aut non omnino aut minus commode geritur; quaeque in ponderibus atque mensuris, et nummorum impressionibus vel aestimationibus, sua cuique civitati et populo sunt propria, et cetera huiusmodi, quae nisi hominum instituta essent, non per diversos populos varia essent, nec in ipsis singulis populis pro arbitrio suorum principum mutarentur (2.25.39).

18. Mark Jordan finds this communal emphasis in the title of the treatise, for *doctrina* presumes the presence of *doctores* (Jordan, "Words and Word," 179).

19. *Deinde ipsa caritas, quae sibi homines invicem nodo unitatis as-*

because of its direct exhortations to love, but because the very processes of reading and studying, of teaching and learning, of giving and receiving signs, binds persons together. United souls are not juxtaposed to one another, as if the teacher remained "outside" the student during the process of teaching, as if they met only at a shared perimeter. Souls overflow and intermingle; Augustine's language suggests that through teaching and learning, souls are united in an image of the perichoretic life of the Trinity.[20]

On the other hand, signification also presupposes agreement about the meaning of signs. A word evokes a thought, or communicates the motions of the soul, only if the hearer or reader is already playing the same language game as the writer or speaker.[21] Signs mean something

---

tringit, non haberet aditum refundendorum et quasi miscendorum sibi-met animorum, si homines per homines nihil discerent.

20. In a famous statement in *Contra Faustum* 19.11, Augustine argues that "Men cannot be brought together (*coagulari homines possunt*) in the name of any religion, whether true or false, without being associated by means of some shared visible symbols or rituals" (*signaculorum vel sacramentorum visibilium consortio colligentur*). Augustine is here speaking specifically of religious communities, but his point is wider: Augustine cannot envision a community of any kind that is not bound together by common signs.

21. Jackson rightly points out, against Markus, that for Augustine "will" determines the *occasion* for a *signum datum*, not its *meaning* ("Theory of Signs," 14). We give signs voluntarily, but the meaning of what we give is not what we will it to be but is pre-determined by

to somebody, and the somebodies who agree on meanings constitute a linguistic community.[22] Augustine notes that even the same sound can have different significances in different languages. "Beta" is the name of a letter in Greek, but a vegetable in Latin ("beet"). He concludes, "all these meanings . . . derive their effects on the mind from each individual's agreement with a particular convention. As this agreement varies in extent, so do their effects. People did not agree to use them because they were already meaningful; rather, they became meaningful because people agreed to use them" (2.94).[23] Signification presupposes community, a compact, covenant, or federation in meaning. *Signa data* are sociologically qualified, as it were, at both ends: They are only signs to those who share things common to a community, and for those who know the meanings of the signs, particular uses of signs mingle souls together. Augustine's treatment of signs thus yields a logos-based sociology, a socio-*logos*.

Semiosis and Sin

---

the code we are using.

22. As Markus (*Signs and Meanings*, 115) puts it.

23. *Sicut ergo hae omnes significationes pro suae cuiusque societatis consensione animos movent, et quia diversa consensio est, diverse movent; nec ideo consenserunt in eas homines, quia iam valebant ad significationem, sed ideo valent quia consenserunt in eas.*

Augustine employs his covenantal conception of semiotics to diagnose the evils of pagan superstitions. In Book 2 of *de doctrina*, he lays out a classification scheme for pagan learning. [24] In his proto-Ramist fashion, he first distinguishes between things humanly instituted and things divinely instituted. Natural sciences, logic, and history are divinely instituted, since humans discover such things by investigating objective realities (2.121). He subdivides humanly-instituted subjects into superstitious and non-superstitious learning. He has little to say about non-superstitious pagan learning, except to explain that this category includes conventions of acting, some techniques of representation in the visual arts, and fictional romances.

He is more interested in superstitious practices, which he defines as those that concern "making and worshipping of idols, or the worshipping or the created order or part of it as if it were god, or if it involves certain kinds of consultations or contacts about meaning arranged and ratified with demons (*pacta quaedam significationum cum daemonibus placita atque foederata*), such as the enterprises involved in the art of magic, which poets tend to mention rather than teach" (2.74).[25] Astrologers, for example,

----

24. I am relying here on Markus, *Signs and Meanings*, chapter 5.

25. The whole passage reads, *Superstitiosum est quidquid institutum est ab hominibus ad facienda et colenda idola pertinens vel ad colendam sicut Deum creaturam partemve ullam creaturae vel ad consultationes et*

tell the truth about the position of the stars but enslave people foolish enough to enter into a *pactum* of meaning with them: "when free people go to see such an astrologer, they pay money for the privilege of coming away as slaves of Mars or Venus, or rather all the stars" (2.79).[26] More dangerously still, astrologers end up contracting their clients to demons. Simply "because they involve signs instituted by human presumption, [these practices] must be classed among those contracts and agreements made with devils" (2.86).[27]

Augustine's analysis can be applied more broadly. Sensible appearances become meaningful signs because a community determines that these appearances will stand for certain motions of the soul. Sharing meanings requires a prior participation in the community. If that community is instituted in pride, then agreement in the

---

pacta quaedam significationum cum daemonibus placita atque foederata, qualia sunt molimina magicarum artium, quae quidem commemorare potius quam docere assolent poetae. Ex quo genere sunt, sed quasi licentiore vanitate, haruspicum et augurum libri (2.20.30).

26. Nam quisque liber ad huiusmodi mathematicum cum ingressus fuerit, dat pecuniam ut servus inde exeat aut Martis aut Veneris vel potius omnium siderum, quibus illi qui primi erraverunt erroremque posteris propinaverunt, vel bestiarum propter similitudinem vel hominum ad ipsos homines honorandos imposuerunt vocabula (2.21.32).

27. Quare istae quoque opiniones quibusdam rerum signis humana praesumptione institutis ad eadem illa quasi quaedam cum daemonibus pacta et conventa referendae sunt (2.22.34).

meanings that community assigns means making a pact with the prideful. Even if we discount demonic influence, becoming fluent in the semiotic system of the city of man involves making a pact, and a *pax*, with that city-without-peace.

To grasp the deeper sources of the distortion of signification and culture, we need to move outside *de doctrina Christiana* and attend to the linguistic analogy Augustine uses to describe the *motus animi* in *de Trinitate*. While exploring the doctrine of the Trinity, Augustine suggests an analogy between the Father who begets a consubstantial Word and the human soul that begets an "inner word" begotten from the soul by an act of will or love. This word is pre-cultural, prior to any of the specific codes of signification used in human societies. As John Cavadini points out, the linguistic image that Augustine uses implies that knowing is always willing, that an act of will intervenes between the mind and its inner word: "one can never simply reproduce one's knowledge in an unmediated fashion. It has to be 'spoken,' even interiorly, that is, in the inner *verbum*, begotten in a particular act of will, in a particular kind of love or intention."[28] Because the will is corruptible, the inner word also is corruptible, so that even before it comes to ecstatic expression in an

---

28. Cavadini, "The Quest for Truth in Augustine's *De Trinitate*," *Theological Studies* 58 (1997), 437.

exterior word it is already a lie, an act of self-deception, a distorting mirror of the soul.

Semiotic codes can become so corrupted that even a more pure inner word suffers distortion as it comes to expression. Cavadini again: "The inner word, as presignificatory, has a kind of vulnerability to deformation when even the gestures, not to mention the words, in which it is forced to express itself, are contextualized by sign systems which have encoded in them the preference for power over justice."[29] A Roman might want to talk about or practice virtue, but the Roman cultural code leaves open only one possibility—virtue is domination, of enemies or of passions. Peaceable virtue is not an option, nor is feminine virtue. As soon as the Roman utters *virtus*, or makes some recognizable virtuous gesture, he is in a cultural pact with power, gender injustice, and violence. To take a more contemporary example: A Presidential candidate might wish to be an advocate of justice, but the pre-existent code of Presidential electioneering channels his words and gestures toward, say, the goal of satisfying potential voters and donors.

Let me sum up what I have sketched so far: Given signs communicate what is in the soul to others, and thereby signs promote the mingling of souls that is community. Signs also presuppose a compact or covenant

---

29. Ibid.

among the sign-users that is not only a pragmatic necessity but a religious or quasi-religious bond. Communication of minds and union of souls takes place not only through language, teaching, and learning, but through gestures, clothing, money, and all the other necessary human institutions that Augustine lists. Cultures, for Augustine, are complexes of signification, which are not only functional but communicative in the deepest sense. (In this, Augustine stands closer to Mauss than Durkheim.) Semiotic processes of culture both presuppose a community of meaning and, ideally, cultivate a perichoretic communion of souls.

But Augustine is, as always, aware of perverse desires and habits that ruin human existence, and he links the ruination of social life to the ruination of signification. Idolatrous and superstitious signs involve users in compacts with demons, since they agree with demons in attributing demonic significance to the signs. (I form a pact with demons if I agree that Scorpio in the house of Saturn is an omen of evil.) Even without demonic involvement, signifying systems, and the consensus on which they are founded, can be distorted by sin, because every one of our interventions in public discourse incarnates a prior interior word that arises from a corrupt will. Further, semiotic systems can become so perverse that it is virtually impossible to express even a good inner word without corruption. The city of man, with its love of self and lust of domination, is the product of these distortions: The city of man rests on a pact of falsehood, its public discourse and culture expresses the inner lust for power that is fallen humanity's characteristic stance, and its signifying systems are infused with that same lust for power, and preform the way the motions of the soul can be expressed.

If the city of God is to take some hold in the world, renewal of the soul will not suffice. Given the distortions of our signifying codes, the best heart cannot break out in true speech and act; his best intentions will be coopted by the regnant signifying system. Augustine must argue either that redemption takes place solely within the ascetic soul that stands in protest against culture as such (which is an admission that culture itself is beyond redemption); or he must argue that the signifying systems themselves can be renovated and made conducive to just community.

Augustine takes the latter course, but with difficulty. He describes the shift from the Old to the New as a redemption of signs, such that the people of the New Covenant possess a semiotic system within which peace, justice, truth, and love may come to linguistic and cultural expression. But once this temporal sequence is introduced, Augustine's theological sociology begins to waver.

Semiosis in Redemptive History

One obvious way that sin disrupts the signifying process is that it has produced a diversity of languages that prevents communication and communion. In *de doctrina* 2.8-9, Augustine refers to the incident at Babel, where "wicked men justly received incompatible languages." Ultimately, God used even this for the salvation of man. The linguistic challenges that attend the interpretation of Scripture in a polylinguistic world humble us so that, faced with its profundities and puzzles, we are thrown back to communion with our fellows, back to the give-and-return of conversation (2.10).[30] Babel's divisions thus have the ultimate effect of reuniting human society in mutual dependence.

But the redemption of signs takes place mainly in the transition from Old to New Covenants. For Augustine, the differences between Christianity and paganism and between Christianity and Judaism are semiotic differences. Jews under the Old Testament system were in subjection to *signa*, albeit *signa utile*. The institutions of Israel were an unusual type of *signa* in that the Jews had no idea what the *res* of their *signa* was (*nescientes quo referrentur*). Yet, they were useful signs because they signified the new covenant, and as the Jews used these signs in the igno-

---

30. *Sed multis et multiplicibus obscuritatibus et ambiguitatibus decipiuntur qui temere legunt, aliud pro alio sentientes; quibusdam autem locis quid vel falso suspicentur non inveniunt, ita obscure dicta quaedam densissimam caliginem obducunt. Quod totum provisum esse divinitus non dubito, ad edomandam labore superbiam et intellectum a fastidio renovandum, cui facile investigata plerumque vilescunt* (2.6.7).

rance of faith they progressed toward that goal (3.22).[31]
Their fall was also semiotic. They erred in adhering to
the "spiritual slavery" of interpreting "signs as things,"
so that they became "incapable of raising the mind's eye
above the physical creation so as to absorb the eternal
light" (3.21).[32] At least Jews were better off than pagans,
who set their affection on signs of falsehoods and became
infatuated not by signs of reality but by empty signs that
led away from the true God. Their bondage was far worse
than the Jews (3.28).

Christian freedom means liberation from both the
useless signs of pagans and the useful signs of the Jews.
When the gospel confronts pagans, it does away with useless signs altogether. A Christian "attends to or worships
a useful sign, one divinely instituted, and does realize its
force and significance, does not worship a thing which is
only apparent and transitory but rather the thing to which

---

31. *Quae tamen servitus in Iudaeo populo longe a ceterarum gentium more distabat, quandoquidem rebus temporalibus ita subiugati erant ut unus eis in omnibus commendaretur Deus. Et quamquam signa rerum spiritalium pro ipsis rebus observarent, nescientes quo referrentur, id tamen insitum habebant, quod tali servitute uni omnium, quem non videbant, placerent Deo* (3.6.10).

32. *Sed si: Sabbatum audierit, verbi gratia, non intellegit nisi unum diem de septem, qui continuo volumine repetuntur; et cum audierit: Sacrificium, non excedit cogitatione illud quod fieri de victimis pecorum terrenisque fructibus solet. Ea demum est miserabilis animae servitus, signa pro rebus accipere, et supra creaturam corpoream oculum mentis ad hauriendum aeternum lumen levare non posse* (3.5.9).

all such things are to be related" (3.29).[33] In confronting Judaism, the gospel does not destroy signs but elevates to the realities to which they always pointed. Augustine does not mean that Christianity liberates from signs as such. The church's signs are fewer and simpler (3.31), but they are still signs, and the proper use of Christian signs leads to the thing.

By proper use of useful Christian signs, the corruptions caused by misuse of signs in paganism and Judaism are healed. The New Covenant restores semiosis, liberating from the idolatrous misuse of signs, from the compact with demons involved in idolatry and superstition, from the useful but limited signs of Israel. Because there is a revolution at the semiotic level, and not merely in the soul, culture can be redeemed. Given Augustine's expansive understanding of signs earlier in *de doctrina*, we can extrapolate from this to an Augustinian theology of semiotic, and hence social, salvation.

This discussion, however, raises difficult problems for Augustine's theory of signs, and for the understanding of culture that accompanies it. It is not clear, for starters, why the Jews were culpable for their "enslavement" to useful signs. Augustine presupposes that we need to know a thing before we can even recognize a

---

33. *Quam ob rem Christiana libertas eos quos invenit sub signis utilibus, tamquam prope inventos, interpretatis signis quibus subditi erant, elevatos ad eas res quarum illa signa sunt, liberavit.*

sign as a sign, much less what the sign stands for. The *res* is the horizon for understanding the *signum*. But if the Jews were ignorant of the *res* to which their *signa* pointed, then how can their enslavement be blameworthy? How could they avoid taking their signs as the things? Augustine deals with this problem briefly, and unsatisfactorily, when he says that "it is better to be dominated by unknown but useful signs than to interpret them in a useless way" (3.32).

More fundamentally, a palpable discomfort runs through Augustine's treatment of the signs of the New order. He cannot deny such signs exist, or that they are useful for bringing us to the real thing. Yet he struggles to explain why the church still uses signs at all. Since Jesus' resurrection, "[W]e are not oppressed by the tiresome necessity of attending to signs, even the signs which we now understand" (3.31[34]), which sounds like a brief for elevation above signification as such.[35] But if the New Covenant takes us from signs, then it takes us from communal life, from the intermingling of souls, from the semiotic processes of human culture. Augustine does not of course draw this conclusion, but instead speaks of the

---

34. *Hoc vero tempore posteaquam resurrectione Domini nostri manifestissimum indicium nostrae libertatis illuxit, nec eorum quidem signorum, quae iam intellegimus*, 3.9.13.

35. This of course is no isolated statement; see Ando, "Signs, Idols and the Incarnation," esp. 32-38.

few, simple, inspiring holy signs of the apostolic tradition (3.32[36]). Gears are grinding as he does so. Once temporality is introduced into the equation—once we consider the transition from Old to New—then the materials Augustine provided for a theology of social redemption—a soteriological sociology, or a sociological soteriology— seem to liquefy and begin to slip through our fingers.

Initially, this impression is deepened by Augustine's discussion of *usus* and *fruitio*, which is embedded in a multi-layered metaphor of *peregrinatio*. When we have examined that metaphor a bit more closely, however, we will find that it helps us out of our impasse and solidifies (if it doesn't entirely clarify) Augustine's social account of salvation once again.

The Pilgrimage of Interpretation

For Augustine, "enjoy" (*frui*) means, "to enjoy something is to hold fast to it in love for its own sake," whereas "to use something is to apply whatever it may be to the purpose of obtaining what you love" (1.8).[37] Augustine has no sooner introduced this distinction than he imag-

---

36. *Pauca pro multis eademque factu facillima et intellectu augustissima et observatione castissima ipse Dominus et apostolica tradidit disciplina*, 3.9.13.

37. *Frui est enim amore inhaerere alicui rei propter seipsam. Uti autem, quod in usum venerit ad id quod amas obtinendum referre, si tamen amandum est* (1.4.4).

ines himself, with his readers, on a pilgrimage toward a homeland:

> Suppose we were travelers who could live happily only in our homeland, and because our absence made us unhappy we wished to put an end to our misery and return there: we would need transport by land or sea which we could use to travel to our homeland, the object of our enjoyment. But if we were fascinated by the delights of the journey and the actual traveling, we would be perversely enjoying things that we should be using; and we would be reluctant to finish our journey quickly (1.8).[38]

Augustine returns repeatedly to this image throughout the opening book of *de doctrina*. In order to enjoy the fullness of the Trinity, who is the one to be enjoyed, "our minds must be purified so that they are able to perceive that light and then hold fast to it." This purification is "a

---

38. *Quomodo ergo, si essemus peregrini, qui beate vivere nisi in patria non possemus, eaque peregrinatione utique miseri et miseriam finire cupientes, in patriam redire vellemus, opus esset vel terrestribus vel marinis vehiculis quibus utendum esset ut ad patriam, qua fruendum erat, pervenire valeremus; quod si amoenitates itineris et ipsa gestatio vehiculorum nos delectaret, conversi ad fruendum his quibus uti debuimus, nollemus cito viam finire et perversa suavitate implicati alienaremur a patria, cuius suavitas faceret beatos* (1.4.1).

trek, or a voyage, to our homeland" (1.22).[39] Jesus' resurrection gives us hope, and reminds us that "He has already given us so much of his spirit to support us in our journey" (1.32).[40] Most dramatically,

> given that we are on a road—in spiritual, not spatial terms—and one blocked as it were by thorny hedgerow, which flourishes through the evil influences of our earlier sins, could he who chose to lay himself down as the way by which we could return have done anything more generous and merciful than to forgive the converted all their sins and, by being crucified for us, pull out the firmly fixed barriers to our return? (1.34).[41]

Sapientia is our destination; we would dine in the house of wisdom. Yet, *Cum ergo ipsa sit patria, viam se quoque*

---

39. *Quam purgationem quasi ambulationem quamdam et quasi navigationem ad patriam esse arbitremur. Non enim ad eum qui ubique praesens est locis movemur, sed bono studio bonisque moribus* (1.10.10).

40. *Quibus autem verbis dici aut qua cogitatione capi potest praemium, quod ille in fine daturus est; quando ad consolationem huius itineris de Spiritu suo tantum dedit, quo in adversis vitae huius fiduciam caritatemque tantam eius, quem nondum videmus habeamus* (1.15.14).

41. *Porro quoniam in via sumus, nec via ista locorum est, sed affectuum, quam intercludebat quasi saepta quaedam spinosa, praeteritorum malitia peccatorum, quid liberalius et misericordius facere potuit, qui se ipsum nobis qua rediremus, substernere voluit, nisi ut omnia donaret peccata conversis et graviter fixa interdicta reditus nostri pro nobis crucifixus evelleret?* (1.17.16).

nobis fecit ad patriam—"although it is actually our home-land, it has also made itself the road to the homeland" (1.23; 1.11.11). Wisdom has made Himself the way as well as the destination.

This journey metaphor does a good bit of work for Augustine. Above all, it integrates *res uti* and *res frui*. The transit from one to the other is the transit through this earthly life on the way to a heavenly destination, the *patria* of the blessed. Along the way, the saints are not to be distracted by the delights of the pilgrimage, but to use those things that are to be used to reach enjoyment of the thing to be enjoyed. Augustine introduces the distinction of *usus* and *fruitio* as part of the discussion of signs, and it is clear that *signa* are among the *res uti* and not the *res frui*. So the journey motif applies as much to the *transitus* from sign to thing as it does from this life to the next. Every sign is a road sign, pointing us toward the destination. And this *transitus* is also the progress from Old to New Covenant, from useful signs that are not to be clung to for their own sake to enjoyment of the thing itself.

This deepens the problems identified in the previous section, for it implies that signs are purely instrumental to the achievement of the thing. What happens when we have gotten home and no longer need the road signs? If signs as such drop away, are we not left again with an aso-cial eschatology and hence, ultimately, an asocial soteriol-ogy? Does salvation take a social form only in this world, but not in the next? Is it possible to tease from Augustine an account of signs that shows they are integral to life *in patria* as well as *in via*?

Rudiments of such an account emerge when we follow Augustine's somewhat torturous efforts to fit human beings into his *uti/frui* scheme.[42] Should we enjoy one another, or use one another, or, somehow, both? This, Augustine says, is a "*magna quaestio*." He initially concludes that other human beings are to be "used." He cannot say otherwise. If my neighbor is an end in himself, then he is the source and form of the happy life, which cannot be. So Augustine must say that the love of neighbor must come under the category of *uti*.

Yet already *usus* begins to take on a more-than-instrumental force. He cannot say we use one another in the same sense that we might use a tool. He pursues this by reflecting on the fact that we are commanded to love our neighbor, not to use him. Speaking of self-love, he writes, "[I]f he loves himself on his own account, he does not relate himself to God, but turns to himself and not to something unchangeable. And for this reason it is with a certain insufficiency that he enjoys himself, because when totally absorbed and controlled by the unchangeable

---

42. As O'Donovan has shown, Augustine's *usus* and *utilitas* do not necessarily carry the purely instrumental, or even exploitative, meaning that the English equivalents tend to have for us; see "*Usus* and *Fruitio*," 368-371.

good he is a better man than when his attention leaves it (1.41)."[43] But it is possible to love oneself *not* on one's own account. Loving God with whole heart, soul, and strength, he concludes, does not annul other loves, but incorporates them into an all-encompassing love, so that

> any other object of love that enters the mind should be swept towards the same destination as that to which the whole flood of our love is directed. So a person who loves his neighbor properly should, in concert with him, aim to love God with all his heart, all his soul, and all his mind . . . he relates his love of himself and his neighbor entirely to his love of God (1.43).[44]

---

43. *Si autem se propter se diligit, non se refert ad Deum, sed ad seipsum conversus non ad incommutabile aliquid convertitur. Et propterea iam cum defectu aliquo se fruitur, quia melior est cum totus haeret atque constringitur incommutabili bono, quam cum inde vel ad seipsum relaxatur* (1.22.21).

44. *Haec enim regula dilectionis divinitus constituta est: Diliges, inquit, proximum tuum tamquam teipsum, Deum vero ex toto corde, ex tota anima, ex tota mente, ut omnes cogitationes tuas et omnem vitam et omnem intellectum in illum conferas, a quo habes ea ipsa quae confers. Cum autem ait: toto corde, tota anima, tota mente, nullam vitae nostrae partem reliquit quae vacare debeat et quasi locum dare ut alia re velit frui, sed quidquid aliud diligendum venerit in animum, illuc rapiatur quo totus dilectionis impetus currit* (1.22.21). Later statements make it clear that the neighbor is to be enjoyed in this sense. In *Contra Faustum* 22.78, while defending the wars of Moses as acts of obedience to God against the Manichean attack on the OT, he notes that the evil

Augustine ultimately brings the use-in-love and enjoyment into close connection (1.79): Enjoying someone or something is "very close to that of using someone or something together with love."[45] The object of love prop-

---

that we recoil from is injustice. This recoil occurs when the natural order of the soul is disordered: "This injustice is seen in every case where a man loves for their own sake things which are desirable only as means to an end, and seeks for the sake of something else things which ought to be loved for themselves. For thus, as far as he can, he disturbs in himself the natural order which the eternal law requires us to observe. Again, a man is just when he seeks to use things only for the end for which God appointed them, and to enjoy God as the end of all, while he enjoys himself and his friend in God and for God. For to love in a friend the love of God is to love the friend for God." The command to love neighbor is defined as "enjoyment in God." Similarly, in *de Trinitate* 9.13, the distinction between *uti* and *frui* is not made in terms of God and everything else, but whether something is below us or on par with us: "Now the creature is not to be loved, but if that love is related to the creator it will no longer be covetousness but charity. . . . Now a creature can either be on a par with us or lower than us; the lower creature should be used to bring us to God, the creature on a par should be enjoyed, but in God. Just as you ought to enjoy yourself not in yourself but in him who made you, so too with the one whom you love as yourself. Let us then enjoy both ourselves and our brothers in the Lord." At times, he can even speak of "enjoyment" of creation, such as the free atmosphere of the high mountains (*de Trin.* 9.11).

45. *Quod si non addidisset in Domino, et te fruar tantum dixisset, in eo constituisset spem beatitudinis suae. Quamquam etiam vicinissime dicitur frui cum dilectione uti. Cum enim adest quod diligitur, etiam delectationem secum necesse est gerat. Per quam si transieris eamque ad illud ubi perma nendum est retuleris, uteris ea et abusive, non proprie diceris frui. Si vero inhaeseris atque permanseris, finem in ea ponens*

erly brings pleasure to us, but this pleasure that the object of love brings to us should be related to our "permanent goal." We enjoy our neighbor not in a proper but in a transferred sense.

Introducing the category of love into the pilgrimage motif—which, it must be remembered, is both an image of the Christian life and of interpretation of signs—helps recover the social dimension of signification that earlier seemed to be slipping away. Mark Jordan points to this:

> What secures the use of any expressive sign is its being positioned in a hierarchy, so that through it one can move towards the top-most member of the hierarchy. This was suggested obliquely in the distinction between *signa naturalia* and *signa data*. A natural sign has equal ontological "weight" with that of which it is the sign. Smoke is no less or more important a thing than fire. The same is true for other causally connected indicators. But in the case of *given* signs, the sign is an artifact subordinated both conceptually and really to the given of the sign. One might say, in search of an Augustinian definition, that an intentional sign is the kind of thing which starts a motion

---

laetitiae tuae, tunc vere et proprie frui dicendus es. Quod non faciendum est nisi in illa Trinitate, id est summo et incommutabili bono (1.33.37).

towards what it signifies and, mediately, towards whomever employs it as a sign.[46]

All signs are road signs, posted along the way toward the end of the journey. Signs are also magnets, drawing the soul on journey toward its destination. That is because signs are signs coming from love drawing the recipient toward love. Given signs are gifts expressing the love that moves the soul of the giver and arousing love for the giver in the one who receives.

Signs of Love

We learn both *signa* and *res*, but Augustine subordinates signs to things in a temporal/spatial sequence. We take note of and pass by the sign in order to reach the thing to which the sign points us, the thing the sign brings to mind. But what propels us past the signs? Why not say of the fascinating *signa* of this world, "Stay, thou art so fair"?[47] Augustine answers in terms of an erotic epistemology, an epistemology of *caritas*.

---

46. "Words and Word," 186.

47. For years, with Augustine's "until they rest in thee" in mind, I taught my students that Goethe is the great Romantic anti-Augustinian, since Goethe presents restlessness as the proper state of human existence. But the *peregrinatio* motif brings Augustine very close to Goethe. Augustine would have resisted Mephistopheles' temptation as strenuously as Faust. Augustine could have echoed Faust's words: "Werd ich zum Augenblicke sagen: Verweile doch! du bist so schoen!

Rowan Williams has suggested that "the most original and interesting feature" of Augustine's work is the link
he forges between language and "what he has to say about
beings who 'mean' and about the fundamentally desirous
nature of those beings." Though this linkage appears in
de doctrina, R. A. Markus notes that it comes to fuller expression in *de Trinitate* 10.[48] There, Augustine asks what
is going on when we desire to know something we do
not understand, or attempt to break through a difficult
or obscure sign to the thing it signifies. We cannot desire
and love something of which we are ignorant, so the pull
cannot come from the thing itself. What then do we desire when we desire to understand what we don't know?
Augustine's answer is

> It must be that he knows and sees by insight in
> the very sense of things how beautiful the disci-
> pline is that contains knowledge of all signs; and
> how useful the skill is by which a human society
> communicates perceptions between its members,

Dann magst du mich in Fesseln schlagen, Dann will ich gern zu-
grunde gehn!"

48. Markus's discussion of this linkage was most helpful; *Signs and
Meanings*, 110-114. See also Williams, "Language, Reality, Desire,"
139; and William Babcock, "*Caritas* and Signification in *De doctrina
Christiana* 1-3," in Duane W. H. Arnold and Pamela Bright, eds., *De
Doctrina Christiana: A Classic of Western Culture* (Notre Dame, IN:
University of Notre Dame Press, 1995), 145-63.

since otherwise an assembly of human beings would be worse for its members than any kind of solitude, if they could not exchange their thoughts by speaking to each other (10.1.2).[49]

Markus calls this a "quest for transcendence," but that is true only in a specific sense. Love for universal knowledge of signs draws us on, but beyond that is love for human society served by signs. The transcendence that the student seeks is not the transcendence of contemplation but a transcendence of self, and of one's particular community, by inclusion in a universal community. This becomes even clearer in two other passages:

What one observes in the light of truth is what a great and good thing it would be to understand all the languages of all peoples, and so to hear nobody as a foreigner, and to be heard by no one as such either. The loveliness of such knowledge

---

49. Translation of Edmund Hill (New City Press). *Quid ergo amat nisi quia nouit atque intuetur in rationibus rerum quae sit pulchritudo doctrinae qua continentur notitiae signorum omnium; et quae sit utilitas in ea peritia qua inter se humana societas sensa communicat ne sibi hominum coetus deteriores sint quauis solitudine si cogitationes suas conloquendo non misceant?*

is now perceived in thought, and the thing so known is loved (10.1.2).[50]

And,

surely no one is so totally indifferent to this kind of knowledge that when he hears an unknown word he does not want to know what it is, and does not ask if he can and find out. When he does ask he is of course being studious to find out, and he appears to love something unknown, which is not the case. There is that form in contact with his consciousness which he knows and considers, in which is manifested the loveliness of linking minds together by hearing and exchanging known vocal sounds; it stimulates a certain studiousness in the man, who is indeed asking about something he does not know, but at the same time observing and loving a form he knows to which that something belongs (10.1.2).[51]

---

50. *Conspicit namque in luce ueritatis quam magnum et quam bonum sit omnes omnium gentium linguas intellegere ac loqui nullamque ut alienigenam audire et a nullo ita audiri. Cuius notitiae decus cogitatione iam cernitur amaturque res nota.*

51. *Nam cuius rei adipiscendae spem quisque non gerit, aut tepide amat aut omnino non amat, quamuis quam pulchra sit uideat. Quocirca quia omnium linguarum scientia fere ab omnibus desperatur, suae gentis quisque maxime studet ut nouerit. Quod si et illi ad perfectum percipien-*

Desiring to know is desiring to join a community of knowers. Seeking to know is an act of love. Study is not a bid for epiphanies enjoyed in cloistered isolation. Study is a bid for universal, mutual, hospitality. What we love when we seek to know what is unknown is, for Augustine, simply the church.

Understood in this context, the pilgrimage transit from sign to thing is not a movement away from society, but toward society, toward communion, expansively toward community, toward the most expansive of communities. The pilgrimage of knowledge—of semiosis, of Christian living, they are all one—is not just a movement toward communion with the God who is both the way and the end of the pilgrimage, but a journey toward all those who are in communion with the God who is both the way and the end of the pilgrimage. Like the faltering hart of the Psalm, we are drawn past signs by a yearning love for a universal community of meaning, for the splendid city where Babel has been reversed by Pentecost.

---

dae se non sufficere sentit, nemo tamen tam desidiosus est huius notitiae qui non cum audierit incognitum uerbum uelit nosse quid illud sit et si potest quaerat ac discat. Quod dum quaerit utique in studio discendi est et uidetur amare rem incognitam, quod non ita est. Species namque illa tangit animum quam nouit et cogitat in qua elucet decus consociandorum animorum in uocibus notis audiendis atque reddendis, eaque accendit studio quaerentem quidem quod ignorat, sed notam formam quo id pertineat intuentem et amantem.

Conclusion

Ambiguities remain, however. Is the communion in love that signs draw us to, and to which we pass when we use signs rightly, itself mediated by signs? Does the pilgrim finally cross a threshold from this world where souls are mingled through the mediation of signs into the city where souls mingle beyond signs, beyond language? Do the pilgrims who arrive at the homeland *talk* to one another? And what of all the cultural semiosis that Augustine describes? Is any of that retained in the life of the resurrection? We will have bodies, Augustine says; but will they be *clothed*, and, if so, will the clothing *communicate*? We will have hands; will we gesture in ways that presuppose a common code of meanings? We will have renewed tongues, but will we use them to pour out the motions of our souls to one another? Men will be redeemed, communing in love with God and one another. To that extent, society is redeemed. But will semiosis, that is, *culture*, be redeemed?

The ambiguity is undoubtedly there, and could be removed by a more robust (Hamannian) appreciation of the fundamental goodness of language. But it is an ambiguity, and a blessed one. Augustine, remarkably, overcame the Plotinian assumption that body, sign, culture were themselves the product of a fall.[52] If he did not quite

---

52. Cavadini, "Quest for Truth," 436.

put the pieces together, Augustine at least gave us most of the pieces we need for a theology of cultural redemption, a social account of salvation. It is his great achievement to have arrived at ambiguity.

MODERNITY AND THE "MERELY SOCIAL": TOWARD A SOCIO-THEOLOGICAL ACCOUNT OF BAPTISMAL REGENERATION

Sacramental theology was for a long time the ugly stepsister of theology, confined to the final—often unfinished—volume of the *magnum opus,* locked in the dingy basement. In recent decades, however, it has become increasingly clear that the concerns of sacramental theology are close to the heart of the problematics of modern Christianity and modern civilization generally.[1] Ecumenical discussions have focused on the triad of "Baptism, Eucharist, and Ministry," guided by the correct belief that finding a consensus here will go a long way toward heal-

---

1. See, for example, the essays on the Eucharist in *Modern Theology* 15:2 (April 1999).

ing divisions within the church. Luther poured out much of his early polemical fury against the Roman sacramental system, and Lutherans broke from the Reformed, and both separated from Anabaptists, because of differences concerning the sacraments. More subtly, one of the deep roots of modern secularism was the early modern disruption of the delicate union of *signum* and *res* that characterized Western theology after Augustine. To put it simplistically but usefully, the dissociation of sensibility characteristic of modernity began at Marburg.

Sacramental theology began to take on these global dimensions when it was recognized that affirmations about sacraments are affirmations *in nuce* about how religion impinges on cultural life. Theology's recognition of this connection has been aided significantly by the introduction of models and categories from the cross-disciplinary subject of ritual studies as well as concepts from contemporary philosophy and semiotics into sacramental theology. My attention in this chapter is on the first of these trends, which examines the Christian sacraments in the light of the anthropological theories of van Gennep, Victor Turner, Mary Douglas, Edmund Leach, and others. In several respects, ritual theory provides a welcome corrective to myopic tendencies of traditional liturgics and sacramental theology, especially as these have been treated since the Reformation. Anthropology situates rites within a community's concrete social relations and power structures, which, translated to theology, means that sacramental theology is firmly located in ecclesiology. Moreover, anthropology often attends to the surface of a rite's actions, materials, sounds, and movements, and thus restores some of the patristic and medieval sensitivity to the multivalent symbolisms of washing, breaking, eating, of water, bread, and wine. Sacramental theologies influenced by ritual studies have thus been able to develop Rahner's and Schillebeeckx's insistence that sacramental efficacy is an efficacy of *signs* and *symbols* rather than a quasi-physical or a moral causation. Reflecting on Christian sacraments in the fresh contexts provided by these disciplines opens wide ecumenical vistas, and lays a pathway toward the reunion of sign and thing, and with that for the first steps toward a reunified vision of creation and redemption.

It would be theological malpractice of a high order, however, to suppose that cultural anthropology is an entirely benign tool for sacramental theology. Two problems must be addressed. First, social scientific models and theories are not theologically innocent, and theologians must beware the alien freight that is sometimes hidden deeply within the hold. Below, I examine some of the questionable methodological and substantive cargo that may be smuggled in under cover of "science." Second, anxious to avoid sociological reductionism, some of the same theologians who make sophisticated use of social science and philosophy perpetuate traditional but questionable concepts that social scientific models (among other things) have helped to undermine. In this connection, I will focus especially on the work of Louis-Marie Chauvet, and use a critique of his work as a springboard for an exploratory reformulation of the concept of "baptismal regeneration." More generally, by working my way *through*—rather than simply working *with*—concepts from ritual studies, I hope to position a stone or two of an ecumenically viable and theologically robust foundation for sacramental theology.

Ritual and Reality

Methodologically, some theologians treat the social sciences as theologically neutral foundations upon which to construct theological conclusions. Kenan Osborne claims that once a phenomenological approach to the Sacraments produces an "initial understanding," *then* "biblical, historical, and liturgical approaches to the sacrament fall into place."[2] Similarly, Worgul borrows the "correlation" method of David Tracy to find the "real foundation for sacraments within concrete human existence."[3] Bernard Cooke, rather old-fashionedly, repeatedly implies that

---

2. Kenan B. Osborne, "Methodology and the Christian Sacraments," *Worship* 48 (1974), 536–49.

3. George S. Worgul, *From Magic to Metaphor: A Validation of the Christian Sacraments* (New York: Paulist, 1980), 31–33.

theology must adjust to the certain deliverances of science.[4] "Larger" concerns of anthropology thus position theology. If John Milbank is right that the social sciences are an alternative, even heretical, theology, then these assumptions are far too credulous.[5]

More substantively, ritual studies privilege certain biases of modernity. As Talal Asad and Catherine Bell have observed,[6] there is no obvious natural line of demarcation between "symbolic" and "functional" acts, a distinction that tarnishes the brilliance of Louis-Marie Chauvet's massive *Symbol and Sacrament.* For Chauvet, liturgy takes place on the far side of a "symbolic rupture" from the everyday, and is thus "beyond the useful-useless distinction" because it "creates an empty space with regard to the immediate and utilitarian." Whatever worshipers may gain from the liturgy, "rituality functions at *another level,* the level of symbol," which permits "a space for breathing, for freedom," for "the intense experience of the *letting go* of our theoretical knowledge, our ethical

---

4. Bernard J. Cooke, *The Distancing of God: The Ambiguity of Symbol in History and Theology* (Minneapolis, MI: Fortress, 1990).

5. John Milbank, *Theology and Social Theory: Beyond Secular Reason* (Oxford: Blackwell, 1990).

6. Talal Asad, *Genealogies of Religion: Discipline and Reasons of Power in Christianity and Islam* (Baltimore, MD: Johns Hopkins, 1993), 55–79; Catherine Bell, *Ritual Theory, Ritual Practice* (New York, NY: Oxford University Press, 1992), 69–74.

'good works,' our personal 'experiences' of God" so that we can be opened to grace.[7] Ritual opens out a (noumenal?) "symbolic order" that is "completely different from that of immediately experienced reality."[8]

Many societies do not, however, share this dichotomy. Asad points out that medieval monks understood the daily office as an intrinsic element in a program of *paedeia,* not as "expressive" or "symbolic" actions occupying a realm "beyond useful and useless." Hugh of St. Victor's notion that sacraments effect *humilitatio* and *exercitatio* shows that he was not operating with a functional/symbolic dualism. By imposing changing bodily postures and movements, Hugh argues, liturgy corrects the "bad changes" that result from sin and inscribes a Christian choreography, training the worshiper to dance life virtuously.[9] On the far side of Chauvet's rupture, one trembles

---

7. Louis-Marie Chauvet, *Symbol and Sacrament: A Sacramental Reinterpretation of Christian Existence,* trans. Patrick Madigan and Madeleine Beaumont (Collegeville, MN: Liturgical Press, 1995), 337–38.

8. Chauvet, *Symbol,* 113, quoting from E. Ortigues, *Le discours et le symbole.* That this dualism is fundamental to Chauvet's work is indicated by his rigorous distinction between the logics and levels of marketplace and symbolic exchange (106–7, 111). Surely, as in the phenomenon of buying "status symbols," the two interpenetrate so complexly that talk of "levels" is misleading.

9. Hugh of St. Victor, *On the Sacraments of the Christian Faith,* trans. Roy J. Deferrari (Cambridge, MA: Medieval Academy of America, 1951), 1.9.3; 156–158; cf. Asad, *Genealogies,* 77–79.

to ask what "everyday" life looks like, once scoured of symbol. And the closest answer seems to be, very much like the modern secular West. Chauvet's dualism is founded on and thus helps to perpetuate the secular structures of modernity.

Ritual theory privileges modern biases also in theorizing about the functions, patterns, or features of "ritual in general." Undeniable "family resemblances" exist among rites from widely varying times and places, but, working with the Kantian form/content dualism that infects sociology and anthropology generally, ritual theory often abstracts a static form from different ritual contents.[10]

---

10. For Durkheim, whatever the specific actions done or words spoken or symbols manipulated, and whatever the participants *believe* they are doing, what is *really* taking place is the reanimation of social bondedness. Likewise, van Gennep's rite of passage pattern can become a Procrustean bed into which many different sequences of action are forced; van Gennep is explicit about his interest in the "essential significance" of rites rather than particular actions (*The Rites of Passage*, trans. Monika B.Vizedom and Gabrielle L. Caffee [London: Routledge & Kegan Paul, 1960], 191). Mary Douglas warns against dismissing "ritualism," apparently without regard to the particular rituals being dismissed (*Natural Symbols: Explorations in Cosmology*, 2nd ed. [London: Barrie and Jenkins, 1973], esp. ch. 2). Ronald Grimes notes, "Although Turner's theory is certainly not archetypalist in either a Jungian or Eliadean sense, it aims at a high level of cross-cultural, transtemporal generalization" (*Beginnings in Ritual Studies*, rev. ed. Studies in Comparative Religion [Columbia, SC: University of South Carolina Press, 1995], 155). There is, to be sure, a countervailing emphasis among anthropologists on the particularities of the words, gestures, objects, colors, and other specific features that make up particular rituals.

Applied to sacraments, this method reduces the Christian interpretation of a rite to a religious gloss on more basic natural institutions or sequences of action; anthropology isolates the container, while Christianity pours in the medicine—and the Victorine allusion is deliberate.

David N. Power, for example, suggests that ritual imitates bodily acts. "Remote action" (moving away from, looking at) is the basis for rites of alienation; copulation is the natural foundation for rites of bonding; and digestion is the basis for rituals of fusion that blur individual identities.[11] Yet, these bodily actions are not "raw" experiences but are always already encoded and suffused with particular intentions. "Moving away" out of embarrassment or revulsion is a different act from "moving away" out of respect or deference; sex is always already charged with symbols and gestures that in turn are em-

---

11. David N. Power, *Unsearchable Riches: The Symbolic Nature of Liturgy*, A PuebloBook (Collegeville, MN: Liturgical Press, 1984), 88–89. This dual structure is of a piece with Power's claim, following Suzanne Langer, that communication and experience are lodged in bodily action prior to language, which intervenes at some second stage to "transform" experience and objectify it (68, 84). Chauvet seems to be operating with similar assumptions when he says that liturgy brackets theory and discourse in favor of sheer symbol, and hints at the possibility that ritual, even though embedded in a tradition, can be performed "before any words" (*Symbol*, 338–339, 342). Rites, however, are always performed by people who have already spoken about the rites being performed, and they almost always include speech acts. Not to mention that speech is itself a bodily act.

bedded in a particular set of cultural beliefs and practices; and every meal has to be arranged in *some* manner, so that there is no "eating *as such*" but only "eating *in this or that way.*" In short, what Power treats as "natural" bodily acts are already cultural and ritual acts, and thus cannot serve as a foundation for ritual. Similar objections can be brought against Michael Lawler, who defines sacraments as "prophetic symbols" that raise literal realities to the "representative-symbolic" level at which Christian meanings come into play. Marriage, according to Lawler, has a "natural level" meaning of "union of this man and this woman" but as a representative symbol becomes suitable to "proclaim, realize, and celebrate in representation" Christ's union with the church—as if *marriage* could exist in the slightest degree outside a representative-symbolic matrix![12]

Abstract formalism is only part of the problem here. Against Power and Lawler, I have insisted that no pre-lin-

---

12. Michael G. Lawler, *Symbol and Sacrament: A Contemporary Sacramental Theology* (New York: Paulist Press, 1987), 52–53. For Chauvet, rites always function in a space of "liminality," symbolically set apart from the "everyday," and thus at the level of "signifying and the pattern it forms" rather than at the "level of the signified and ideational 'contents'" (*Symbol*, 326). Even if these "levels" can be distinguished, any intelligible response to a "signifying pattern" requires some recognition of "contents": otherwise, the pattern is no pattern but kaleidoscopic chaos. "It was lovely and moving, but I have no idea what it was about" is not, surely, the hoped-for response to the church's worship.

guistic, pre-semiotic, or pre-ritual human life exists. If this is the case, then some language and semiosis are already encoded in the activities and institutions that correspond to Christian sacraments. By introducing Christianity at a secondary level, "on top" of "natural" actions, theology again collaborates with secularism in refusing to allow the Christian coding of reality to enter constitutively into the definition of actions or social institutions. Sacramental theology is thus recruited into the force that "polices the sublime" and keeps religion in its proper, privatized place.[13] If the gospel merely pours content into preexisting forms, it cannot transform, cannot burst the wineskins.[14]

Worgul goes to an unusual extreme, combining Levi-Strauss and Turner to describe the efficacy of the Eucharist. Having portrayed human life as a set of binary oppositions, he claims that ritual enables passage from the "bad pole" to the "good pole," from death to life, and that each transition passes through a moment of Buberian, egalitarian *communitas*. Strong experiences of *commu-*

---

13. Milbank. *Theology*, ch. 5.

14. Historically, the church did not merely raise marriage to the level of a prophetic symbol, but transformed the inner dynamics of family life, destroying the Roman *pater-familias*, the primacy of clan and blood vengeance, and the cult of the ancestors. Recording thus took place in the basic meaning of "family" and hence in the basic meaning of the ritual of marriage.

nitas keep a culture stable, while weak *communitas* can lead to disintegration.[15] Worgul claims that the Eucharist is an example of this process, but though the Eucharist no doubt effects a passage from death to life, the path does not run through *communitas*. Undifferentiated *communitas* has nothing to do with the church, which is precisely a differentiated community, one *body* of many members. Be that as it may, Worgul's anthropological revision of eucharistic theology does not provide any "deeper" insight into how the Eucharist works than theological explanations. To say, similarly, that baptism is a "rite of passage" is *not* to arrive at some more basic level of description but merely to re-describe what the New Testament calls "death and resurrection with Christ," "the washing of regeneration," "crossing of the Red Sea."[16] Redescription can have the valuable heuristic function of highlighting unnoticed features of a rite, but the *theological* description must remain fundamental. Anthropological redescription

15. Worgul, *Magic to Metaphor,* 185–193. In a sense, Worgul's point is the sheerest tautology: A community whose members have strong ties to one another will be more stable than one where ties are weak.

16. It is a separate question whether the category of *rites de passage* is a useful or coherent one. Milbank sees Turner's emphasis on liminality as a secular effort to marginalize religion by confining it to sublime moments of transition, he also suggests that cultural boundaries are constituted by symbol and ritual, and therefore ritual functions are more to form boundaries than to provide safe passage across boundaries that are simply "there" *(Theology,* 122–123).

forces typology to the margins, so that Christian rites are interpreted without reference to the patterns and categories of redemptive history.[17] The prolegomena to Christian sacramental theology is no longer a "treatise on the sacraments of the Old Law" but a "treatise on the rites of the Ndembu."

No Church without Baptism

Questions concerning the efficacy of baptism have long divided Christians. Many Protestants fear that talk of "baptismal regeneration" imputes an almost magical power to water, while Catholics and Orthodox accuse Protestants of robbing baptism of any efficacy at all. In seeking to move beyond this impasse, social scientific categories are both helpful and harmful. To illustrate this, I will examine Louis-Marie Chauvet's discussion of baptismal efficacy, showing that he imports secular assumptions into his account. Along the way, I will be developing a positive account of baptismal efficacy that will expose how Protestant-Catholic differences on this question are differences within a common, and flawed, framework.

Chauvet's discussion of baptismal efficacy relies to a large extent on categories from anthropology, semiot-

---

17. By vindicating the rationality of "primitive" prohibition and taboo, anthropology can also reinforce a flattened hermeneutic in which the holiness restrictions of Israel are retained in some form by the church (cf. Power, *Unsearchable Riches*, 90–91).

ics, and linguistic philosophy. Comparing the sacraments with speech acts, however, Chauvet warns that grace is *"irreducible* to any explanations," and baptismal grace in particular cannot be reduced *"theologically* to the symbolic efficacy of a language act." This caution is necessary lest theology dissolve into anthropology and become "only a variant within the social sciences." Thus, "it is one thing to be proclaimed a son or daughter for God and brother or sister for others in Jesus Christ, to be recognized as such by the group, and to be authentically so on the *social level*; it is quite another to be so on the *theological level* of faith, hope, and charity." Distinctions of this sort are central to Chauvet's work, manifested in a pervasive contrast of Christian identity and salvation.[18]

Despite its surface plausibility, his distinction between "sociological" and "theological" is erroneous in at least two ways. Ontologically, Chauvet assumes that "language acts" and, presumably, other social and cultural processes are secular realities, not permeated with religious significance. Even membership in the church, thus, might, for Chauvet, be merely "social." Especially in the church, however, this is *never* the case. Chauvet's reminder that church members may be dissembling, though correct enough, is beside the point. A dissembling member is not a "social" Christian but a "false son" or "unfruitful

18. *Symbol,* 425, 439, 443.

branch," and this is a theological fact with eternal consequences. Based on this ontological assumption, Chauvet implies that social science can provide an adequate account of immanent social mechanisms, but theology must be trundled out to account for grace. But if social reality is not secular, if every immanent process has a transcendent dimension, then an a-theological sociology cannot give an adequate account of any social process.

Moreover, if, as Milbank has powerfully put it, sociology is an alternative theology, and if theology is *the* social science, then a theological account *is* sociological, and vice versa. If the social sciences are already theologically committed, then theology cannot supplement them but must revise, perhaps radically, sub-orthodox or heretical social scientific descriptions. The apostle Paul did not believe that pagan feasts were "secular": Rather, they take place at the "table of demons." With much of the tradition, both Protestant and Catholic, Chauvet's treatment of baptismal efficacy assumes a conception of personal identity such that the interior self is ontologically fundamental. Since this self is untouchable by social roles and rituals, baptism cannot effect a truly "ontological" change but can only skim the surface of personality. For Chauvet, sacraments can affect "identity" or "social" standing but not "theological" status or "salvation." The way round this obstacle is to abandon the ancient soul imprisoned in the body and its modern counterpart, the Cartesian ego, or, to put it differently, to challenge the effort to mark an absolute boundary between inner and outer.

A "narrative" conception of personal identity provides a corrective here.[19] At a social level, any particular baptism is, as Alasdair MacIntyre implies, an event in the history of baptism, which is to say, a moment in the church's story.[20] Baptism immerses a person in that history. Identities are formed at the intersection of various narratives of which one is a part (of family, community, nation, and so on), so that when baptism embeds one's story in that of the church, his identity is objectively modified. To "I am an American, or Scot, or Chinese" is added "I am a member of the Christian church"; one's "forefathers" now include not only Washington, Robert the Bruce, or Mao but Abraham, Isaac and Jacob; the story that once began, "my father sailed to the Cape from Amsterdam," now begins, "my father was a wandering Aramean." At an individual level, identity is bound up with the events of one's life and his (selective) memory of those events. Roles acquired and significant actions done become part of my "record," a story that marks my difference from others and traces the continuity of *my* life through time. Objectively, baptism makes me a member

19. See Stanley Hauerwas and Gregory L. Jones, eds., *Why Narrative? Readings in Narrative Theology* (Grand Rapids, MI: Eerdmans, 1989).

20. "Virtues, the Unity of a Human Life, and the Concept of a Tradition," in Hauerwas and Jones, eds., *Why Narrative?*, 100.

of Christ's body, and this becomes an episode in the story of who I am. Subjectively, the baptismal narrative into which I am submerged may break violently against the story that, before baptism, identified me, forcing what may be a painful re-evaluation of my past and producing a revised self-image.[21]

In this framework, it is possible to rehabilitate the notion that baptism imprints an "indelible character." Baptism irreversibly plants my story in the story of the church, for even if I renounce her, my renunciation is part of her history. As a facet of individual identity, baptism is equally permanent, for one is never unbaptized.[22] A baptized man can renounce Christ, turn persecutor of the church, reject everything he once confessed, forget his baptism. Having once passed through the waters, however, his every action thereafter, including those that are wholly inconsistent with his baptismal identity, are actions of a baptized man. Forgetfulness of baptism is the culpable forgetfulness of the baptized. Even those who leave the Father's house are sons, however prodigally they may squander their inheritance in riotous living.

In short, what is ontologically fundamental is not the naked "I" laid bare by stripping away layers of accidental

---

21. George W. Stroup, *The Promise of Narrative Theology* (London: SCM, 1981), 95.

22. Wolfhart Pannenberg, *Systematische Theologie, Band* 3 (Göttingen: Vandenhoeck & Ruprecht, 1993), 268.

cultural clothing, any more than God is the "bare mini-mum" of deity that remains after we peel off his attributes, word, and works. Rather, the ontologically fundamental self, what makes me uniquely me, is a complex that in-cludes the roles, stories, actions and events of my life; the individual and his world are not hermetically sealed from one another, but mutually defining. Thus, while it is true that I am a husband, it is equally important to see that I *am* a husband. "Husband" is not an accident inhering in an essential unmarried self but one of the roles that makes up my identity. Importantly, I am a husband because I have gone through the ceremony of marriage. Rites, by placing us in new roles, vesting us with new clothes, and imposing new sets of obligations and rules, effect an "on-tological" transformation, a change in who we are, who we think we are, and who others think we are. Just in this way, baptism clothes us with Christ, and these clothes remake the man.

"Baptismal regeneration" may thus be defined in terms of the new identity, tasks, relationships, and priv-ileges that are conferred through the baptismal rite. To Catholics and Orthodox, this may at first blush seem an inadequate account of "regeneration." In addition to all these "merely social" or "merely psychological" tran-sitions, they will want to insist, baptism also effects a "spiritual" rebirth. Though I am using "regeneration" in a different way than theology has historically employed the term, my argument is that to raise the objection of reductionism is to remain entrenched in questionable categories. (Protestant denials that baptism is efficacious, of course, assume the same framework; for Protestants, baptism cannot "regenerate" precisely because its efficacy is limited to an external cultural dimension.) As argued above, it is simply impossible to give a completely a-theological account of anything at all. Despite its pretenses, the methodological atheism of the social sciences is *not* an absence of theology but the promotion of a false theology. Thus, this formulation of baptismal regeneration is not a thin soup of sociology but thick theological stew.

Let me attempt to unpack that assertion. First, this formulation assumes a theological account of "identity." Baptism effects a transition, as Rowan Williams puts it, not only in the regard of men but in the "gaze of God," and this makes us "new creations" in the deepest possible sense. Identity, Williams suggests, is enmeshed with relations in community, but our most fundamental belonging is to the community of Adam or of Christ, and therefore our basic identity is not constituted by social or cultural factors, but by the transcendent "regard of God upon *us*."[23]

---

23. Rowan Williams, "Sacraments of the New Society" in David Brown and Ann Loades, eds., *Christ: the Sacramental Word* (London: SPCK, 1996), 90–94.

The baptized is no longer regarded as "stranger" but born again as a "son of the house." Chauvet notwithstanding, prying apart social and theological "levels" is simply impossible. On the other hand, a psychological or sociological account of identity that leaves out one's belonging to Adam or Christ is leaving out the most fundamental source of identity. It is not merely an incomplete account but fundamentally and radically mistaken.

Socio-theological consideration of the nature of the church leads to a similar conclusion. No group's existence as group is either temporally or logically prior to its common practices. Thousands may be addicted to Peanuts comics, but these teeming multitudes do not form a Peanuts fan club until they have declared the club exists, established membership fees and entry requirements, instituted rites and procedures (including the secret handshake), and adopted club identities (Charlie Brown, Lucy, Linus, Snoopy, etc.). The club as club exists only in and through these institutions and practices. Likewise, theoretically, any number of isolated individuals may sincerely believe that Jesus is Lord without forming a church. The church as a recognizable human community exists only in the common confession of Christ by her members, obedience to the Word, liturgical practices, fellowship and mutual aid, and formal and informal procedures of correction and forgiveness. If the Spirit dwells in the church as church, he dwells in the people organized and constituted by these practices. Baptism is one of the practices without which the church does not exist. Initiation is thus not so much a doorway through which one passes into the house as the act by which one becomes part of the house; it is not passage toward membership so much as the first act of membership, and therefore the first contact with the Spirit who circulates through the body (cf. Acts 2:38; 1 Cor. 12:12–13). Baptism into membership in the community of Christ therefore also confers the *arrabon* of the Spirit, and in this sense too is a "regenerating" ordinance. There can be no "merely social" membership in *this* family.

Chauvet's discussion distinguishes between Christian identity, membership in the visible social entity of the church on the one hand, and salvation on the other. This too is a dualism that must be radically challenged as being based on the same modernist dualisms examined above. Salvation is not an entity, substance, or power that floats free of human persons in concrete situations. Rather, salvation is "adjectival": Persons, communities, and, in a sense, the nonhuman creation are or will be saved; or, if salvation is nominal, it applies in fullness only to the eschatological order. A saved person is one who, redeemed in Christ from sin and death, lives as God created him to live, walking with God, submissive to his rule. A saved people consists of the redeemed whose communal life is conformed to the New Covenant under the Lord Christ.

Salvation in its fullest sense is eschatological; only at the end will death be swallowed up in victory and "God's will be done on earth as it is in heaven." Yet because the church is on the path toward this eschatological consummation, she anticipates, to the extent that she conforms to the will of Christ, the final peace of the kingdom. The church as a concrete historical community is thus not merely the means of salvation but the already partially realized goal. To approach from another angle: Adam was created to be priest and king, so a saved person is one restored, through Christ, to this Adamic status and task; the eschatological people is the kingdom of priests (Rev. 1:5–6; 5:9–10; 20:6). By baptism into the royal priesthood of the church, one is incorporated into the race of the Last Adam. It is thus not correct that the Spirit first saves and then at some second stage equips for ministry. Living the life of salvation *is* ministering in God's house; as baptism authorizes and deputizes to such ministry, it grants a share in the life of salvation.[24]

---

24. Bringing together the arguments of the two preceding paragraphs, we can also address the issue of the "necessity" of baptism, a question best answered, as Aquinas realized, in a corporate rather than individual frame of reference (cf. *ST* 3a.61.1). Within this context, baptism is not merely a pointer to but a necessary part of the *now* of eschatological salvation. Without her practices, the church would not be the saved people of God because she would not exist at all as a recognizable human community. And that would mean that salvation is not a historical reality. Since it is one of the divinely authorized practices by which the church exists as church, baptism is necessary

How is baptism connected to the eschatological "not yet"? Baptism does not guarantee an eternal standing among the people of God, for the baptized may be removed from the house and cut off from the Table. Yet, baptism is not irrelevant to eternal salvation; though baptism "by itself" does not guarantee a standing, baptism never is "by itself" but always a step on a pathway. Perseverance to the end of the pathway, the mark of eschatologically saving faith, is, as Augustine insisted, a gift of grace, which, being grace, is gratuitously distributed as God pleases. Yet, this grace is distributed through means, so that what we bring under the heading of "the grace of perseverance" are the concrete ways God holds close and brings nearer, baptism among them. Baptism holds us close by admitting us to the Table, where we feed on Christ in the Spirit; by putting us within hearing of his life-giving Word; by joining us to people who encourage, exhort, and comfort. Through continual baptismal *anamnesis,* we stir ourselves to faithfulness in edifying the body and gratitude for the gift of Christ. In baptism, we are inducted into ministry in God's house, and continuing in that ministry is the way of salvation. Clothed in the crucified Christ, the baptized enters the path of suffering service and living sacrifice whose destination is a weighty and glorious house, the brightness of endless day.

---

to her existence; and since the church is the site where salvation has occurred and is occurring, baptism is necessary for salvation.

'Merely social'?

Arguing with Chauvet has led to a view of baptismal efficacy that is not quite Protestant and not quite Catholic.
Using concepts of ritual theory, we have come to formu-
late the "regeneration" effected in baptism in "sociological" terms: Baptism inducts us into the community of
Christ, confers a new identity, and imposes new responsi-
bilities. But this "sociological" account is, I have argued,
equally a theological account. For the task of the baptized
is service to the Lord in his house, his identity is "child of
God," his privileges include fellowship at his Table. This
is the "new life" effected by the "waters of regeneration."
These are "merely social" facts only if one assumes that
this house is not really God's house and this Table not
really his Table.

But that, of course, is simple unbelief.

CHAPTER NINE

WOMB OF THE WORLD: BAPTISM AND THE PRIESTHOOD OF THE NEW COVENANT IN HEBREWS 10:19–22

Historically, "baptismal regeneration" has referred to the spiritual transformation of an individual through the rite of Christian baptism. In addition to theological objections from some Christian traditions, the basis of this doctrine has been questioned on philological grounds. The Greek term underlying "regeneration" (παλιγγενεσία, cf. Tit. 3:5), can have a broader significance than in sacramental theology. Stoic philosophy speculated about cosmic regenerations (παλιγγενεσίαι) following periodic conflagrations (ἐκπυρώσεις), and Matthew 19:28 shows the word could be used in a cosmological sense in first-century Judaism and the early church.[1] For some, this cosmic connotation undermines the use of Titus 3:5 as a baptismal text, for how can baptism be a washing that brings cosmic renewal?

In this chapter, I attempt to answer this question by examining one aspect of the New Testament typology of baptism. From Tertullian's second-century treatise *De baptismo,* it has been a truism of liturgical commentary that Christian baptism fulfills the priestly ordination rite of the Old Testament (Exod. 29; Lev. 8–9) and thus initiates into the New Covenant priesthood. After seeking to demonstrate that this ancient typology finds biblical confirmation in Hebrews 10:19–22, I shall examine how baptism functions in this passage as an efficacious sign producing a change in the distribution of household ministry that requires a corresponding change in law. I assume Menahem Haran's definition of "priest" as a "temple servant" or "personal minister" to God in his house, and also Philip Peter Jenson's conception of Israelite religion as a structure of "graded holiness."[2] Ac-

---

1. Martin Dibelius and Hans Conzelmann, *The Pastoral Epistles*, Hermeneia (Philadelphia, PA: Fortress Press, 1972), 148. Spicq's comment is apt: "Le choix même du mot palingénésie suggère qu'il faut lier étroitement la régénération individuelle du néophyte à la nouvelle ère du cosmos inaugurée par Jésus-Christ" (*Les Epîtres Pastorales*, Etudes Bibliques [Paris: Gabalda, 1969], 653).

2. Menahem Haran, "Priests and Priesthood," in *Encyclopaedia Judaica* (Jerusalem: Keter Publishing House, 1972), XIII, 1069–86; Philip

cording to Jenson, "P" imagined Israel as a concentrically arranged community radiating from the tabernacle, its ranks marked out, among other things, by clothing, food, and access to or exclusion from holy environments. Within Israel, the fundamental division was between priests and people, and this division was actually constituted by ordination (Exod. 29, Lev. 8–9). By instituting this continuum, ordination, along with the construction of the tabernacle, formed Israel's antique order. The "eighth" day of Aaron's ordination was the first day of a new socio-religious cosmos. If, therefore, baptism fulfills Aaronic ordination, if baptism does now what ordination did then, we have reason to suspect that it reconstructs the religious landscape. The baptismal formation of a new priestly community, historically extending the veil-rending work of Jesus' death, challenges and remaps antique Israelite topography.

Proving that a New Testament writer is engaging in "innerbiblical interpretation" of an Old Testament rite or text is difficult. Having established that Hebrews 10:19–22 refers to Christian baptism, my argument will proceed according to the following logic. Under the Mosaic system, ordination, as applied to a man, produced a priest with certain obligations and privileges. New Testament writers might indicate that baptism fulfills ordination in

Peter Jenson *Graded Holiness: A Key to the Priestly Conception of the World*, JSOT Sup, no. 106 (Sheffield: JSOT Press, 1992).

several ways. First, one might explicitly assert that baptism has replaced ordination, but we have no such statement in the New Testament—hence the difficulty. Second, a text might state that baptism produces priests, but again we lack such an explicit proposition. Third, if a text states that baptism confers one or several priestly tasks and privileges, it follows that the baptized has become a priest and that baptism has the same function in the church as ordination had in Israel, that is, initiating priests. Therefore, baptism fulfills and replaces ordination. I argue that Hebrews 10:19–22 states precisely that baptism confers priestly privileges.[3]

Baptism Makes Priests

In 10:22, the writer to the Hebrews encourages his readers to "draw near" confidently, having "our hearts sprinkled from an evil conscience and our bodies washed with pure water" (ρεραντισμένοι τὰς καρδίας ἀπό συνειδήσεως πονηρας και λελουσμένοι το σῶμα ὕδατι καθαρῷ). My first concern here is to decide whether this is a baptismal text. Most commentators believe it is. A prominent exception to this consensus is Markus Barth, who presents two arguments that ultimately become one.[4] On Barth's read-

---

3. I do not mean that ordination is the only rite that baptism fulfills and replaces. It also fulfills circumcision and the other washings of the Levitical system.

4. Markus Barth, *Die Taufe—Ein Sakrament? Ein exegetischer Beitrag*

ing, Hebrews 7–10 does not encourage establishment of a new cult or priesthood but announces that the death of Christ fulfilled the whole Old Testament system. Anything added to this unique act casts doubt on its sufficiency. Barth, secondly, distinguishes "objective" and "subjective" dimensions of the Old Testament system; the first refers to sacrifices as means of expiation, and the second to rites of sprinkling and washing that applied expiation to individuals. Hebrews 10:22 can be a baptismal text only if these dimensions of the Levitical system are separated, such that Jesus' death fulfills the "objective" aspect while the rites and ceremonies of the church fulfill the "subjective." Hebrews, Barth argues, teaches instead that the cross fulfills and terminates both the objective and subjective.[5] Thus, Barth interprets "washing" as the power of the cross erupting into the church's life, and "body" as the "whole man."

Barth's very Barthian arguments prove too much, undermining a reference to a rite of baptism not only in Hebrews 10 but virtually anywhere in the New Testament. On Barth's premises, baptism as an act of repentance seems to cast as much doubt on the sufficiency of

---

zum Gespräch über die kirchliche Taufe (Zürich: Evangelischer A.G. Zollikon, 1951), 473–79.

5. "Er bleibt nichts, aber auch gar nichts mehr aus dem alttestamentlichen Kult zu erfüllen oder fortzusetzen. In Christi Tod ist alles, alles ein für allemal erfüllt" (Barth, *Die Taufe,* 477).

the cross as baptism understood as a sacramental application of redemption.[6] Contrary to Barth, Hebrews does envision an ecclesiological fulfillment of Old Testament rites and institutions: sacrifice, specifically, is offered in the church's praise and good works (Heb. 12:28–13:17). Augustine is thus closer to the spirit of Hebrews when he insists that the charity, signs and rites of the *totus Christus,* as much as the historical work of Jesus, fulfill the Old Testament. Exegetically, Barth fails to do justice to the language of the text. Hebrews speaks of "pure water," but Barth prefers the more abstract "Waschung" or "Reinigung." For Barth, when the writer says "bodies washed with pure water," he means that what are not really bodies are not really washed by what is not really water.

Though not following Barth, Attridge muses on what he sees as an abrupt turn in the argument of Hebrews.[7] He describes the transition from first to second

---

6. A. J. M. Wedderburn reckons that an extreme cruxomonism renders baptism "superfluous as such" and requires one to "de-sacramentalize" or spiritualize the passages that speak of baptism as a saving event (*Baptism and Resurrection: Studies in Pauline Theology against its Graeco-Roman Background,* WUNT, no. 44, [Tubingen: J. C. B. Mohr, 1987], 65–66)

7. Harold W. Attridge, "The Uses of Antithesis in Hebrews 8–10," in George W. E. Nickelsburg with George W. Mac Rae, eds., *Christians among Jews and Gentiles Essays in Honor of Krister Stendahl on his Sixty-fifth Birthday* (Philadelphia, PA: Fortress Press, 1986), 1–9 (9), *idem, The Epistle to the Hebrews,* Hermeneia (Philadelphia, PA: Fortress Press), 288–89.

covenants as a shift from external and physical to internal and spiritual realities but finds this trajectory surprisingly disrupted by the writer's insistence that the bodily death of Jesus inaugurates the spiritual covenant. Baptism in 10:22 poses similar perplexities: how can a physical and external rite initiate into an internal and spiritual covenant? Attridge's surprise, however, arises only because he has imposed categories alien to Hebrews. First and second covenants differ as "flesh" and "conscience," but it is a mistake to transpose this into internal/external, as if the two dualisms were equivalent. The first covenant was not flawed because it depended on bodies but because its cleansing agent was the blood of bulls and goats rather than the blood of a sinless man. As much as the first, the second covenant is concerned with bodies—with Jesus' bodily self-offering and with the bodily consecration and living sacrifice of his people. Physical and corporate aspects of the Christian life are evident in the following verses (10:24–25), which warn against alienation from the public assembly of worship and good works. Neither Barth nor Attridge, therefore, convincingly undermines the majority opinion that baptism is the ritual that qualifies a people to draw near to the heavenly sanctuary.[8]

---

8. If the washing is baptism, two further questions arise. First, what is the relationship between the baptismal "washing of bodies" and the "sprinkling of the heart and conscience"? Nils A. Dahl suggests that baptism is "the application of the work of Jesus to the individual"

What, then, is the source of the imagery? Fleming-

and thus the sprinkling of the heart identifies the "inner significance" of the reality that baptism ritually signifies ("A New and Living Way: The Approach to God According to Hebrews 10:19–25," *Int* 5 [1951], 401–12 [407n27]). P. E. Hughes, along similar lines, points to parallels with 1 Peter 3 to show that baptism is more than outward cleansing (*A Commentary on the Epistle to the Hebrews* [Grand Rapids, MI: Eerdmans, 1977], 412). Second, the sanctuary Christians enter is a "heavenly" sanctuary (9:24; 10:19), but how can baptism qualify for entry into heaven? There are a few possible responses here. On the one hand, Hebrews envisions the church also as the "house" of God (3:6; 10:21), and it has been argued that the contrast of heaven/earth in Hebrews is not so much spatial (up/down) as temporal (old/new) (Ulrich Luck, "Himmlisches und irdisches Geschehen im Hebräerbrief," *Novum Testamentum* 6 [1963], 192–215). Thus, the writer assures his readers that they "have come" to the heavenly Jerusalem by their entry into the church (Heb. 12:22). Incorporation into the heavenly people is equivalent to entering the heavenly sanctuary. This response, however, may assume an eschatological realization that goes beyond what Hebrews envisions. Thus, on the other hand, one might distinguish between "drawing near" and "entering." Baptism qualifies the baptized to "draw near" to the sanctuary, sets him or her on the pathway and gives confidence that the journey will be accomplished, but does not confer entry. This formulation preserves an eschatological horizon for the entry into the Most Holy Place, which would literally be accomplished not at baptism but at death or the Second Coming of Jesus. Without denying that such an eschatological tension is at work in Hebrews, however, several factors suggest that there is an "already" dimension to the entry to the Most Holy Place. The sharp contrast between the restricted access of the Mosaic system and the free access of the New Covenant, the reference to the way inaugurated "through the veil," and the later insistence that believers have come to the heavenly Zion all support the conclusion that the entry is not wholly future. Baptism, with the incorporation into the heavenly people that this implies, is a ritual ton represents the majority view: "The background of this language is to be found in the Old Testament passages describing the consecration of priests. They needed to be purified from 'uncleanness' by being sprinkled with sacrificial blood (cf. Exod. 29:20–21; Lev. 8:23, 24, 30), and also to be washed with water."[9] Details of the text support this conclusion. Christ's blood is definitely the agent for cleansing the heart and conscience. Most of the other uses of sprinkle (ῥαντίζω) in Hebrews refer to sprinkling blood (9:19, 21–22; 12:24), and even the reference to the water containing the ashes of the red heifer (9:13) is not an exception, since the heifer's blood was burned and mixed with the water (Num. 19:5). Throughout the letter, the blood of Christ is alone sufficient to purify the conscience (συνείδησις; 9:9, 14; 10:2). To draw near, one must come under blood and water—a comparatively rare combination in Levitical law but found in the ordination rite (Exod. 29:4, 21; Lev. 8:6, 30).[10] Hebrews 10:22 describes baptism with imagery borrowed from ordination.

---

qualifier for present entrance. See further discussion in John Dunnill, *Covenant and Sacrifice in the Letter to the Hebrews* (Cambridge: Cambridge University Press, 1992), 146–48, and John M. Scholer, *Proleptic Priests: Priesthood in the Epistle to the Hebrews*, JSNT Sup, no. 49 (Sheffield: JSOT Press, 1991), 91–103.

9. W. F. Flemington, *The New Testament Doctrine of Baptism* (London: SPCK, 1948), 98.

10. Two other rites combine blood and water as cleansing agents cleansing from skin disease and from corpse defilement (Lev. 14:6–7,

But the text goes further to show that "baptism fulfills and replaces ordination." Sprinkled and washed, believers are qualified to enter through the "veil" (10:20; καταπέτασμα), a reference to the veil separating the Holy Place from the Most Holy Place (cf. 6:19; 9:3).[11] Some commentators conclude that the Old Testament background is the High Priest's entry to the Most Holy Place on the Day of Atonement.[12] Atonement is prominent in the context (e.g., 9:24), and the writer contrasts the restricted access under the Old system to the confident approach of the New, yet the Day of Atonement is not the immediate reference in 10:19–22. The High Priest washed before entering the Holy of Holies (Lev. 16:4; cf.

Num. 19:5, 9, 17–19).

11. In the Mosaic tabernacle, a veil separated the Holy Place from the courtyard, but several considerations make it certain that 10:20 refers to the "second" veil that separated the two portions of the tent. Elsewhere in the letter the word is used to refer to the "second veil." In 6:19, the Christian hope is an anchor for the soul that passes behind the καταπέτασμα where Jesus has entered, and it is clear that Jesus has entered as High Priest into the true Most Holy Place, fulfilling "once for all" (ἅπαξ) the annual entry of the Aaronic High Priest (9:7, 11). Moreover, in 9:3, the writer has explicitly referred to the "second veil" (δεύτερον καταπέτασμα). Finally, Attridge points out that though καταπέτασμα sometimes refers to the first veil in the LXX, the inner veil is always translated with this word (Attridge, *Hebrews*, 184).

12. James D. G. Dunn, *Baptism in the Holy Spirit: A Re-Examination of the New Testament Teaching on the Gift of the Spirit in Relation to Pentecostalism Today*, Studies in Biblical Theology, 2nd series, no. 15 (London: SCM Press, 1970), 213.

Exod. 30:20), but he was sprinkled with blood only at his ordination.

William Lane suggests that 10:22 refers to the blood and water of the Sinai covenant (cf. 9:18–22).[13] Though undoubtedly included in the text's allusive web, the Sinai covenant does not strictly fit the bill. Israel was constituted a "royal priesthood" by the sprinkling of blood (Exod. 19:6; 24:1–8), but even then no lay Israelite was permitted to touch the mountain, or, later, to enter the tent or approach the veil. One might rescue Lane's interpretation by observing that the writer conflates the Sinai covenant with the ordination of the priests and the erection of the tabernacle. This "confusion" underwrites what 10:19–22 implies, that the dual structure of the first covenant—a narrow priestly covenant within the larger national covenant—no longer exists. All those baptized and sprinkled with the blood of Christ have privileges of access beyond those of Israel's High Priests.[14] Thus, baptism is the rite

---

13. William Lane, *Hebrews 9–13*, WBC, 47B (Dallas, TX: Word, 1991), 287.

14. Attridge *(Hebrews,* 288) and James Moffatt *(A Critical and Exegetical Commentary on the Epistle to the Hebrews*, ICC [Edinburgh: T. & T. Clark, 1924]) deny that the writer intends to teach the priesthood of believers, but it is difficult to know how he could have made the point more clearly. For the contrary opinion, see Ernest Best, "Spiritual Sacrifice: General Priesthood in the New Testament," *Int* 14 (1960), 273–99; Darrell J. Pursiful, *The Cultic Motif in the Spirituality of the Book of Hebrews* (Lewiston, NY: Mellen Biblical Press,

that confers the privilege of access through the veil (one of the set of priestly privileges). Ordination conferred the same privilege under the Old Testament system by making priests. If baptism makes priests, baptism plays the same role in the church that ordination played in Israel. It follows that baptism fulfills and replaces ordination.

Undifferentiated Priesthood for Undivided Sanctuary

To see the wider implications of baptism to priesthood, we need to examine some threads of the epistle's argument. Though the identity and historical setting of the writer and original recipients of the letter to the Hebrews are subjects of considerable and unresolved debate,[15] the writer gives a theological description of his situation by using several metaphors. The first covenant is growing old and becoming obsolete (8:13). Metaphorically the church finds herself at Kadesh Barnea, having left Egypt behind, she must choose, like Israel, between entering to conquer and shrinking back (Heb. 3–4).[16] Some of the book's descriptions are "apocalyptic," indicating that a new world is coming into existence. Earthquakes shake

---

1993), 128, 132–33; and especially Scholer, *Proleptic Priests.*

15. For summaries of the issues of authorship, recipients, and setting, see William Lane, *Hebrews 1–8*, WBC, 47A (Dallas, TX: Word, 1991), lvii–lxvi, and Attridge, *Hebrews,* 1–13.

16. Albert Vanhoye, "Longue marche ou acces tout proche? Le context biblique de Hébreux 3, 7–4, 11," *Biblica* 49:1 (1968), 9–26.

heaven and earth, toppling what can be shaken so that the unshakable kingdom alone remains (12:26–27). A new age (αἰών) has come and is coming. The Son is rolling up and changing the "garments" of heaven and earth (1:10–12), for he is the one through whom God made the ages (αἰῶνες) (1:2).

That these "garments" and "shakable things" include the institutions of the "first covenant" is evident from the first lines of the epistle, where the author contrasts the filial word with the Torah spoken through angels (1:1–2; 2:1–4; cf. Gal 3:19). Though the apocalyptic language is metaphorical, it is nonetheless theologically weighty, implying that the changes in sanctuary, priesthood and law detailed in the rest of the letter are so radical that they can be described with the imagery of cosmic destruction and renewal. In this sense, the letter to the Hebrews, despite its distinctiveness, joins with the rest of the New Testament in announcing that, in Christ, there is a new creation.[17]

The exhortation of 10:19–22 springs from this new situation. Several structural features and allusions indicate that this admonition concludes the entire discussion

---

17. For further discussion of the New Testament's use of apocalyptic language with reference to political, religious and cultural transformations, see G. B. Caird, *The Language and Imagery of the Bible* (Grand Rapids, MI: Eerdmans, 1980), 243–71, and N.T. Wright, *Jesus and the Victory of God* (London: SPCK, 1996), 320–68.

of priesthood, covenant and sacrifice from the previous chapters. Quotations from Psalm 110 and Jeremiah 31 in Hebrews 10:12–17 form an *inclusio* with the quotations in 8:1, 8–12,[18] suggesting that 10:19–22 is based on the material of 8:1–10:18. But the allusive web stretches more widely. As G. H. Guthrie has pointed out, 10:19–22 is similar in both content and structural significance to 4:14–16. Guthrie designates these units "overlapping constituents," since each serves both as conclusion to the preceding section and as introduction to the following section. Reference in 4:14 to Jesus as "high priest" and the word ὁμολογίας form a concluding *inclusio* with 3:1, and close out 3:1–4:16.

At the same time, 4:14–16 introduces the themes that dominate the large section from 5:1 to 10:18. Guthrie suggests that 10:19–25 has a similar structural role, drawing implications from the section beginning with 5:1 and also introducing the exhortations that conclude the epistle. In content, too, 4:14–16 and 10:18–25 are parallel; both exhort believers confidently to "draw near" (προσερχώμεθα) because of the priestly ministry of Jesus. Thus, the two passages form the frame surrounding the

18. Attridge, "Uses of Antithesis," 1–5, *idem, Hebrews,* 279, James Swetnam, "Form and Content in Hebrews 7–13," *Biblica* 55:3 (1974), 333–48 (335). Lane (*Hebrews 9–13,* 279) points out that the change to direct address in 10:19 also marks a seam in the text.

central chapters of the epistle.[19] Beyond this, the combination of "confidence" (παρρησία) and "house" (οἶκος) in
10:21–22 reaches back to 3:6, which identifies Jesus as
"son" (υἱός) rather than "priest" (ἱερεύς) over the house.
The author's address to his readers as "brothers" (ἀδελφοί)
in 10:19 takes up the "holy brothers" (ἅγιοι ἀδελφοί) of
3:1, which in turn concludes the discussion of the brothers of Jesus (2:11, 17). Thus, 10:19–22 is the opening of a
hortatory passage that draws implications from the entire
preceding argument.

How the pathway leads to this destination is not,
however, self-evident. Indeed, the exhortation does not
seem to follow from the preceding argument at all. The
typological argument of the previous chapters seems to
establish only *Christ's* right of entry into the heavenly
sanctuary. It seems entirely reasonable to argue that Jesus, the greater Aaron, entered the heavenly sanctuary
alone—to cleanse his people to be sure, but not to take
his people in. Such a construction would avoid some glar-
ing discontinuities between the Yom Kippur ritual and
its fulfillment. Under the law, the High Priest was utterly alone in his approach to the Most Holy Place (Lev.
16:17) and, Calvin's hints notwithstanding,[20] Israel was

19. G. H. Guthrie, "The Structure of Hebrews: A Textlinguistic Analysis" (PhD. diss., Southwestern Baptist Theological Seminary, 1991).
For a summary of Guthrie's work, see Lane, *Hebrews 1–8,* xc–xcviii.

20. John Calvin, *Commentaries on the Epistle of Paul the Apostle to the*

not even represented by the stones of the High Priest's breastplate (Exod. 28:15–30), for on the Day of Atonement he wore linen garments, not the mixed garments of his daily ministry (Lev. 16:4). If Jesus takes a multitude into the inner sanctuary, he shatters the whole rite. To fulfill the law properly, Jesus must enter alone.[21] On this view, the second covenant transposes the themes of the first to a higher key, but the melodic and harmonic structure remains entirely intact.

Hebrews 10:19–22, however, offers a more creative variation on the Levitical theme, apparently leaping from the argument concerning Christ's priesthood to the conclusion that not only Christ but all Christians may enter the "sanctuary" (ἅγια). Presumably, the author believed he laid the groundwork in the first ten chapters. Like most foundations, this one is nearly invisible to superficial observation, though no less secure for that. Some digging is required.

First, the epistle opens with four chapters in which the themes of priesthood, sanctuary and sacrifice figure very little. Jesus is High Priest (2:17), but this title apparently bobs up from some deep current, and it is immedi-

---

Hebrews, trans. John Owen (Edinburgh: Calvin Translation Society, 1853), 234.

21. John Brown suggests that 10:19 refers to the entry of Jesus, not believers, into the heavenly sanctuary (*An Exposition of Hebrews* [London: Banner of Truth Trust, 1961], 455).

ately submerged for two more chapters, only to resurface just as suddenly in 4:14. The focus of the opening chapters is the restoration in Christ of Adamic dominion over the creation. A careful reading of Hebrews 2, however, reveals that the priestly title of 2:17 has been prepared for by several terms that carry, *inter alia,* Levitical connotations. The crown in 2:9 seems to make Jesus a king, but Israelite High Priests too wore crowns (Exod. 28:36–38; Lev. 8:9) and Jesus' connection with the priest-king Melchizedek is a leitmotif throughout the letter.

According to 2:10, Jesus "brings many sons to glory," a turn of phrase that, in Hebrews, may well have a priestly resonance. Though the specific reference of glory (δόξα) is to the eschatological state of believers, entrance into glory, for both Christ and His people, is envisioned elsewhere in Hebrews as entrance into the Most Holy Place, where the glory is enthroned above the cherubim (8:1–2; 9:11, 25; 10:19). Jesus' purpose in tasting death was to bring his sons and brothers to glory in the heavenly sanctuary, to crown them with priestly (and royal) honor. To accomplish this, he had to be "perfected" (τελειῶσαι, 2:10), a verb used in the LXX to translate the technical ordination phrase, "fill the hand" (מלא יד).[22] Hebrews

---

22. In the LXX, τελειῶσαι is used absolutely of ordination only at Leviticus 21:10, leading many commentators to suggest that the word did not connote "ordain" for first-century writers and readers. David Peterson, who has done the most extensive study of perfection in

2:11 further describes Jesus as the Sanctifier who shares a common origin (ἐξ ἑνός) with those he sanctifies, so that together Sanctifier and sanctified might form a holy fraternity (3:1), analogous to the Aaronic community of "holy ones" (cf. Exod. 29:1). Incarnation in this passage forges a quasi-familial connection between Jesus and the brothers consecrated to stand to serve with him. Thus, giving him the title of "High Priest" is appropriate (2:17).

Underlying the argument of Hebrews 2–3, more-over, is the "Shiloh pattern," named for the events recorded in 1 Samuel 1–4. The priestly family of Eli had become incurably corrupt, and Yahweh threatened to remove the "house" of Eli, to set up the "house" of another priest, and to desolate his own "house." At the same time, he

---

Hebrews, argues for a "vocational" sense, so that Jesus is perfected in that he is qualified to act as redeemer. This qualification includes but is not limited to priesthood (*Hebrews and Perfection: An Examination of the Concept of Perfection in the Epistle to the Hebrews* [Cambridge: Cambridge University Press, 1982], 26–30, 70–73). I am satisfied with Peterson's "vocational" reading of the term, so long as the priestly resonance is heard. Moisés Silva notes that Leviticus 21:10 indicates that the "head word" ("fill") of the phrase ("fill the hand") might take on the meaning of the whole phrase, but cautions against reading the full phrase into every use of the word ("Perfection and Eschatology in Hebrews," *WTJ* 39:1 [1976/77], 60–71 (61). While agreeing with Silva's linguistic point, it seems reasonable to suppose that in the presence of the semantic catalysts of sacrifice, priesthood and sanctuary that are so abundant in Hebrews, the word will undergo an alchemical transformation. Meaning arises from literary context, and not merely from lexical context.

promised a "faithful priest" who would minister in a purified sanctuary (1 Sam. 2:27–36; 3:10–14). Soon after,
Eli and his sons died, and the Philistines took the ark into
captivity. Under Solomon, Yahweh established a new set
of houses—the priestly house of Zadok presiding over the
Jerusalem temple. Judgment on "Shiloh" recurs in the Old
Testament: Jeremiah, a priest from the descendants of Eli
at Anathoth (Jer. 1:1; cf. 1 Kings. 2:26–27), warned that
what had happened to Eli and Shiloh would be repeated in the destruction of Solomon's temple and removal
of its unfaithful priests (Jer. 7:12–14). As in the first instance, however, this warning came with the promise of
a restored house and a new priestly family, fulfilled in the
restoration temple and the High Priest Joshua (Zech. 3).

"Shiloh" has its place in the typological imagination of the early church. In the early chapters of Luke,
John and Jesus are twin Samuels announcing the coming
judgment upon the temple and its corrupt leadership.[23] If
they warn of the destruction of "Shiloh," however, they
also promise the formation of a new priesthood and the
construction of a new house. This typology is operating
in Hebrews 2–3. Hebrews 2:17 contains a virtual quotation from 1 Sam. 2:35, describing Jesus as a "faithful"

---

23. See further, Eric Burrows, *The Gospel of the Infancy, and Oth-
er Biblical Essays*, Bellarmine Series, no. 6 (London: Burns Oates &
Washbourne, 1940); René Laurentin, *Structure et théologie de Luc I–
II*, Etudes Bibliques (Pans Gabalda, 1957).

High Priest, and 3:6 indicates that he is the Son over the "house" of those sons who have been brought to glory. Since Jesus is a sanctified priest, it follows that his household is a priestly house and he is a new Zadok, who, not coincidentally, bears the name of the High Priest of the restoration. From the very first chapters of Hebrews, the establishment of a new priesthood, a new house of housekeepers, is presented as the goal of Jesus' ministry. When the author later reminds his readers that they have a "great priest over the house" (ἱερέα μέγαν ἐπὶ τον οἶκον, 10:21), he is assuring them that they may enter the house since they have become a holy brotherhood (3:6) through and under their High Priest.[24] For the writer of this letter, the "apocalyptic" costume change of heaven and earth involves a change not only of "law" and "covenant" but of priesthood.

Hebrews 7 provides another cornerstone of the argument by showing that this new priestly house is no longer confined to a single tribe or class but encompasses the whole people of God. Throughout the discussion of the mysterious figure of Melchizedek, the focus of the writer, despite some traditional etymologizing of his name and

---

24. G. M. M. Pelser ("A Translation Problem Heb 10:19–25," *Neotestamentica* 8 [1974], 43–53 [49]), L. Floor ("The General Priesthood of Believers in the Epistle to the Hebrews," *Neotestamentica* 5 [1971], 72–82 [75]), and Dahl ("A New and Living Way," 406), all interpret οἶκος in 10:21 as "household," contra Lane (*Hebrews 9–13*, 276).

titles, is fixed on the superiority of this priest to Aaron. He teases this conclusion out of Genesis 14 in several ways. In stressing Melchizedek's lack of genealogy, the author is not being "playful,"[25] nor is he offering a glaringly fallacious *argumentum ex silentio*. Silences are significant in the midst of surrounding noise; holes in the text are noteworthy if one expects higher ground. And silence concerning the ancestry of a priest is, for both Jew and Greek, nothing short of revolutionary, for "fleshly" descent from the founder of the house was required for many priesthoods of the ancient world.[26] Dispensing with the genealogical qualification challenges the whole system of graded holiness.

The author also supports his brief for the superiority of Jesus' priesthood by referring to Abraham's payment of tithes to Melchizedek. Because Abraham is the "patriarch" and acknowledged head of all Israel, his homage through gift to Melchizedek indicates that Levi and Aaron too are subordinate to the Melchizedekan priest. This much is on the surface of the text, but the harmony

---

25. *Pace* Attridge, *Hebrews,* 187.

26. See Mary Beard and John North, eds., *Pagan Priests* (London: Gerald Duckworth, 1990); Jules Martha, *Les sacerdoces athéniens,* Bibliothèque des Écoles Françaises d'Athènes et de Rome, no. 26 (Paris: Ernest Thorin, 1882); Leopold Sabourin, *Priesthood: A Comparative Study,* Supplements to Numen, Studies in the History of Religions, no. 25 (Leiden: E. J. Brill, 1973).

beneath the surface comes from the narrative of Numbers 16–18, in which Korah, Dathan and Abiram attempt to seize Aaron's priesthood (Num. 16), Yahweh confirms Aaron's election as priest by causing his staff to bear fruit in his presence (Num. 17), and he institutes a tithe system in which the Levites collect a tenth from Israel and passed on a tenth of their tenth to the priests (Num. 18). The tithe system mentioned in Heb. 7:5, then, was set up to confirm the Aaronides' exclusive standing in the holy place. Institutionalized gift-giving traced the contours of religious and social order, and the tithe system also reinforced gradations in food rights, for only Levites could eat from Israel's tithes and only priests from the tithes of the Levites (Num. 18:10, 18). Tithing fortified the partitions separating Israelite from Israelite, showing that some from Abraham's loins were closer to Yahweh's house and table than others from the same loins (Heb. 7:5, 10). The argument of Hebrews 7 is less fanciful and more daring than some have dreamed, for, by leveling distinctions within Abraham's seed, the writer seems to take his stand with Korah against the priestly privileges of Aaron.

Consensus concerning the book of Hebrews is difficult to come by, but I suspect that scholars unanimously agree that Korah did not write Hebrews. Yet, this background clarifies the implications of Melchizedek's reappearance. The "change in law" is, in Hebrews 7, mainly a change in qualifications for priestly standing (cf. νόμος in 7:12, 16). Under the old system, priestly privilege was dependent on genealogy, but the Melchizedekan priest is qualified by resurrection (7:16), and therefore voids the fleshly "law." Christ holds a priesthood that transcends ancient distinctions, a priesthood to which not only lay Israelites but even Abraham paid homage. When Melchizedek appears, all the seed of Abraham bows with the patriarch; before Melchizedek, the seed of Abraham is one and undivided. It follows that access to and ministry in the house, once a privilege of those who received tithes, is now extended to all who join Abraham in giving gifts to Melchizedek.

Given the structural analogy of temple and people in the old system, one would expect that an undifferentiated priesthood would minister in an undivided sanctuary, and this is precisely what we find. Hebrews 10:19 states that those who have sprinkled hearts and washed bodies are permitted confidently (ἔχοντες...παρρησίαν) to draw near to the holy place (τὰ ἅγια). τὰ ἅγια corresponds to the Most Holy Place, since v. 20 encourages the readers to enter by the way that Jesus has made through the veil (καταπέτασμα). Thus, the baptized are now in the position of the High Priest. Continuing to think of "Holy" and "Most Holy," however, misses the point of ch. 9, which hinges on the contrast between the "first" and "second," terminology that, applied to the chambers of the tabernacle, is unique to this author.[27] This distinction is initially applied not to the tabernacle but to the covenant (8:7, 13). Though translators are correct to supply "covenant" (διαθήκη) in 9:1, this emendation misses the subtlety of the author's presentation. "The first" (ἡ πρώτη) in 9:1 prepares for the same phrase in 9:2, this time applied to the "tent" (σκηνή): "first" tent rhymes with "first" covenant. This creates a fruitful ambiguity at 9:18, where the author asserts that even "the first" (ἡ πρώτη) was not inaugurated without blood. Again, most translations emend "covenant," but the Greek raises the question "the first *what*?," and the author's answer is that the initiation of the "first" involves both cutting a covenant and constructing a sanctuary (cf. 9:19–21).[28] We should also take note of the rare verb ἐγκαινίζω, used in the New Testament only in Hebrews 9:18, where it describes the "inauguration" of the covenant, and in 10:20, where it refers to the "opened" way into the sanctuary.[29] Covenant and sanctuary are inseparable: a new covenant remodels the holy place.

---

27. Lane, *Hebrews 9–13*, 219.

28. Hebrews 9 combines the inauguration of the covenant (Exod. 24) with the erection of the tabernacle (Exod. 40), though according to the chronology of Exodus these events were separated by the better part of a year (Exod 19:1, 40:17). Theologically, however, the author is quite correct that the inauguration of the Sinai covenant includes the erection of the tabernacle.

29. Cf. Pelser, "A Translation Problem," 47, 49.

Having established this homology between covenant and sanctuary, the writer is prepared to offer his summary of the significance of the Mosaic tabernacle. It shows that the way into the ἅγια has not been manifested "as long as the first tent has standing" (ἔτι πρώτης σκηνῆς ἐχούσης στάσιν, 9:8). In context, the "first tent" is the "holy place" (vv. 2, 6), but through the play on "first" and "second" in the preceding verses, the first tent becomes a parable (παραβολή) for the entire dissolving first covenant. This is so because the Mosaic tabernacle (and the similarly structured temple of Solomon) architecturally embodied the exclusion of the "sons" from glory. While the first tent had standing, only those qualified by fleshly descent from Aaron might draw near to stand to serve. Hebrews announces that the "first" no longer has standing, since the "second" has appeared and the "time of reformation" has begun at the consummation of the ages.[30] While the first tent blocked the "way" (ὁδός), the Melchizedekan Priest has eliminated the first tent and made a ὁδός, so that the new undifferentiated priestly fellowship might minister in an undivided house.

---

30. In the background, doubtless, is the rending of the veil that, according to the synoptic accounts, took place at the time of Jesus' death, which in principle ended the divided sanctuary and therefore the divided Israel the sanctuary represented (Matt. 27:51; Mark 15:38; Luke 23:45). See Brown, *Hebrews,* 386; F. F. Bruce, *Commentary on the Epistle to the Hebrews,* The New London Commentary on the New Testament (London: Marshall, Morgan & Scott, 1964), 246.

Hebrews 12:28–13:17 spells out the nature of household ministry as love for brothers, hospitality, sexual purity, generosity, offering praise, and eating the Eucharistic flesh denied to Aaronic priests. Hebrews makes clear that these facets of ecclesial life have a priestly character. Christ's blood cleanses the conscience from dead works in order to prepare for "service" (λατρεύειν) to the living God (Heb. 9:14). While the LXX distinguishes consistently between λειτουργία ("priestly ministry") and λατρεία ("worship" in a general sense, including both priests and people), in Hebrews this distinction is effaced and the λατρ-word group is normally used to describe priestly service in the tabernacle (8:5; 9:1, 6). Thus, when 9:14 uses this terminology to refer to Christian service, it means that Christ's blood cleanses consciences specifically to qualify for priestly ministry.[31] The new priesthood is not a wholly undifferentiated community: The Pauline image of the body, in which the church is harmony of difference rather than a blank unity, matches Hebrews' vision of each member exercising some facet of priestly ministry in Christ's house. Nor is the priestly community egalitarian in every respect, for among the necessities of housekeeping are ministries of government, administration and leadership (Heb. 13:7, 17). No member, however, may lay claim to privileged entry rights into the house or ex-

---

31. H. Strathmann, "λατρεύω, λατρεία," *TDNT,* IV, 59–65.

clusive rights at the table. Every member equally stands to serve, hands filled to sacrifice and to feast.

Baptism Remakes the World

Against this backdrop, we return to the baptismal reference in Hebrews 10:22. Because it fulfills and replaces the ordination rite, baptism is the ritual enactment of the gospel of Hebrews. Through his unique sacrifice and his entry into the heavenly sanctuary, Jesus has shaken the old covenant house and the aftershocks are global in scope. Baptism temporally and geographically extends his disruption of heaven and earth. By its very form, baptism fulfills the old ordination rite, administering the once-for-all priestly bath to those outside the lineage of Aaron, and thus enacts the promise and threat of Shiloh: formation of a new priestly house crowned and enthroned together with Melchizedek, the dissolution of priestly gradations within the seed of Abraham, the end of genealogical qualification for priests, and the replacement of the divided sanctuary. As first-century Jewish converts, once divided into priests and laymen (cf. Acts 6:7), were baptized, a homogeneously priestly people emerged, and as Gentiles were bathed, ancient divisions between Jew and Greek eroded as well. Baptism formed a new nation out of the old, molding the eschatological race of the Last Adam, the kingdom of priests. It is the efficacious sign of the clothing change of heaven and earth, destroying antique Israelite order and remapping the terrain. It is the "washing of παλιγγενεσία." Baptism is not only the womb of the church, but of the world.

CHAPTER TEN

CHRISTS CHRISTENED INTO CHRIST: PRIESTHOOD AND IMITATION IN AUGUSTINE AND AQUINAS

Baptismal anointing(s) and investiture have frequently been interpreted in the light of Old Testament installation of priests, kings, and prophets. From Tertullian's *De baptismo* through the scholastics, in both the Eastern and Western churches, this has been a common theme of baptismal theology, and continues to be prominent in Catholic and Orthodox and, to a lesser extent, Anglican and Lutheran reflection on initiation.[1] Though this typol-

---

1. See the texts in Paul Dabin, *Le sacerdoce royal des fidèles dans la tradition ancienne et moderne* (Brussels: L'Editions Universelles, 1950); Thomas M. Finn, *Early Christian Baptism and the Catechumenate,* 2 vols, Message of the Fathers of the Church 5–6 (Collegeville, MN: Liturgical Press, 1992). For discussions of the rites involved, see especially Leonel Mitchell, *Baptismal Anointing* (Notre Dame, IN: University of Notre Dame Press, 1978); Gabriele Winkler, "The Orig-

ogy is frequently noted in recent work, the wider redemptive-historical and ecclesiological issues have not received so much attention nor have differences of emphasis and formulation always been sufficiently recognized. In his useful collection of documents, Paul Dabin is so insistent on finding a moral unanimity in the tradition that he obscures significant differences both in theological formulation and in liturgical practice.

In an effort to fill these gaps somewhat, this chapter will examine the use of these themes by Augustine and Aquinas, who represent two of the key moments in the Western development of this theological construct. After an exposition of each, I will enumerate some differences between them and briefly indicate some of the ecclesiological issues at stake.

Augustine

One can be misled about Augustine's baptismal theology by exclusive attention to his polemical treatises.[2] Against

---

inal Meaning of the Prebaptismal Anointing and Its Implications" in Maxwell E. Johnson, ed., *Living Water, Sealing Spirit: Readings on Christian Initiation* (Collegeville, MN: Liturgical Press, 1995), 58–81.

2. Among works on Augustine's baptismal theology, see Peter Cramer, *Baptism and Change in the Early Middle Ages, c. 200–c. 1150*, Cambridge Studies in Medieval Life and Thought (Cambridge: Cambridge University Press, 1992), 87–129; J. C. Didier, "Saint Augustine et le baptême des enfants," *Revue des études augustiniennes* 2

the Pelagians, he insists that infant baptism is incoherent
except upon the assumption that infants require remission of sins; against the Donatists, he claims that, though
it can exist and be administered outside of the fellowship
of the Christ's Body, it cannot exist or be administered
rightly. In the Pelagian dispute, Augustine seems to reduce baptism to exorcism;[3] in the second, baptism seems
bound up with a mechanistic ecclesiology. In both cases, however, these conclusions are mistaken. Against the
Donatists, Augustine urges that schismatics cannot ad-
minister baptism rightly because by definition they lack
caritas, in the absence of which all virtue and knowledge
is a clanging cymbal; the *ecclesia* of *nulla salus extra eccle-
siam* is the community of faith and love.[4] With regard to

(1956), 109–29; N. M. Haring, "The Augustinian Axiom: *Nulla Sacramento Injuria Facienda Est,"* *Mediaeval Studies* 16 (1954), 87–93;
idem, "One Baptism: An Historical Study of the Non-Repetition
of Certain Sacraments," *Mediaeval Studies* 10 (1948), 217–19; A.
Houssiau, "L'engagement baptismal," *Revue théologique de Louvain*
9 (1978), 145–50; J. Patout Burns, "Christ and the Holy Spirit in
Augustine's Theology of Baptism" in Joanne McWilliam, ed., *Augustine: From Rhetor to Theologian* (Ontario: Wilfrid Laurier University
Press, 1992), 161–71. F. Van der Meer, *Augustine the Bishop* (London: Sheed and Ward, 1961), 347–87, gives a vivid description of
fifth-century baptismal procedures, including selections from Augustine's baptismal sermons.

3. So Cramer, *Baptism and Change,* 87.

4. See, for example, Augustine's use of the parable of the ungrateful
steward, whose debts, previously forgiven, "returned with redoubled

Pelagius, Augustine's use of baptism must be seen against the background of the Pauline thematic of the two Adams. This, first, implies a solidarity of all human beings in sin and, second, makes remission of sin one aspect of the baptismal transfer from Adam to Christ.

This context brings us to the heart not only of Augustine's baptismal theology but of his ecclesiology, and arguably of his entire theology.[5] Karl Adam long ago

---

force upon his head" because of his refusal to forgive his brother (*De baptismo* 1.12 [20]).

5. For a bibliography on Augustine's ecclesiology, see Émilien Lamirande, "Un siècle et demi d'études sur l'ecclésiologie de saint Augustin: Essay bibliographique," *Revue des ètudes Augustiniennes* 8 (1962), 1–125, and Michael A. Fahey, "Augustine's Ecclesiology Revisited," in McWilliam, ed., *From Rhetor to Theologian,* 173–81. Among the works consulted for this essay were Emile Mersch, *Le Corps Mystique du Christ: Études de théologie historique,* 2nd ed. (Paris: Desclèe de Brouwer et Cie, 1936), 2:35–138; Fritz Hofmann, *Die Kirchenbegriff des hl. Augustinus: In Seinen Grundlagen und in Seiner Entwicklung* (Munich: Max Huber, 1933); Robert F. Evans, *One and Holy: The Church in Latin Patristic Thought* (London: SPCK, 1972), 65–128; Michel Reveillard, "Le Christ-Homme, tête de l'Eglise: Étude d'ecclèsiologie selon les *Enarrationes in Psalmos* d'Augustin," *Recherches augustiniennes* 5 (1968), 67–94; Karl Adam, *Saint Augustine: The Odyssey of His Soul* (London: Sheed and Ward, 1932); Jeremy Duquesnay Adams, *The Populus of Augustine and Jerome: A Study in the Patristic Sense of Community* (New Haven, CT: Yale University Press, 1971), 17–69; Gerald Bonner, "Augustine's Concept of Deification," *Journal of Theological Studies* 37 (1986), 369–86; Yves Congar, *L'Église de saint Augustin à l'époque moderne,* Histoire de Dogmes 3 (Paris: Éditions du Cerf, 1970), 11–24.

suggested that the crucial consequence of Augustine's development from neo-Platonism to Christianity was a growing appreciation of the soteriological significance of the humanity of the Christ. The progress of his thinking was closely related to his developing conceptions of sin and grace. As his recognition of the radical sinfulness and weakness of human nature grew more profound, he realized that what sinners need is not repair but a "new nature," "a completely new foundation and a new root," which, Augustine believed, is only possible through incorporation into the "new and sinless humanity" of the God-man. Thus, "this real, essential union of our humanity with the new man, Christ, is the sum and climax of Augustine's teaching regarding redemption," and Adam suggests that the primary interest of his entire theology is a "fundamental conception of Christianity as a vital union of all the redeemed with the new man who is Christ."[6] Baptism incorporates into this new human nature.[7]

---

6. Adam, *Saint Augustine*, 44–48. See the similar statement of Vetter, quoted by Mersch, *Corps Mystique*, 45nI: "Le mystère du corps du Christ est le mystère central dans la théologie augustinienne." Mersch (84–138) marshals abundant evidence of the pervasiveness of this theme in Augustine's writings and sermons. What little Augustine says about deification is connected with the basic idea of incorporation into Christ: see Bonner, "Augustine's Concept of Deification," 369–86.

7. Adam, *Saint Augustine*, 45–46; Bonner, "Augustine's Concept of Deification," 383. Ambiguities concerning the relation of the bap-

From this angle, we can understand how Augustine employs the links between Christian initiation and priesthood. To be sure, he nowhere systematically sets this out. References scattered throughout his writings reveal a consistent and detailed picture, but the occasional nature of the references must not be forgotten. Augustine's thought, especially when he is teaching from biblical texts, operates by what Frances Young calls a method of "overlay."[8] Augustine can hardly mention one aspect of this paradigm without bringing the others immediately into play, and the various images and themes rapidly pile up. To set out his teaching as a series of arguments

---

tized to the elect arise particularly in Augustine's disputes with the Donatists and Pelagians. By insisting in his controversy with the Donatists that baptism is conferred even among schismatics, though they derive no benefit from it, he darkened the shadow that already fell between *sacramentum* and *res*, between the *communio sanctorum* and the *societas sacramentorum*, and with his further attention to the problems of grace and perseverance in his polemics against Pelagius, the shadow darkened further. Nonetheless, Augustine never doubted the efficacy of the sacraments, the promise that those baptized in the Catholic church were incorporated into Christ. See R. Prenter, "Metaphysics and Eschatology in the Sacramental Theology of St. Augustine," *Studia Theologica* 1 (1948), 5–26; Van der Meer, *Augustine the Bishop*, 628n67; Hofmann, *Kirchenbegriff*, 353–72; Evans, One *and Holy*, 92–107.

8. Frances Young, "From Analysis to Overlay: A Sacramental Approach to Christology" in David Brown and Ann Loades, eds, *Christ the Sacramental Word: Incarnation, Sacrament and Poetry* (London: SPCK, 1996), 40–56.

and propositions, then, necessarily distorts somewhat the fundamental intertwining of these themes in Augustine's own teaching. Yet, for analytical purposes, it is useful to expound the doctrine in a more formal fashion than Augustine himself did.

Augustine's habit of connecting initiation to priesthood is not merely ornamental, nor is it part of some superficial allegorization of the baptismal liturgy. It is instead directly implied by his fundamental Christology, ecclesiology, and baptismal theology. Indeed, Augustine's Christology can be described as an explication of the meaning of the "chrism" by virtue of which Jesus is the Christ: *Christus a chrismate dictus est, id est, ab unctione.*[9] The chrism by which Jesus is Christ is the Holy Spirit. Augustine rhapsodizes on the mystery of Psalm 45:7, that God should have anointed God, and concludes that such an anointing could not be by a visible sign but only by an inner, spiritual anointing.[10] In his commentary on Psalm 149, Augustine immediately moves to explain the "chrism" of Christ by reference to Old Testament types. As the kings and priests of the Old Testament were anointed, so Christ is anointed *vero* as both King and Priest. This dual office is basic to his work of redemption: As King, he fights for us, defeating Satan in the cross,

---

9. *Enarratio in Psalmum* 149; *PL* 37:1952–53.

10. Ibid. 44 (45); *PL* 36:505–6.

and as Priest he offers himself as sacrifice and intercedes before his Father.[11]

In *De Trinitate* 15.46, Augustine again points out that the Spirit is the unction that makes the Christ. Here, however, he insists that the Anointed One is not the only one anointed. The unction of initiation signifies that *donum gratiae* that came on Christ at his baptism in the form of a dove, but in that baptism the anointing of the entire body is manifested.[12] Christ is not Anointed One except as he is *totus Christus,* head and body, savior and church, husband and bride.[13] The anointing of the Christ, as pictured in Psalm 133, flows from the head to the beard and garments. All who are included in the Anointed are themselves anointed; all in Christ are Christ's and christs. Indeed, "Christ" is a title for the corporate person constituted by head and body; in a typical passage, he writes that *omnes quippe unctos ejus chrismate, recte christos possumus dicere: quod tamen totum cum suo capite corpus unus est Christus.*[14] Augustine makes the same move from a pneumatological Christology to a pneumatological ecclesiology in his comments on Psalm 104:15. Just as Christ's

---

11. Ibid. 149; *PL* 37:1952–3.

12. *PL* 42:1093.

13. See Mersch, *Corps Mystique*, 84–138.

14. *De civitate Dei* 17.4; *PL* 41:532.

face shines with the oil of grace and holiness, so too do
the faces of those who coming to him accept his grace.[15]

From this, it is a very small step to recognizing that
those who share the chrism of the Christ share in the
offices and ministries that his chrism confers. Comment-
ing on Revelation 20:6, Augustine notes that the promise that all will be priests to the Father and Son is appli-
cable to all Christians, not only to clergy: "as we call all
believers Christians on account of the mystical chrism,
so we call all priests because they are members of the one
Priest."[16] In a sermon fragment preserved by John the
Deacon, Augustine moves more directly from Old Testament priestly anointing to the anointed people of the
new covenant: *Tunc enim unus sacerdos ungebatur; modo
Christiani omnes unguntur.*[17] Old Testament anointings
prefigure the royal priesthood of the church.[18] Given the
totus Christus doctrine, to say that the typological anointings prefigured the church is virtually equivalent to saying that they prefigured Christ.

These various strands—christological, ecclesiological, typological, and eschatological—come together in a
classic passage:

---

15. *Enarratio in Psalmum* 103 (104); *PL* 37:1370.

16. *De civitate Dei* 20.10; *PL* 41:676.

17. *De Calendis Januarius contra paganos; PL* 39:1734–35.

18. *Sermo* 351.5.12; *PL* 39:1548–49.

Et solus tunc ungebatur rex, et sacerdos: duae istae illo tempore unctae personae. In duabus personis praefigurabatur futurus unus rex et sacerdos, utroque munere unus Christus, et ideo Christus a chrismate. Non solum autem caput nostrum unctum est, sed et corpus ejus non ipsi. Rex autem est, quia nos regit et ducit; sacerdos, quia pro nobis interpellat (Rom. viii, 34). E quidem solus ille sacerdos talis extitit, ut ipse esset etiam sacrificium. Sacrificium obtulit Deo non aliud quam seipsum. Non enim inveniret praeter se mundissimam rationalem victimam, tanquam agnus immaculatus fuso sanguine suo redimens nos, concorporans nos sibi, faciens nos membra sua, ut in illo et nos Christus essemus. Ideo ad omnes Christianos pertinet unctio: prioribus autem Veteris Testamenti temporibus ad duas solas personas pertinebat. Inde autem apparet Christi corpus non esse, quia omnes ungimur: et omnes in illo et Christi et Christus sumus, quia quodammodo totus Christus caput et corpus est.[19]

This entire passage is built on a temporal contrast between what was the case *tunc* and what is true *nunc*.

---

19. *Enarratio in Psalmum* 26, 11.2; PL 36:199–200. Dabin, *Sacerdoce royal*, 99, comments that this passage "est si fondamental qu'il est repris, sous une forme ou sous une autre, par les représentants les plus autorisés de la tradition occidentale."

Elsewhere, too, Augustine emphasizes the *mutatio sacerdotii* from Israel to the church, figured in various ways in the Old Testament. The newness of the new is a novel distribution of royal and priestly privilege, which is marked by anointing. *Tunc* the unction was restricted to two personages, and Augustine seems initially to be heading toward an affirmation that *nunc* the unction is more widely administered. Instead, surprisingly, he notes a restriction: what is prefigured in the *duae personae* of the Old Testament is the *futurus unus rex et sacerdos.* The two point to One who combines the two, and that One alone rules and leads, sacrifices and intercedes. But the narrowing of the unction from two to one is ultimately for the purpose of its extension to all, since *non solum autem caput nostrum unctum est, sed et corpus ejus nos ipsi,* or, more briefly, because the One has made the many *concorporans sibi.* The unity of head and members is remarkable: *in illo* (i.e., in the Head) *et nos Christus essemus and omnes in illo et Christi et Christus sumus. Quodammodo* in the final clause indicates Augustine's desire to protect the priority and unique priesthood and kingship of the Head but the affirmation of the inseparability of the *totus Christus* is bold. It is in this christological and ecclesiological context that Augustine understands the extension of the Old Testament anointings to all believers. What *tunc* pertained to only two, *nunc* is granted to *omnes Christianos.*

The eschatological dimension of this passage is no less important: to the *tunc* and *nunc,* there is added a *futurus,* of which the present is a figure. The whole passage is a comment on the title of Psalm 26, which, in Augustine's Latin Bible was, "Of David, before he was anointed." The Psalm is the anointed believer's cry of longing for the presence of God. Believers, already anointed *in sacramento,* are like David, yet to be anointed. Unction is not merely a conferral of a static position but impels forward, leading the anointed ones to desire a future fullness of the oil of gladness. Augustine hears the same voice in Psalm 118 (119:81), where the *regale sacerdotium* strains *avidissime ac vehementissime* toward a good not yet granted.[20]

It is not always clear whether Augustine is referring to a sacramental rite or to the invisible operation of the Spirit. Overall, both are in Augustine's sights, and it is clear in certain passages that a share in the spiritual anointing and priesthood of the Anointed Priest is conferred by baptism and/or chrism. The comments on Psalm 26 make explicit reference to anointing *in sacramento* by which one comes to share in the chrism of Christ.[21] In *De Trinitate* 15.46, he explains that the visible oil signifies the invisible anointing Christ received at his baptism. Initiation confers the priestly right to access to the temple,

---

20. *Enarratio in Psalmum* 118 (119); *PL* 37:1557.

21. *PL* 36:200.

as Augustine demonstrates in a richly layered discussion of Psalm 132. In that Psalm, the priests are said to be clothed in salvation, and since Christ alone is salvation, the psalmist anticipates the sartorial baptismal imagery of Galatians 3:27. Augustine links this with the following image of the budding horn of David. Horns represent spiritual height, which is attained by following the example of John the Baptist, who did not call attention to his own ministry but pointed to the greater One who baptized with the Holy Spirit. Saints and priests exult not in their own good, but because everything of theirs that is good is not of themselves but of the One who baptizes. The baptized may therefore boldly approach the temple, not by their own merits but because they have received a baptism not of human beings but of the One by whom the horn of David is raised up.[22]

Baptism is also implicitly identified as the rite of initiation into the priestly people in Augustine's anti-Pelagian tract, *De peccatorum meritis et remissione.* He cites a series of New Testament passages to establish that only the sheep of God are saved, and that one is made a member of the flock through baptism. This applies to infants as well: *de ovibus ejus non esse incipiunt parvuli, nisi per baptismum.*[23] In the following section, he cites a series of

---

22. *Enarratio in Psalmum* 132; *PL* 37:1728.

23. 1.27 (40); *PL* 44:132.

passages from 1 Peter to show that infants remain in darkness unless they are adopted into the people of God, who offer the sacrifice of praise to the One who brought them from darkness into light. In view of the previous section, it is clear that the transition from outside to within the flock and royal priesthood is effected by baptism.

What does it mean to be a "Christian," one who shares the royal and priestly anointing of Christ? For Jesus, being a priest meant preeminently sacrificing himself, and since the church's priesthood is merely a share in that of the Head, her priesthood takes the same form.[24] Through the only-begotten Priest the church offers her multifaceted sacrifice: by defending the truth to the point of shedding blood, by cultivating the fires of holy and pious love, by keeping appointed feasts as a memorial of Christ's saving work, by a sacrifice of humility and praise.[25] Augustine, however, understands these specific acts of sacrifice as moments in the return to God through incorporation into the new Adam. Sacrifice is not merely "giving up" something, nor a collection of fragmented activities. Rather, it is *omne opus, quod agitur, ut sancta soci-*

---

24. On the idea of sacrifice in Augustine, see Joseph Lecuyer, "Le sacrifice selon saint Augustin," *Augustinus Magister* (Paris: Etudes Augustiniennes, 1954), 2:905–14; Bernard Quinot, "L'influence de L'Épître aux Hébreux dans la notion augustinienne du vrai sacrifice," *Revue des etudes augustiniennes* 8 (1962), 129–68.

25. *De civitate Dei* 10.3; *PL* 41:280.

etate inhaereamus Deo, relatum scilicet ad illum finem boni, quo veraciter beati esse possimus. Sacrifice is not simply an act to which God responds favorably by inviting the sacrificer to fellowship with himself; in Christ, sacrificial acts are themselves the steps by which the sacrificer returns. The whole life of the church is a sacrificial participation in the ascending sacrifice of Christ, the *sacerdos magnus.* Because her sacrifice is in union with that of her Head, the church not only continually offers sacrifice but also is sacrificed.[26] For Augustine, the sacrifice of the Christian is both active and passive, inner and outer, and takes place both in the sanctuary and in the marketplace.

Sharing in the sacrificial priesthood of Christ is particularly manifested in sharing the bread and sacrifice of the eucharist. At the close of *De civitate Dei* 10.6, Augustine subtly moves from the general sacrifice that encompasses the whole life of the church to the focused eucharistic sacrifice. Christ offered himself in the form of a servant, and thereby indicates that true sacrifice is the sacrifice of humility. Augustine cites Romans 12:3–6, which explains the exhortation to offer oneself as a living sacrifice in terms of "not thinking of yourself more highly than you ought." True sacrifice is humble promotion of the unity of the body, as each seeks not his own but the other's good: *Hoc est sacrificium Christianorum:*

---

26. Ibid. 10.6; *PL* 41:283–84.

multi unum corpus in Christo. And this unity is, in turn, manifested liturgically by sharing one loaf. Eucharist is not here a propitiatory sacrifice, yet it is sacrificial as the liturgical performance of the whole-life sacrifice of the church.

Augustine insists that sacrifice is the work of the whole people, yet he does not ignore the importance or position of the ordained priesthood.[27] He entered the Catholic church in part as a result of his search for stable authority, and he could describe ordination as the indelible "sacrament of conferring baptism."[28] Pastors exercise their authority not *in se* but *in corpore Pastoris,* and even evil bishops have the right to be obeyed.[29] Without ministers, human beings neither become Christians nor live

---

27. On Augustine's view of the ordained priesthood, see Cardinal Michele Pellegrino, *The True Priest: The Priesthood as Preached and Practiced by Saint Augustine* (Langley, UK: St Paul Publications, 1968); Maurice Jourjon, "L'évêque et le peuple de Dieu selon saint Augustin" in Henri Rondet, et al., *Saint Augustin parmi nous* (Paris: Xavier Mappus, 1954), 151–78; H. E. J. Cowdrey, "The Dissemination of St. Augustine's Doctrine of Holy Orders during the Later Patristic Age," *Journal of Theological Studies* 30 (1969), 449–54. On the importance of *auctoritas* in Augustine's thought and experience generally, see Peter Brown, *Augustine of Hippo* (London: Faber and Faber, 1967), 216, 238, 278, 310–11.

28. *De baptismo* 1.1.

29. Jourjon, "L'évêque," 166, 173–74.

Christian lives.[30] For all his emphasis on authority and on the necessity of office, however, Augustine wrote little about ordination or the privileges of the priesthood, and episcopal presidency at the eucharist does not play a large role in his thought. His mind instead was full of wonder at the unity of leaders and people in the one Priest, the fundamental equality of bishop and people as sheep and servants of God, manifested in his repeated motto, *praesumus, sed si prosumus.*[31] Authority is in rendering service, so that, though the service may take the form of discipline and command, it has always in view the unity and peace of the church. Exercise of authority is a particular form of the Christian sacrifice offered in different ways by all the baptized.

In the way he weaves together initiation, priesthood, and sacrifice, Augustine displays a grasp of the astonishing novelty of the Christian *ecclesia,* the common share of the whole community in the chrism of the Anointed Priest, and its basic divergence from ancient models of community, whether Jewish or pagan.

Thomas Aquinas

One can say with only mild exaggeration that contemporary Roman Catholic ecclesiology and the whole thrust

---

30. Pellegrino, *True Priest*, 73.

31. Ibid., 59ff.

of Vatican II was inspired by rigorous efforts to rescue Thomistic ecclesiology from his polemical Counter-Reformation interpreters.[32] Careful studies of Thomas have revealed a remarkably "spiritual" or "theological" conception of the church that stood in sharp contrast to the juridical or institutional model that dominated Catholic theology after the sixteenth century. These studies have also revealed that the church has a much higher profile in Thomas' theology than might be assumed, given the lack of a separate treatise *De ecclesia*. Indeed, that absence may not be a sign of Thomas's lack of interest in the church but of the pervasiveness of ecclesiology.[33] In Yves Con-

---

32. On Thomas's ecclesiology, see Yves Congar, "The Idea of the Church in St. Thomas Aquinas," *The Thomist* 1 (1939), 331–59; idem, *L'Église de saint Augustin*, 232–41; idem, *Thomas d'Aquin: sa vision de théologie et de l'Église* (London: Variorum Reprints, 1984), 159–73, 523–42; Avery Dulles, *A Church to Believe in: Discipleship and the Dynamics of Freedom* (New York, NY: Crossroad, 1983), 149–69; Thomas Grabmann, *Thomas Aquinas: His Personality and Thought* (New York, NY: Longmans, Green, and Co. 1928), 173–81; John Mahoney, "The Church of the Holy Spirit in Aquinas," *Heythrop Journal* 15 (1974), 18–36; Mersch, *Corps Mystique*, 158–252; Colman E. O'Neill, "St. Thomas on Membership of the Church," *The Thomist* 27 (1963), 88–140; George Sabra, *Thomas Aquinas' Vision of the Church: Fundamentals of an Ecumenical Ecclesiology* (Mainz: Matthias-Grunewald Verlag, 1987). Dulles notes (165) that only Augustine is cited more often that Thomas in *Lumen Gentium*.

33. See Sabra, *Thomas Aquinas' Vision*, 20–33, for a review of the various historical and theological explanations for the absence of a separate treatise. Several scholars have suggested that the "mystical body"

gar's description, the whole of *sacra doctrina* is concerned
with eternal life, which consists in the knowledge of God,
and that which leads to eternal life, a division of subject
matter that matches the Cappadocian division of theology and economy and the alternative Thomistic definition
of theology as centrally concerned with the divinity and
humanity of Christ. The church is the means by which
the knowledge of God is acquired. In other terms, the
Summa is about the *egressus* from God and the *regressus*
to him, and the church is cast in the role of return to
God, so that the whole of the second part of the *Summa*
is ecclesiology.[34]

Following Augustine, Thomas insists that Christ's
human nature is the pathway of return to God. Thomas'
contribution is to develop two related points. First, he defines Christ's humanity more precisely as an instrumental
cause of the return to God. Thomas does not conceive
of the instrumentality of the flesh in relation to the incarnation alone, but to the whole work of the incarnate
Christ. Specifically, the mystical body is born from the
side of Christ on the cross, as Eve was born from the

---

is the central concern of Thomas' entire theological project. See the
quotation from Kaepeli in Congar, "Idea of the Church," 358, and
the similar statement in John T. Dittoe, "Sacramental Incorporation
into the Mystical Body," *The Thomist* 9 (1946), 470.

34. Congar, *L'Église de saint Augustin*, 234; idem, *Thomas d'Aquin*,
524; Dulles, *A Church to Believe in*, 150.

side of Adam. This definition of Christ's humanity as a conjoined, animate instrumental cause of the redeemed community is developed in the context of the second principle, the scholastic notion of the grace of the Head. As Head, Christ in his humanity contains the fullness of all graces and infuses them into his body. There are various levels and degrees of membership in the body; in one sense, all human beings are reckoned as either actual or potential members, but those are members particularly who are united to Christ in glory, by love, or by faith.[35] Returning to God requires union with the head through faith and love.

Though in his essential conception of the church Thomas does not have in view juridical and institutional structures, he does see them as necessary for union with the mystical body. To understand his reasons for this it is necessary to bring into the discussion his teaching on the New Law, which has been recognized as a key element of his ecclesiology (1a–2a.106–8). The basic principle of the New Law, Thomas says, is the grace of the Holy Spirit. Yet there are externals in the New Law, as there were under the old. These externals dispose the faithful to receive the grace that comes by the Holy Spirit. Thus, the institution of the church, its governmental structures, disciplinary mechanisms, and sacraments are the scaffolding that en-

---

35. Mersch, *Corps Mystique*, 163–240.

ables the realization of the mystical body, which is the communion of the faithful in the grace of the Holy Spirit. The institution of the church is a "veil and vehicle" of the mystical body.[36]

We reach a similar conclusion if we follow Thomas' liturgical theology, which is inseparable from his understanding of the transition effected by Christ from the Old Law to the New.[37] Through the work of his incarnation, Jesus "has ushered in the worship or rite of the Christian religion by offering himself up as an oblation and sacrifice to God" (3a.62.5). The work of Christ on the cross, thus, must be seen as preeminently a priestly act of worship that inaugurates and sets a pattern for a new form of worship. Congar argues that the emphasis of this sentence should be placed on *seipsum:* in contrast to the offering of bulls and goats, Jesus has inaugurated true worship, which is defined as self-offering to God.[38] Interior sacrifice of the whole self is the chief and true act of worship whereby the creature pays fit homage to

36. Congar, "Idea of the Church," 359.

37. Thomas no more has a treatise on the liturgy than on the church, but like ecclesiology, his liturgical theology is profoundly woven into the fabric of his theology. See Liam G. Walsh, "Liturgy in the Theology of St. Thomas," *The Thomist* 38 (1974), 557–83; Christopher Kiesling, "The Sacramental Character and Liturgy," *The Thomist* 27 (1963), 385–412.

38. Congar, *Lay People in the Church: A Study for a Theology of Laity* (rev. ed.; London: Geoffrey Chapman, 1985), 142–3.

the Creator. Interior sacrifice, however, is complemented and aided by exterior acts; sacrifice must be *duplex* because man is body and soul, and as worshipers perform external acts of reverence, reverence increases so that the interior sacrifice becomes more and more perfect.[39] Christian sacrifice must not merely be external but social and ritual. As Congar explains, "Christ has not simply put an end to positive religions in favour of a purely personal, human, inwardness; he has ushered in a worship and a sacrifice as a *positive, social, institutional religion.*" The whole Christian *cultus Dei* arises from Christ's priestly work in which he is the chief celebrant, the only true priest, but "in the measure that Christ communicates to men the power to celebrate his priestly worship with him . . . he dedicates and deputes them by making them share in his priesthood."[40]

This brings us to Thomas' view of sacramental character.[41] Thomas did not invent this theological construct,

---

39. Barnabé Augier, "Le Sacrifice," *Revue thomiste* 34/n.s. 12 (1929), 198–204.

40. Congar, *Lay People in the Church*, 143–44.

41. There is an extensive literature on sacramental character in Thomas, far more than on other aspects of Thomistic sacramental theology. See B. Thierry D'Argenlieu, "La doctrine de Saint Thomas d'Aquin sur le caractère sacramentel dans les 'Sentences,'" *Revue thomiste* 34/n.s. 12 (1929), 219–33; idem, "La doctrine du caractère sacramentel dans la 'Somme'," *Revue thomiste* 34/n.s. 12 (1929), 289–302; Kiesling, "The Sacramental Character and Liturgy," 385–412; Stephen McCor-

but he made the contribution of linking character with the worship of God and thus with the priesthood of Christ. Sacraments are related to divine worship in one of three ways. The eucharist pertains to the *divinum cultum* by virtue of the action itself, since it is the church's sacrifice. Order pertains to the worship of God in respect of agency, since the ordained are deputed for handing on divine things. Baptism and confirmation, however, pertain to the divine worship with respect to the recipient, "for through it man is given power to receive the other sacraments of the church. Hence baptism is said to be the gateway of the sacraments" (3a.63.6). All sacraments derive their meaning from the eucharist; baptism, confirmation, and penance are ordered to reception of the eucharist, and ordination is ordered to its consecration and administration. Not every sacrament imprints character on the soul, but only those that assign a particular place in the worship of God and are once-for-all rites: that is, baptism, confirmation, and ordination (63.6).

"Character" is variously defined. It is *quoddam signum distinctivum,* which, given the following explanation, is to be understood as a sign whose purpose is to distinguish one thing from another (63.1). Responding to the objection that character cannot be a sign imprinted

---

mack, "The Configuration of the Sacramental Character," *The Thomist* 7 (1944), 458–91; G. Thils, "Le pouvoir cultuel du baptisé," *Ephemerides Theologicae Lovanienses* 15 (1938), 683–89.

on the soul since signs are available to the senses, Thomas uses *character* interchangeably with *signaculum* (translated as "seal"), and says that the terms can be applied analogously to anything that figures another thing or distinguishes one thing from another (reply 2). In 63.3, Thomas cites a longer and more theologically full definition, also used by Albertus Magnus:

> Character is a distinctive mark deriving from the eternal character and imprinted upon the rational soul, setting the seal of the Trinity which creates and re-creates upon the created trinity an image of it, and distinguishing the sealed from the unsealed in terms of the state of faith belonging to the former.

Character, then, is not a visible mark but an invisible effect of the sacramental rite. For those sacraments that confer character, the latter is *res et sacramentum*, being *res* in regard to the outward sign, but *sacramentum* in regard to inward grace (63.3; 63.6).

Sacramental character becomes somewhat clearer from the illustrations that Thomas employs. Foremost among these is a military analogy: just as soldiers were marked with a physical sign when they were deputed for a particular task, so the Christian is marked by a spiritual character as a deputation for his task (63.1). Coins, too, are marked by a character that designates them for commercial use (63.3). Thomas also sees character as a sort of consecration, analogous to the sanctification of buildings, altars, and other inanimate objects.[42] He conflates these illustrations with a trinitarian use of "character," derived from the New Testament. After quoting the longer definition cited above, he points out that the "eternal character" from which the character of the soul is derived is Christ himself (citing Heb. 1:3). As a soldier is configured to the commander by the character he receives, so the one who receives the sacrament is configured to Christ.

Importantly, Thomas speaks of character as a seal by which one is deputed to *(deputatur)* and given the *auctoritas* necessary to fulfill a task related to the *cultus Dei.* He situates character in the "powers" of the soul (as opposed to the essence or passions of the soul), because "everything which is designed to lead to an act is to be attributed to a power," and character is designed to lead to an act. In this same section, Thomas rejects the idea that baptismal character most nearly pertains to grace, arguing instead that baptism is most nearly connected to the acts of divine worship (3a.63.2). By the performance

---

42. Arguing for the indelibleness of sacramental character, he notes, *nam ecclesiae vel altaris manet consecratio semper, nisi destruatur* (63.5). More generally, *character se habet ad animam in qua est, sicut consecratio ad resconsecratas* (63.6). Those sacraments that imprint a character *homo sanctificatur quadam consecratione* (63.6).

of the external sacraments of baptism, confirmation, and orders, one is given a power and ability to perform certain acts in the worship of God. This power is an instrumental one that Thomas explicitly compares to the instrumental causality of the sacraments, so that the recipient becomes a "tool" or, more technically, a separated, animate instrument of Christ.

What kinds of actions does character empower? Worship, Thomas says, consists of the exchange of divine things, whether giving or receiving, and a "certain power" is necessary for both of these, an active power for *traditio* and a passive power for reception (3a.63.2). Baptism, as the "gateway of the sacraments," conveys the passive power to receive the sacraments, while ordination confers the active power for handing over; alternatively, the baptized are active to perfect themselves, the ordained to perfect others. By the sacramental character of ordination, the priest becomes an instrument of Christ, so that when he speaks the words of institution, the bread and wine are consecrated to become the body and blood of Christ. By the sacramental character of baptism, which is strengthened by confirmation, the lay person is empowered to receive the grace offered in the sacrament. Though Thomas initially distinguishes grace and character, then, the imprinting of character is in service to the reception of grace, as the institutions and sacraments of the church are in service to the formation and perfection of the mystical body.

Both the power of giving and receiving divine things derive from participation in Christ and, because the rites of the *cultus Dei* are derived from the priesthood of Christ the configuration to Christ conferred by sacramental character is specifically to his priesthood. Thus, "a configuration to his priesthood is imparted to the faithful through the sacramental characters which are nothing else than a certain kind of participation in the priesthood of Christ deriving from Christ himself" (63.3). Christ alone has full power of priesthood, and by participation in him the faithful and the ordained come to share in different ways in his power and in the things pertaining to divine worship. For this reason too, sacramental character is as permanent as the priesthood of Christ, which is eternal (63.5). Yet, though the characters of ordination and baptism have the same root in the priesthood of Christ, Thomas distinguishes the two fairly sharply.[43] Ordination confers the power of *traditio,* and

---

43. On Thomas's view of ordination, priesthood, and episcopacy, see Joseph Lecuyer, "Les étapes de l'enseignement thomiste sur l'épiscopat," *Revue thomiste* 57 (1957), 29–52; Noel Molloy, "Hierarchy and Holiness: Aquinas on the Holiness of the Episcopal State," *The Thomist* 39 (1975), 198–252; R. P. Marie-Joseph Nicolas, "La doctrine de S. Thomas sur le sacerdoce," *Studitomistici* (Rome: Pontificia Accademia Romana di S. Thomasso d'Aquino, 1974), 2:309–28. J. Perinelle, "La doctrine de S. Thomas sur le sacrement de l'ordre," *Re-*

elsewhere Thomas treats ordination as conferring power to consecrate the Eucharist.

Discontinuities

Several of the basic elements of the Augustinian model are found in Aquinas: the christological foundation, the notion that baptism confers a share in the priesthood of the Priest, and the implication that those who are baptized into this priesthood have a place in the sacrifice of the *cultus Dei*. It is difficult to determine how significant is Thomas's failure directly to designate the baptized as "priests." Yet, there are substantive differences. First, Thomas distinguishes, in a way not apparent in Augustine, between the royal priesthood of the faithful manifested in lives of faith, hope, and love, and their deputation, through baptismal character, to act receptively in the worship of God. Thomas never uses the royal priesthood texts, particularly 1 Peter 2:9–10, when speaking about the effects of baptismal character, though he does so on other occasions when he has the "spiritual" priesthood of the faithful in view. For Augustine, there is no evidence of such a distinction; royal priesthood is enacted both in lives of sacrifice and in liturgical participation, with the Eucharist as precisely the ritualization of the ecclesial sacrifice of humility, unity, and love.

---

vue des sciences philosophiques et théologiques 19:2 (1930), 236–50, has a particularly lucid summary of Thomas's teaching on these subjects.

Second, Thomas distinguishes far more sharply between the effects of ordination and baptism than Augustine does. According to Michele Pellegrino, Augustine
never speaks of his status as priest or bishop as something
that brings him closer to Christ, but for Thomas a specific
configuration to Christ is conferred by ordination. Furthermore, Thomas, typical of post-Gregorian theologians,
defines the ordained priesthood in terms of power. To be
sure, he recognizes, as fully as Augustine, that the authority of the minister in the church is exercised in service, but
the specifically eucharistic power of the ordained priest
has a profile in Thomas that it never assumes in Augustine. Significant also is Thomas's distinction between active and passive participation in the worship of God, the
restriction of the baptismal priesthood's liturgical activity
to "receiving" what the ordained priest "hands over." Augustine does not obliterate the difference between official
and general priesthood, but when he speaks of the sacrifice it is the whole church—bishop and people—that
both offers and is offered. For Augustine, the transactions
of liturgy take place between the Body of the Priest and
the Father; for Aquinas, the priest stands on the side of
the Head, so that transactions take place also between different portions of the body.

Finally, the typological framework of Augustine's
theology is noticeably absent. This is doubtless partly
due to the differences in universe of discourse between

a late antique African and a thirteenth-century school-man, but the absence of the typology significantly alters the overall picture. In Augustine, there is a clear temporal movement from *tunc* to *nunc* which stretches ahead to a fulfillment in the future. In Thomas, however, this movement is flattened and the picture is more static as a result; when he does refer to the priesthood of the Old Testament, he sees it fulfilled in Christ and further in the ordained ministry of the church. The broader implications of this shift are significant. For Augustine, the church intervenes in history as the eschatological community partly because it embodies a hitherto unknown universal distribution of priesthood. The above discussion suggests that for Augustine the universal administration of chrism is part and parcel of the redemption accomplished by the Christ. For Aquinas, and for Roman Catholic theology even after Congar, the novelty of this community, and hence the novelty of the gospel of the kingdom, is seriously obscured.

WHAT'S WRONG WITH TRANSUBSTANTIATION? AN EVALUATION OF THEOLOGICAL MODELS

The doctrine of the real presence of Christ in the celebration of the Eucharist is a classic case of theological deadlock. Accusations of rationalism, speculation, and outright heresy are tossed back and forth by all sides. Both Lutherans and Reformed theologians accuse Roman Catholics of teaching a physical and local presence of Christ. Roman Catholics and Lutherans accuse the Reformed of rationalizing (away) the mystery of the real presence, while the Reformed charge that both the Lutheran doctrine and the Roman Catholic doctrine of transubstantiation are founded on and entail extrabiblical speculation. Reformed theologians charge Lutherans with teaching a localized presence, while the Lutherans deny that they teach that Christ's presence in the Eucharist is local. The Reformed counter that the Lutherans have equivocated on the meaning of "local."[1] Similar examples of deadlock could be multiplied, many of them centering on apparently minute issues.[2] In many cases, the debates have been framed in such a way that it seems impossible to get around the obstacles, and one is tempted to search for a safe place among the Eastern Orthodox, far above the fray.[3]

In this chapter, I focus on a small part of this debate, namely, the Reformation challenge to the Thomistic doctrine of transubstantiation.[4] Even this fragment

---

1. For a typical orthodox Lutheran evaluation of the Reformed position, see John Theodore Mueller, *Christian Dogmatics* (St. Louis, IL: Concordia Publishing Company, 1955), 509–20. Charles Hodge provides a typical Reformed discussion of the Lutheran doctrine in *Systematic Theology*, vol. 3 (Grand Rapids, MI: Eerdmans, 1986), 661–77.

2. In fact, the issues are anything but minute. As Edward Schillebeeckx points out, sacramental theology reveals the decided differences between Catholic and Protestant conceptions of reality (*The Eucharist* [New York: Sheed & Ward, 1968], 79).

3. The Orthodox Church affirms the real presence of Christ, but eschews speculation about the mode of Christ's presence.

4. An essential work on this question is Charles Herbert Stinson, "'Substantia Corporis': A Study of the Philosophical Semantics and Terminology in Latin Christian Dogma with Special Reference to the

of the total picture is enormously complicated, so this chapter has been restricted to an examination of the positions of three representative theologians. I first describe the doctrine of transubstantiation as it was given classic formulation by Thomas Aquinas,[5] seeking particularly to determine underlying theological and philosophical motivations and models. Then, I sketch the responses of Martin Luther and John Calvin to the Roman doctrine. My purpose is to show how Calvin's handling of transubstantiation (and of the Lutheran doctrine) shifted the entire context of the debate, providing for a more biblical doctrine of the Eucharistic presence that at the same time does justice to the legitimate concerns of other theological traditions.

Eucharist: From Tertullian's Time to the Berengarian Controversy" (Ph.D. dissertation, Columbia University, 1971).

5. It is true that the concept of transubstantiation predates Aquinas. Still, Thomas's defense of the doctrine is rightly considered classic. Schaff stated simply that "The doctrine of the sacraments, as expounded by Thomas is, in all particulars, the doctrine of the Catholic Church" (*History of the Christian Church: Volume V: The Middle Ages, AD 1049–1294* [1907; repr., Grand Rapids, MI: Eerdmans, 1981], 671). Though this does not accurately describe the contemporary situation, Thomas's doctrine still provides the starting point for Roman Catholic discussions of the real presence. See, for example, Schillebeeckx, *The Eucharist*.

Thomas Aquinas[6]

Thomas's doctrine itself is well-known. According to his formulation, by the priest's consecration, the entire substance of the bread and the wine is converted into the entire substance of the body and blood of Christ. Yet, the accidents, or empirical properties, of the bread and

---

6. Among the useful works that treat Thomas's doctrine of the real presence, several theological encyclopedias include helpful overview articles: Engelbert Gutwenger, "Transubstantiation," in *Sacramentum Mundi: An Encyclopedia of Theology*, vol. 6 (New York, NY: Herder and Herder, 1970), 292–95; Joseph de Ghellinck, "Eucharistie du XIIe siècle en occident," *DTC*, vol. 5 (1913), 1233–1302; E. Mangenot, "Eucharistie du XIIe au XVe siècle," *DTC*, vol. 5 (1913), 1302–26. A standard Protestant treatment may be found in E. Kattenbusch, "Transubstantiation," in *The New Schaff-Herzog Encyclopedia of Religious Knowledge*, vol. 11 (New York, NY: Funk and Wagnalls, 1911), 494–501. Still useful is Darwell Stone, *A History of the Doctrine of the Holy Eucharist*, vol. 1 (London: Longmans, Green, 1909), 323–33. More recent treatments may be found in Burkhard Neunheuser, *Eucharistie in Mittelalter und Neuzeit* (Handbuch der Dogmengeschichte; Freiburg: Herder, 1963), 40–43; P. R. Rupprecht, "Der heilige Thomas und das Leidensgedächtnis in der Eucharistie," *TQ*, vol. 118 (1937), 403–36; Karl Rahner, *Schriften zur Theologie*, vol. 4 (Einsiedeln: Benziger, 1967), 357–85; James F. McCue, "The Doctrine of Transubstantiation from Berengar through Trent: The Point at Issue," *HTR*, vol. 61 (1968), 400–402; E. Schillebeeckx, *The Eucharist,* 54–63; Paul Henry Jones, "The Mode of Christ's Eucharistic Presence: An historical archaeology and ecumenical proposal" (Ph.D. dissertation, Vanderbilt, 1988). Unavailable to me was G. Reinhold, *Die Lehre der örtlichen Gegenwart Christi in der Eucharistie bei Thomas von Aquin* (Vienna, 1893), which is to my knowledge the only book-length treatment of the question.

wine remain, even after the substance has changed. The remaining accidents of bread and wine are subject to corruption and even provide physical sustenance, despite the fact that they are "substanceless." The obvious difficulty with this formulation is to explain how accidents can remain unchanged when the substance on which the accidents depend has undergone a complete conversion. Thomas's answer was that, by the power of God, the accident of "dimension" acts as something of a substitute substance in which the other accidents inhere.[7]

Our concern is not to examine Thomas's doctrine of transubstantiation as such, but to ask how and why he came to a doctrine that seems, on the face of it, quite bizarre. Several contextual factors must be noted if we are to interact fairly with Thomas's explanation and defense of the real presence and transubstantiation.

Thomas came at the culmination of several centuries of debate on the Eucharistic presence. The writings of the Fathers are remarkable for their lack of debate on Eucharistic doctrine. Beginning in the ninth century, however, a series of heated Eucharistic debates rocked Western Christendom.[8] By Thomas's time, many of the issues had

---

7. Stone, *A History of the Doctrine of the Holy Eucharist*, vol. 1, 330.

8. For discussions of the debates that formed the background to Thomas's doctrine, see Stone, *A History of the Doctrine of the Holy Eucharist*, vol. 1 (1909), 216–322; McCue, "The Doctrine of Transubstantiation from Berengar through Trent," 385–97; Neunheuser,

long been resolved. Already in the eleventh century, Eucharistic doctrine had been polarized into symbolic and realistic traditions. Moreover, both the word and the concept of transubstantiation were already in current usage well before the thirteenth century.[9] Berengar's forced re-

---

Eucharistie in Mittelalter und Neuzeit; Josef Rupert Geiselmann, *Die Eucharistielehre der Vorscholastik* (Paderborn, 1926); Geiselmann, *Die Abendmahlslehre an der Wende der christlichen Spatantike zum Frühmittelalter: Isidor von Sevilla und das Sakrament der Eucharistie* (Munich: Max Hueber, 1933); Jaroslav Pelikan, *The Growth of Medieval Theology (600–1300)* (Chicago: University of Chicago Press, 1978), 74–80; John F. Fahey, *The Eucharistic Teaching of Ratramn of Corbie* (Mundelein, IL: St. Mary of the Lake Seminary, 1951); Egil Grislis, "The Manner of Christ's Eucharistic Presence in the Early and Medieval Church," *Consensus* 6 (October 1980), 3–14; and Hans Jorissen, *Die Entfaltung der Transsubstantiationslehre bis zum Beginn der Hochscholastik* (Münster: Aschendorff, 1965). On the eleventh-century conflict in particular, see Allan John MacDonald, *Berengar and the Reform of Sacramental Doctrine* (1930; repr., Merrick, NY: Richmond, 1977); R. P. Redmond, "The Real Presence in the Early Middle Ages," *CR* 8 (1934), 442–60, a sharp critique of MacDonald's views; Charles E. Sheedy, *The Eucharistic Controversy of the Eleventh Century* (New York, NY: AMS Press, 1980); and Jean de Mondos, *Lanfranc et Berengar: La controverse eucharistique du XIe siècle* (Louvain: Spicilegium Sacrum Lovaniense, 1971). For the Eucharistic teaching of Albert the Great, Thomas's teacher, see E. Gutwenger, "Substanz und Akzidens in der Eucharistielehre," *ZKT* 83 (1961), 260–94; and Hans Jorissen, "Materie und Forme der Sakramente in Verstandnis Albertus des Grossen" *ZKT* 80 (1958), 26–315.

9. The first use of the term is attributed to Roland Bandinelli (the future Pope Alexander III) in the mid-twelfth century. See Gutwenger in *Sacramentum Mundi* vol. 6, 292; Erwin Iserloh, "Abendmahl III/2: Mittelalter," in *TRE* vol. 1, 92–93; and Pelikan, *The Growth*

cantation in 1079 included an affirmation that the bread
and wine "are substantially converted" into the body and
blood of Christ, and a church council—the Fourth Lateran Council of 1215—had actually employed the term
"transubstantiation,"[10] though for nearly a century after
the Fourth Lateran Council, transubstantiation did not
hold the field unchallenged.[11]

Thus, in seeking to explain the conversion of substance in the Eucharist, Thomas was defending what

---

of Medieval Theology, 203. The notion that there is a "conversion" of
the elements in the Eucharist is of patristic origin, as is the use of the
term "substance." Stinson attributes the introduction of the latter
term to exegetes and popular preachers lacking in philosophical acu-
men (Stinson, "Substantia Corporis," 580).

10. Pelikan, *The Growth of Medieval Theology,* 203–4.

11. McCue, "The Doctrine of Transubstantiation," argues that, despite the use of the term at the Fourth Lateran Council, for almost a
century after the Fourth Lateran no theologian considered transubstantiation as a necessary article of orthodox faith (393). Thomas,
McCue claims, was the first to condemn consubstantiation as heretical and impossible (400–402). McCue also suggests that transubstantiation held its preferred place in the late medieval world because
of a misinterpretation of the decision of the Fourth Lateran Council
(385). See Pelikan's similar comment: Even after the Fourth Lateran,
"Theologians continued to recognize that the fundamental content
of the dogma of transubstantiation was the doctrine of the real presence, rather than a particular philosophical definition of substance
and accident" (*The Growth of Medieval Theology,* 204). Paul Henry
Jones identifies the three chief late medieval theories as consubstantiation, annihilation or succession, and transubstantiation ("The Mode
of Christ's Eucharistic Presence," 140–41).

he understood to be the teaching of the church, and he mounted this defense with the tools that lay close to hand. Predominant among these tools was the philosophy of Aristotle. Though the fact of Aristotelian influence on Thomas's doctrine of transubstantiation is beyond dispute, there is considerable debate about how central Aristotelian categories were in Thomas's treatment. Edward Schillebeeckx, for example, has distinguished three levels of commitment in Thomas's teaching on the real presence,[12] which can be visualized as a series of concentric circles. At the core—the level of dogma—Thomas, along with Bonaventura, "took as their point of departure the distinctive quality of the sacramental presence of Christ's body and blood—that was the biblical dictum, the dogma and therefore the norm for their speculation about this aspect of faith."[13] Second, Thomas affirmed the Catholic doctrine that the elements are converted, that "the

---

12. E. Schillebeeckx, *The Eucharist*, 63.

13. Ibid., 49. Max Thurian agrees that the basic emphasis in Thomas's teaching is the reality of the presence of Christ: "the dogma of transubstantiation has a protective and defensive purpose," namely, "to express the mystery of the real presence in an understandable way to the men of this period." In his appropriate efforts to contextualize Christian doctrine, however, Thomas sometimes "deprived certain truths of their proper evangelical savor, substituting insipid Aristotelianism" ("Toward a Renewal of the Doctrine of Transubstantiation," in *Christianity Divided*, ed. D. J. Callahan et al. [New York, NY: Sheed & Ward, 1961], 197–9).

reality of bread was something quite different after the consecration—it became the body of Christ."[14]

Only at the periphery of his doctrine, in his effort to explain the nature of the conversion, did Thomas introduce Aristotelian categories. Schillebeeckx concludes that "within the Aristotelian framework of thought that prevailed in the Middle Ages, it was impossible to safeguard the distinctively Catholic teaching on Christ's presence in the Eucharist without affirming transubstantiation."[15] It is necessary therefore to distinguish between Thomas's affirmation of Catholic dogma and the philosophical dress in which he clothed it. The dogma is that there is a "fundamental, radical and, in this sense, substantial change of the bread," and it was only in his explanation of the remaining *species* or accidents that Thomas appealed to Aristotle.[16]

---

14. Ibid., 63.

15. Ibid., 59.

16. Ibid., 75. It must be recognized that Schillebeeckx's interpretation of Thomas serves his own theological agenda. While admitting that these three "levels" were inseparable to Thomas himself, Schillebeeckx raises the possibility that modern Catholics might be able to separate the core dogma from its philosophical shell (63). Even the Council of Trent did not sanction Aristotle as an inevitable ontological implication of Catholic dogma (60–61). Schillebeeckx thus proposes that the Eucharistic conversion might be understood as a "transsignification" without undermining the traditional Roman Catholic doctrine. This view has a large following among contemporary Dutch Roman Catholic theologians. See Gutwenger in

Schillebeeckx is correct to emphasize that Thomas developed the doctrine of transubstantiation as part of a defense of the doctrine of the real presence. But he is wrong in his conclusion that Thomas appealed to Aristotle *only* in his explanation of the remaining accidents of bread and wine.[17] In fact, Thomas's understanding of the

---

Sacramentum mundi, vol. 6, 294. P. Schoonenberg argues that the Roman church has never given dogmatic status to any particular interpretation of transubstantiation. Only denials of the real presence have been condemned; a symbolist interpretation that retains the real presence is fully in accord with Roman doctrine ("Transubstanciación: ¿hasta qué punto está determinada históricamente esta doctrina?" *Concilium* 24 [1967], 86–100).

17. It is true that many Aristotelian categories appear in Thomas's discussion of the accidents. Among the questions raised in that connection were the following: "Does the substance of the bread and wine remain in this sacrament after the consecration?" "Is the substance of the bread, after the consecration, annihilated or reduced into one of the four elements?" "Do the accidents of the bread and wine remain?" Aristotelian technical terms abound in these questions: "substance," "accidents," "four elements." (St. Thomas Aquinas, *Summa theologiae*, trans. and ed. Thomas Gilby, vols. 58–59 [New York, NY: Blackfriars and McGraw-Hill, 1975], 3a.75. Throughout, I will use the standard Thomistic shorthand system of reference. All of the references are to the *Summa theologiae*.) Western theologians, of course, had asked questions about the mode of Christ's presence in the Eucharist and the relationship of Christ's historical flesh to the Eucharistic body before the revival of Aristotle. The Eucharistic debates between Radbertus and Ratramnus dealt extensively with these questions. What is worthy of note then is not the fact that Thomas speculated on these questions but his way of posing the questions. Thomas framed the questions in Aristotelian terms.

real presence itself was by his own admission indebted to an Aristotelian philosophy of space and Aristotle's concept of substance. Thomas, for example, argued that the body of Christ cannot be locally present partly because "if a thing is in place, it must correspond exactly with the place in which it is, as Aristotle shows. But the place this sacrament occupies is much smaller than the body of Christ. Therefore, Christ's body is not in this sacrament as in place [*in loco*]" (3a.76.5). Thomas denied that the body of Christ in the sacrament could be visible because "the body of Christ is in this sacrament as if it were just substance." Since substance without accidents is not visible, but "only open to the intellect, the object of which is the essence of things, as Aristotle says," so the body of Christ is not visible (3a.76.7). The body of Christ is present not *per modum quantitatis,* but *per modum substantiae.*[18] Aristotelianism thus controls not only the speculative periphery of Thomas's doctrine, but his explication of the dogmatic core as well; Thomas appealed to Aristotle not only in explaining the accidents but also in explaining the mode of Christ's presence.

The Aristotelian framework of Thomas's thought was manifested in his interpretation of the words of institution, to which he appealed as biblical proof of transubstantiation. He argued that Christ's words "would not

---

18. Raymond Moloney, "Eucharist," in *A New Dictionary of Theology*, ed. J. A. Komonchak et al (Wilmington: Glazier, 1987), 348–49.

be true if the substance of the bread was still there, as the substance of the bread is not Christ's body" (3a.75.3). This argument assumes, however, that the words of institution are a predication about the "substance" of the elements, which in turn assumes an Aristotelian theory of predication. Thus, Thomas's exegesis of the words of institution is convincing only if one accepts the categories that he brings to the text. He intended to prove that the substance of the bread is changed into the substance of Christ's flesh, but in order to prove this he appealed to the words of institution, which contain no explicit mention of the "substance" of anything. The argument is narrowly circular; Thomas assumed what he intended to prove.[19]

Another indication of the role of Aristotle in Thomas's Eucharistic theology emerges in his discussion of the relation between Old and New Covenant sacrifices. He introduced this question as an argument in favor of Christ's presence *secundum veritatem*. Christ cannot be present in a "merely figurative way" because that would be inconsistent with the "perfection of the New Law."

---

19. The editor of the *Summa* recognized that this assumption has been made and appended this footnote to 3a.75.3: "This means this thing, this reality, this substance, underlying the visible appearances, the accidental qualities which are the object of sight and of other senses." This note does indeed appear to have captured Thomas's own thought, and reveals even more explicitly the assumed Aristotelian metaphysic.

The sacrifices of the Old Law contained that true sacrifice which was the passion of Christ, only in a figurative way. . . . It was only right that the sacrifice of the New Law instituted by Christ should have something more, that it should contain Christ himself who suffered for us, and contain him, not merely as by a sign or figure, but in actual reality as well. So it is that this sacrament which really contains Christ himself is, as Dionysius says, the fulfillment of all the other sacraments, in which a share of Christ's power is to be found (3a.75.1).

Thomas claimed that the difference between the Eucharist and the Old Covenant sacraments is a difference between "figure" and "reality" and went on to quote Hebrews 10:1 to support this formulation. To be sure, Hebrews everywhere characterizes the difference between Old and New Covenants as a difference between "figure" and "reality," but it must be seriously questioned whether Hebrews justifies Thomas's particular understanding. The perspective of Hebrews is what has come to be called "redemptive-historical." From the first verses of the epistle, the author emphasizes that the covenants differ because of the final and definitive accomplishment of redemption by the Son. Thomas, reading the text through an Aristotelian framework, read "figure" and "reality" as categories that have reference to substance. For Thomas, something is "substantially" different about the New Covenant sacraments.[20] Thomas was not satisfied to say that there had been an historical transition from anticipation to fulfillment, from one covenantal administration to another; instead, he insisted that there had been a "substantial" change in the very constitution of things. For this reason, Thomas believed it no longer sufficient to speak of the New Testament sacrament as "signs" or "figures."

That the Aristotelian notion of substance is at the heart of Thomas's discussion of the Eucharistic presence is clear. But what did Thomas mean by "substance"?[21] It is clearly wrong to conclude that Thomas taught a "physical presence" of Christ's body. The Eucharistic body of Christ is not apparent to the eyes but only to the intellect, something that hardly can be said of a physical substance. Thomas's distinction between a presence *in loco*

20. Calvin, employing "substance" in a different sense, emphasized that the substance of both Old and New Covenants is Christ (*Institutes of the Christian Religion*, ed. John T. McNeill, trans. Ford Lewis Battles, 2 vols. [Philadelphia, PA: Westminster, 1960], 2.10.2).

21. Thomas surely was not the first to use "substance" to describe the Eucharistic presence. See Stinson, "'Substantia Corporis,'" *passim*. But prior to the revival of Aristotle, "substance" was used in a vague general sense, and contrasted with "figure" or "sign." Thomas used the term in this sense, but also used it in the technical Aristotelian sense in opposition to "accidents." See G. Ghysens, "Présence réelle eucharistique et transsubstantiation dans les définitions de l'Eglise Catholique," *Iren* 2 (1959), 420–35.

and a presence *per modum substantiae* likewise indicates that the presence of the body and blood is not a physical presence. After the consecration, indeed, *no* physical substance remains locally where the accidents of bread and wine appear.[22]

While it is fairly easy to determine what "substance" is not, it is more difficult to determine what it is. In Thomas's understanding, "substance" is a purely metaphysical reality.[23] Jones argues that "substance" is the objective, underlying reality of a thing, neither imaginary nor empirically apparent.[24] Others describe "substance" as the "ultimately existing subject"[25] or "a *quid*/without qualification."[26] The substance is the answer to the question, "What is it?"[27] Neunheuser suggests that by "substance" Thomas meant to teach that the presence of Christ was

---

22. Stinson, "'Substantia Corporis,'" 613.

23. Moloney, "Eucharist," 348–49.

24. Jones, "The Mode of Christ's Eucharistic Presence," 192.

25. Joseph Bobik, *Aquinas on Being and Essence: A Translation and Interpretation* (Notre Dame, IN: University of Notre Dame, 1965), 72.

26. Bernard J. Lonergan, *Verbum: Word and Idea in Aquinas* (Notre Dame, IN: University of Notre Dame, 1967), 25.

27. Herbert McCabe, "The Real Presence," *CR* 49 (1964), 757. According to McCabe, the Council of Trent affirmed that the "physical substance" of Christ's body was present in the Eucharist, but denied that the "physical substance" of Christ's body was physically present (ibid.).

genuine but "spiritual": "in this sacrament the true flesh of Christ is offered to the faithful for food, truly, although not 'carnally,' but 'in a spiritual manner' [*quodam spirituali modo*]."[28] Rupprecht explains Thomas's position in this way: "only the substance of the Body and Blood is offered in the sacrament, but not the body and blood in their whole being,"[29] implying that the "substance" of a thing is something less than the full reality of that thing. Stinson claims that Aquinas gave an entirely novel meaning to *substantia*. From Tertullian to Berengar, *substantia* referred to "a sensory thing; it is a visible, physical reality, spatial and quantitative." Under the influence of Aristotle, Aquinas delocalized, dequantified, and despatialized substance.[30] Because of this "spiritualizing" tendency, the Lutheran theologian Hermann Sasse charged that the

---

28. Neunheuser, *Eucharistie in Mittelalter und Neuzeit,* 40: "in diesen Sakrament das wahre Fleisch Christi den Glaubigen zur Speise gereicht wird, wahrhaft, wenn auch nicht 'fleischlich,' sondern 'in einer geistlichen Weise' (quodam spirituali modo), anders, als wir das von den übrigen Speise hergewohnt sind." The quotation is from the *Summa contra Gentiles,* vol. 4,.61–68.

29. Rupprecht, "Der Heilige Thomas und das Leidensgedächtnis in der Eucharistie," 418: "wird nur die Substanz des Leibes und Blutes im Sakrament geboten, nicht aber Leib und Blut in ihrem ganzen Sein."

30. "'Substantia Corporis,'" 575, 613.

Thomistic doctrine is closer to the Reformed doctrine than either are to Lutheranism.[31]

Thomas's conception of "substance" has played an important role in twentieth-century discussions among Italian Roman Catholic theologians concerning the implications of modern physics for Eucharistic theology.[32] Carlo Colombo has argued that for Thomas "substance" is a purely metaphysical reality, consisting of prime matter and the substantial form. The substance is the "intimate reality" of a thing, and is "transphysical."[33] Filippo Selvaggi, by contrast, replies that the Fathers knew nothing of this abstract metaphysical "substance"; instead, they posited a conversion of the *physical* substance of the bread and wine, while admitting that the appearance of bread and wine remains unchanged. Similarly, the scho-

---

31. Hermann Sasse, "A Lutheran Contribution to the Present Discussions on the Lord's Supper," *CTM* 30 (1959), 35.

32. See the summary of this debate by Cyril Vollert, "The Eucharist: Controversy on Transubstantiation," *TS* 22 (1961), 391–425. Vollert summarizes the contributions of various Italian theologians, including Filippo Selvaggi, "Il concetto di sostanza nel dogma eucaristico in relazione alla fisica moderna," *Gregorianum* 30 (1949), 7–45; Selvaggi, "Ancora intorno ai concetti di 'sostanza sensible' e 'realtà fisica,'" *Gregorianum* 38 (1957), 503–14; Manuel Cuervo, "La transubstanciación según Santo Tomás y las nuevas teorías físicas," *Ciencia tomista* 84 (1957), 283–344; and Antonio Due, "Las especies eucarísticas y las teorías modernas," *Pensamiento* 13 (1957), 347–52.

33. Vollert, "The Eucharist," 395–96.

lastics did not view substance as an invisible "inner kernel" of a thing.[34]

Perhaps the best way to understand Thomas's intention is to ask what he was denying. On the one hand, he challenged the pure symbolism of Berengar. "Substance" protected Thomas's doctrine against the threat of a purely symbolic interpretation of the Eucharistic presence. On the other hand, Thomas was equally intent on combating a crudely materialistic and local presence. He insisted that consubstantiation, one of the popular Eucharistic theories of the late medieval period, was both inappropriate and impossible. It was inappropriate because it conflicted with the veneration of the host, implied that the sacramental food was bodily as well as spiritual, and ran counter to the meaning of the sacrament. It was impossible because it would require the body of Christ to move to many places at once, and would draw Christ down from heaven.[35]

By affirming a "substantial presence," then, Thomas sought to protect his doctrine on both fronts. In short, as Raymond Moloney puts it, "As metaphysical rather than

---

34. Ibid., 402.

35. McCue, "The Doctrine of Transubstantiation from Berengar through Trent," 401–2. Paul Henry Jones argues that Thomas's doctrine of substance permits Christ to be really, though not locally, present; Christ is locally absent, but substantially present ("The Mode of Christ's Eucharistic Presence," 196).

physical, this [substantial] mode of presence avoids the crude materialism of Paschase. As ontological and objective, it avoids the threat of pure symbolism."[36]

Thomas, thus, intended to teach a non-figurative but non-physical presence. Yet, apparently under the force of his Aristotelian framework, he sharply opposed figure and reality. This opinion was implicit in the question, "Is the body of Christ really and truly in this sacrament or only in a figurative way or as in a sign?" (3a.75.1). The polarizing of the issue is significant, as is the prejudicial "only." Christ is *either* really and truly present *(secundum veritatem),* or he is present in a merely figurative way *(solum secundum figuram).* There is no room in Thomas's mind for a doctrine that affirms both the reality of Christ's presence and the symbolic character of the elements.[37]

Continuing debates about the meaning of Thomas's doctrine suggest the likelihood that Thomas's own conception of "substance" was ambiguous. This hypothesis can be tested by comparing Thomas's treatment of two

---

36. Moloney, "Eucharist," 348–49.

37. Russian Orthodox theologian Alexander Schmemann claims in fact that Western theologians went astray in sacramental theology, and indeed in their entire worldview, when they began to distinguish between "figure" and "reality." See *For the Life of the World* (Crestwood, NY: St. Vladimir's Seminary Press, 1973), 135–51. It should be recalled that Thomas was not the first to introduce this sharp distinction. Already in the eleventh-century Eucharistic disputes, the options had become polarized.

related issues: the Eucharistic sacrifice and the veneration of the consecrated elements.

As we have seen, Thomas taught that the Old Covenant sacrifices "contained that true sacrifice which was the passion of Christ," albeit "only in a figure" (3a.75.1). In the New Covenant, Thomas implied, the Eucharist contains the true sacrifice in reality. Elsewhere, Thomas explicitly noted that the difference between the Eucharist and other sacraments is that the Eucharist is both a sacrament and a sacrifice: "This sacrament adds this to the other sacraments, the character of being a sacrifice" (3a.79.7). Moreover, this sacrifice has a propitiatory character. It "has the power of rendering satisfaction" and "suffices of its own quality to satisfy for all punishment" (3a.79.5).

Thomas connected the Eucharistic sacrifice to the historical work of Christ in a complex way. The passion of Christ is "represented" in the sacrament, individualizing the work of Christ so that "the effect of his Passion wrought in the world the sacrament works in a man" (3a.79.1). Thomas also called the Eucharist a "commemoration" of the passion (3a.74.1). In another passage, Thomas stated that "Christ and his Passion are the cause of grace and spiritual refreshment," and through the sacrament this grace is bestowed (3a.79.1). The cross is a *vere sacrificium* and *vera immolatio,* while the Mass is merely an *imago quaedam repraesentativa.*[38]

Thus, though Thomas did teach a Eucharistic propitiation, he also attempted to do justice to the once-for-all nature of the Lord's historical passion and death. What marks Thomas's treatment of the Eucharistic sacrifice, indeed, is his concern to distinguish between the historical death of Christ and the liturgical sacrifice.[39] Though the doctrine of transubstantiation has been abused to defend a literal conception of the Eucharistic sacrifice, this does not seem to have been Thomas's intent. His hesitance with

---

38. Quoted in Josef Jungmann, *The Mass: An Historical, Theological, and Pastoral Survey* (Collegeville, MN: Liturgical Press, 1972), 76. The quotations are from *Summa Theologiae,* 3a.74.4 and 3a.83.1.

39. E. L. Mascall concludes that "St. Thomas was rightly anxious to avoid any suggestion that there is in the Mass a literal slaying of Christ, a literal repetition of Calvary, and . . . in consequence he took refuge in a rather vague notion of the Mass as a commemoration, representation or memorial of the Passion. . . . St. Thomas was quite clear that Christ is really present in the Mass and that by the Mass the fruits of the Passion are communicated to the Church and to the faithful" (*Corpus Christi: Essays on the Church and the Eucharist* [London: Longmans, Green and Co., 1953], 128). See also Stone's compilation of citations on the Eucharistic sacrifice, *A History of the Doctrine of the Holy Eucharist,* vol. 1, 323–28. Jungmann notes that Thomas displays a "certain reserve" in describing the Mass as a sacrifice (*The Mass,* 76). Neunheuser suggests Thomas's doctrine is that the virtue or benefit of Christ's sacrifice is offered in the Mass (*Eucharistic in Mittelalter und Neuzeit,* 40–41).

regard to the Eucharistic sacrifice suggests a "spiritualized" understanding of the body's "substantial" presence.

On the other hand, Thomas argued that Christ must be present *secundum veritatem* because "it would go against the reverence which is accorded to this sacrament if there were another substance present there which ought not to be given the worship of *latria*" (3a.75.3).[40] Elsewhere, Thomas admitted that if Christ were not truly present in the elements, their veneration would be idolatrous.[41] It is noteworthy, first, that in this argument the practice of the church provided the starting point with which Thomas sought to make his doctrine consistent. He did not raise the possibility that the adoration of the elements may itself be suspect. This overt appeal to the practice of the church is especially revealing when we recall Thomas's emphasis on the Eucharistic sacrifice and his agreement with the popular opinion that the Eucharist is the "sacrament of sacraments."

Thomas's defense of the veneration of the consecrated elements, moreover, displays the realistic or physicalist side of Thomas's conception of substance. If Christ is not

---

40. Jones points out that long before the thirteenth century the elements had been detached theologically from the full liturgical context of the Eucharist, and had become cultic objects in themselves ("The Mode of Christ's Eucharistic Presence," 137).

41. Walter Farrell, *A Companion to the Summa*, vol. 4 (New York, NY: Sheed & Ward, 1942), 307.

somehow "contained" in the elements (3a.75.l),[42] then it would be idolatry to bow in worship to them. But how can Christ be "contained" in the sacrament without being present *in loco?* How can Christ be "contained" in the sacrifice without being resacrificed? How can Christ be worshiped in the sacrament without being eaten in the sacrament? While Thomas evidently intended to avoid these implications, it is not clear that he was able to do so.

Thus, it appears that Thomas's own conception of "substance" was ambiguous. In order to protect against a literalistic interpretation of the Eucharistic sacrifice, he stressed the "spiritual" quality of substance. In order to protect the veneration of the host, he stressed the "realistic" quality of the substance.

Aristotelian categories led Thomas inevitably to the question of how the accidents of bread and wine remain in the absence of the substance. In this connection, we discover a final underlying motivation in Thomas's doctrine, namely, his desire to maintain the mysterious nature of the sacramental presence of Christ. He achieved this purpose chiefly by dismissing out of hand every objection to transubstantiation as a manifestation of a lack of faith. He stressed that "the way in which Christ exists in this sacrament is something that cannot be reached

---

42. Stone points out that Thomas did insist that the elements really "contain" Christ (*A History of the Doctrine of the Holy Eucharist*, vol. 1, 328).

by natural power of any created mind" (3a.76.7). To the objection that the accidents cannot remain independent of their substance, he replied that "there is no reason why the common law of nature should not arrange things in one way, yet for a contrary arrangement to be quite in order because of some special privilege of grace." Thus, "although the common order of nature prescribes that an accident should inhere in a subject, we have here, for a special reason and in the order of grace, accidents without a subject" (3a.77.1). Though it does not seem possible for bread and wine to turn into Christ's body and blood, one should not doubt that this is what takes place, for the conversion "is not like any natural change, but is entirely beyond the power of nature and is brought about purely by God's power" (3a.75.4).

This resolution of the issue by an appeal to a nature/supernature distinction cannot, of course, prove the doctrine of transubstantiation as such. After all, one might argue that it would be an even greater display of divine omnipotence if the flesh and blood were to appear sensibly on every altar at each celebration of the Mass. Instead, Thomas's appeal to the utter (arbitrary?) power of God seems to have been a rhetorical device to protect what he had established on other grounds. The effect, however, is to leave anyone who questions the miracle of transubstantiation suspect of limiting the absolute power of

God.[43] It is significant, finally, that the Eucharistic mystery is *not* communion with Christ, but the metaphysical conversion of the elements.

Several conclusions suggest themselves from the foregoing examination:

1. The questions Thomas asked and many of his answers were framed by Aristotelian philosophy. This colored his exegesis of particular biblical passages as well.

2. Thomas at times began with the practice and piety of the church and sought a theological rationale for that practice and piety.

3. Thomas wanted to avoid both a purely symbolic interpretation of the Eucharistic presence and a physicalist interpretation.

4. Thomas polarized figure and reality.

5. Thomas taught that Christ was present substantially in the consecrated elements.

---

43. It is also important to note that wider theological questions are opened up here. Thomas's doctrine of the real presence was firmly embedded in his dualism of nature and grace, so a challenge to transubstantiation constitutes a challenge to an entire worldview.

Luther[44]

In many important respects, Luther broke as decisively with medieval Eucharistic theology as he did with the medieval doctrine of justification. For Luther, Christ's promise of his presence in the Supper is not a statement concerning a metaphysical marvel but simply the gospel.[45] Against both Roman Catholics and the Zurich theologians he stressed that the Supper was pure gift and that its central blessing was the assurance of forgiveness. He perceived in both Thomistic and Zwinglian notions

---

44. Surveys of Luther's doctrine of the Eucharist may be found in Hermann Sasse, *This Is My Body: Luther's Contention for the Real Presence in the Sacrament of the Altar* (Minneapolis, MN: Augsburg, 1959); Paul Althaus, *The Theology of Martin Luther*, trans. Robert C. Schultz (Philadelphia, PA: Fortress, 1966), 375–403; Bernhard Lohse, *Martin Luther: An Introduction to his Life and Work*, trans. Robert C. Schultz (Philadelphia, PA: Fortress Press, 1986); Karl Barth, "Luther's Doctrine of the Eucharist," in *Theology and Church: Shorter Writings (1920–1928)* (New York, NY: Harper & Row, 1962), 74–111; Hans Grass, *Die Abendmahlslehre bei Luther und Calvin: Eine Kritische Untersuchung* (Gütersloh: C. Bertelsmann Verlag, 1954); Albrecht Peters, *Realpräsenz: Luthers Zeugnis von Christi Gegenwart im Abendmahl* (Berlin: Lutherisches Verlagshaus, 1960); and Julius Kostlin, *The Theology of Luther in its Historical Development and Inner Harmony*, 2nd ed., vol. 2 (Philadelphia, PA: Lutheran Publishing Society, 1897), 511–21.

45. Robert H. Fischer, "Luther's Stake in the Lord's Supper Controversy," *Dialog* 2:4 (1963), 57. Luther asked rhetorically of the words of institution, "What is the whole Gospel except an explanation of this testament?" (quoted in Barth, "Luther's Doctrine of the Eucharist," 78).

of the Supper the threat of works righteousness, the danger of considering the Eucharist as something offered and done rather than something received. Even his effort to explain the sacramental union of elements and reality may be understood "not [as] a metaphysical but a religious affirmation that the God-man Jesus Christ has graciously brought his presence to this celebration as a special instance of his self-impartation."[46] By integrating the doctrine of the Supper with the NT gospel of grace, Luther began to write the epitaph for the medieval paradigm of Eucharistic theology.

Even before Luther, the Thomistic doctrine was far from secure. Thomas's solution to the question of the real presence had been, in fact, almost immediately undermined by Duns Scotus and William of Ockham, both of whom returned to an earlier, more realistic and physical conception of substance.[47] This development is crucial

---

46. Robert H. Fischer, "Introduction," *Luther's Works*, ed. Helmut T. Lehmann, 55 vols. (Philadelphia, PA: Muhlenberg, 1961), vol. 37, xix.

47. Stinson, "'Substantia Corporis,'" 614. More generally, Paul Henry Jones comments that in the late medieval world "substance" was often interpreted in a materialistic fashion ("The Mode of Christ's Eucharistic Presence," 210). Both Scotus and Ockham, moreover, considered transubstantiation to be an acceptable opinion, but not the dogma of the church. Scotus considered transubstantiation as philosophically less plausible than consubstantiation (McCue, "The Doctrine of Transubstantiation from Berengar through Trent," 403–7).

for an understanding of Luther, who stands in the Ockhamist rather than the Thomistic tradition.[48]

Though Luther never budged from his insistence on the real presence of Christ's body and blood, his doctrine went through several stages of development. Paul Althaus writes, "The dividing point [in the development of Luther's doctrine] is the beginning of the controversy about the real presence in about 1524. In the first stage, Luther is opposed to Rome; in the second stage, he is opposed to the Enthusiasts and the Swiss."[49] Luther's dispute with the Swiss was a decisive turning point in the Reformation and has been subjected to several insightful examinations.[50] In

---

48. On Luther's debt to Ockham, see Steven Ozment, *The Age of Reform: 1250–1550: An Intellectual and Religious History of Late Medieval and Reformation Europe* (New Haven, CT: Yale University Press, 1980), 238–39. Luther's Eucharistic theology was much more realistic than Thomas's; Luther supported the condemnation of Berengar's "spiritualizing" doctrine and said that in the Supper the teeth of the faithful crush the body of Christ, a description to which Thomas doubtless would have reacted with horror (Sasse, *This Is My Body,* 162).

49. Althaus, *The Theology of Martin Luther,* 375.

50. For explorations of Luther's dispute with the Swiss, see Fischer, "Luther's Stake in the Lord's Supper Controversy," 50–59; Fischer, "Introduction," *Luther's Works,* vol. 37, xi–xxi; Heiko A. Oberman, *Luther: Man between God and the Devil* (New Haven, CT: Yale University Press, 1989), 232–45; Sasse, *This is My Body,* 233–72; and B. A. Gerrish, "Discerning the Body: Sign and Reality in Luther's Controversy with the Swiss," *JR* 68 (1988), 377–95.

this section, however, our focus will be Luther's earlier period, in which he interacted directly with the Roman Catholic doctrine.

In *The Babylonian Captivity of the Church* (1520), Luther attacked the three-fold captivity of the sacrament of communion. He condemned the withholding of the elements from the laity (27–28),[51] the doctrine of transubstantiation, and the Eucharistic sacrifice. Luther considered transubstantiation "less grievous" to the consciences of believers than communion in one kind or the sacrificial conception of the Mass (28).[52] In this early treatise, his main concern with the doctrine of transubstantiation was that it had been laid down as a dogma of the church: "My one concern at present is to remove all scruples of

---

51. Page references are to Martin Luther, *The Babylonian Captivity of the Church,* in *Luther's Works,* vol. 36. Luther never considered communion in one kind to be a central concern, and chastised the Hussites for insisting that the cup *must* be offered to the laity. See Barth, "Luther's Doctrine of the Eucharist," 77; Sasse, *This Is My Body,* 91–93; and Jaroslav Pelikan, *Obedient Rebels: Catholic Substance and Protestant Principle in Luther's Reformation* (New York, NY: Harper & Row, 1964).

52. Barth emphasized that Luther never considered transubstantiation to be heresy: "When he realized that the indirect identity of bread and body could equally well be expressed in a form different from the doctrine of the Roman church, he discarded that form with as little sentiment as one expends discarding an old coat" ("Luther's Doctrine of the Eucharist," 102–3). Sasse notes that Luther saw the idea of the Mass as something offered to God as the most dangerous Eucharistic teaching of Rome (*This Is My Body,* 87).

conscience" (30). Rome had elevated a speculation—a mere opinion—into a binding dogma, and, worse yet, threatened to persecute those who disagreed.[53] "Since it is not necessary to assume a transubstantiation effected by divine power, it must be regarded as a figment of the human mind, for it rests neither on the scriptures nor on reason" (31). Luther thus urged toleration of views other than transubstantiation. No one, he insisted, should be called a heretic for believing that real bread and real wine are present on the altar. All should be at liberty to hold one or the other doctrine without fearing for their salvation (30). Luther's dominant concern here was evidently pastoral, not theological or philosophical.

Luther did, however, voice several philosophical reservations concerning the doctrine of transubstantiation. First, he claimed that it is more probable to hold that there is real bread and wine in the Eucharistic meal than to hold that the substance of bread and wine is entirely converted. It is an "absurd and unheard-of juggling with words" to understand "bread" to mean "the accidents of the bread" (31). Luther affirmed the reality of Christ's presence, while at the same time dispensing with the

---

53. Barth comments that in 1520 Luther's concern was simply for Christian freedom ("Luther's Doctrine of the Eucharist," 102). Stone points out that Luther admitted transubstantiation as an opinion, but not as a dogma (*A History of the Doctrine of the Holy Eucharist*, vol. 2, 11).

"superfluous miracle" of the transformation of the substance and retention of the accidents (29). Luther here was applying Ockham's Razor, trimming off unnecessary elements of the Roman doctrine. The error of Rome lay in the fact that it had speculated beyond the limits of revelation.

Another of Luther's objections to transubstantiation, especially as formulated by Aquinas, was that it was illogical and unphilosophical: the Thomistic doctrine "hangs so completely in the air without support of Scripture or reason that it seems to me he knows neither his philosophy nor his logic" (29). Thomas was ignorant of Aristotle, who taught that the subject and accidents are inseparable, and he should therefore be pitied for attempting to employ Aristotelian philosophy without understanding it (29). Though he called Aristotle a "monster" (33) and laid the blame for the doctrine of transubstantiation on him (31), Luther indulged in some Aristotelian speculation of his own. Aristotle taught that both accidents and substance are subjects, though the substance is the chief subject. If Rome needs transubstantiation to prevent an idolatry of the substance of the bread, it also needs a "transaccidentation" so that the body of Christ is not confused with the accidents. But if the accidents can be erased "by an act of the intellect," the substance can also be transcended without positing a transformation of the substance (33–34). This section of the treatise is best read as Luther's attempt to "answer a fool after his own folly." His argument would then be an attempt to show the absurdity of the Thomistic doctrine. It is as if Luther said, "You want to play Aristotle, I'll give you Aristotle."

When Luther turned to his own views, several other key elements of his doctrine emerged. First and foremost, Luther emphasized that his main concern was to defend the Word of God, that no violence be done to what God has said. The words of institution must be understood in nothing other than their grammatical and proper sense.[54] Believers must cling with "simple faith" to Christ's words, and in response to Aristotelian speculations, must "put aside such curiosity and cling simply to the words of

---

54. In a famous letter, Luther told of his own inclination to abandon the doctrine of the real presence, so as to undermine further the authority of Rome. The words of institution forced him to retain the doctrine: "But I am captured by the Word of God and cannot find a way out. The words are there, and they are too strong for me. Human words cannot take them out of my soul" (quoted in Sasse, *This Is My Body,* 81). Sasse also quotes Luther's 1519 treatise on the sacraments, in which he attacked "those who practice their arts and subtleties to such an extent that they ask where the bread remains when it is changed into Christ's flesh. What does it matter? It is enough that it is a divine sign, in which Christ's flesh and blood are truly present—how and where, we leave to Him" (quoted in ibid., 100). See also Fischer, "Luther's Stake in the Lord's Supper Controversy," 51–52, for a discussion of Luther's insistence on the words of institution over against Zwingli.

Christ."[55] Sasse claims that Luther's "belief in the Real Presence rests solely on the words of Christ."[56]

Alongside his appeal to simple faith in the simple words of Christ, Luther insisted also that the mystery of the sacrament not be explained away. Believers should be "willing to remain in ignorance of what takes place here and content that the real body of Christ is present by virtue of the words" (30). He admitted that he could not understand how the bread is Christ's body, "yet I will take my reason captive to the obedience of Christ [2 Cor. 10:5], and clinging simply to his words, firmly believe not only that the body of Christ is in the bread, but that the bread is the body of Christ" (34). Philosophy cannot explain the mystery. So what? "The Holy Spirit is greater than Aristotle" (34). He asked, "Is it necessary to comprehend the manner of the divine working in every detail?" (33).

In one respect, Luther's argument contains little that Thomas would find objectionable. Like Luther, he insisted that the words of institution prove that Christ's body and blood are really and even "substantially" present

---

55. Sociologically, it would be interesting to examine these appeals in the light of the populist tendencies of the Reformation. Clearly, Luther is allying himself with the people against the magisterium and the university. This is not to impugn his motives; rather, it highlights the pastoral concern and emphasis of the Reformation.

56. Sasse, *This Is My Body*, 107

(though they would differ on the meaning of the latter adverb). Luther's charge that the Roman doctrine undermined the mystery of the present, however, would have carried little weight with Aquinas, who justified transubstantiation precisely as a great mystery, the mystery of mysteries. Thomas did not claim to have explained the mystery of the Eucharist. Indeed, Luther's position could easily be parried by Roman Catholic theologians with the rejoinder that Luther's rejection of transubstantiation indicated that he did not appreciate fully the miracle of the sacrament. After all, Luther himself admitted that he had dispensed with "superfluous miracles." Luther's charges of rationalizing could be met with countercharges of the same character. As long as Luther charged the Catholics with speculation in the sense of going beyond the revelation of Scripture, he was on firm ground. As soon as he began charging them with attempting to explain away the mystery of the Eucharist, he was left without support.

Luther's anti-sacramentarian treatises run along the same lines. The NT speaks of the elements both as "bread and wine" (1 Cor 10:16–17) and as "body and blood" (Matt 26:26–29). Thus, both must be present.[57] Luther attempted to explain the "sacramental union" of the elements with Christ's body and blood by drawing an analogy between the incarnation and the Eucharist. There

---

57. *That These Words of Christ, "This Is My Body," etc., Still Stand Firm Against the Fanatics,* in *Luther's Works,* vol. 37, 29.

are two natures in the one person of the God-man. The humanity is not transubstantiated into the divinity, but both natures are there in their entirety: "This man is God; this God is man." The mystery of the incarnation cannot be grasped by philosophy. So also in the sacrament, it is not necessary to believe in a transubstantiation. Rather, it is sufficient simply to believe that the bread is body and the wine is blood, and vice versa.[58]

Luther did not stop with this basic affirmation, however.[59] In spite of his constant appeals to the "simple meaning," he attempted to define the *mode* of the presence of Christ's body and employed the language of "substance" in his definition.[60] The words of institution imply

---

58. *The Babylonian Captivity,* 35.

59. Cf. the opinion of Sasse: "Luther believes in the Real Presence without trying to build up a theory comparable to the theories of impanation, transubstantiation, consubstantiation or whatever the subtle minds of philosophers and theologians may have devised" (*This Is My Body,* 104). Barth argued that though Luther seemed to prefer the formulation of Peter d'Ailly, "all such precise formulation is for Luther a scholastic question in which he has no interest. He will contend sharply neither against the doctrine of transubstantiation nor for the so-called consubstantiation doctrine; but only *against* those who make out of the former 'a necessary article of faith and law'; and *for* the real presence of the body in the bread" ("Luther's Doctrine of the Eucharist," 102–3). While these statements seem to capture Luther's fundamental intent, it is also true, as we shall see, that he offered philosophical explanations for his doctrine.

60. Fischer calls attention to the paradox that Luther professes to reject philosophy and insists that he need not be able to explain *how*

that "in the Supper we eat and take to ourselves Christ's body truly and physically."[61] More dramatically, Luther maintained at the Conference of Cassell in 1534 that the body of Christ is "divided and is eaten and is bitten with the teeth."[62] The Marburg Colloquy ended when Luther insisted that the statement of union include an affirmation of Christ's "substantial" presence in the Eucharist, an expression that Zwingli rejected.[63]

Luther did not deny that there is also a "spiritual eating": "[Christ] joined both together, the Word and his body, to be eaten spiritually with the heart and physically with the mouth."[64] He also admitted that Augustine called the Eucharistic elements figures and signs, but noted that for Augustine they were signs of something present yet invisible.[65]

Christ is present, yet his works are filled with philosophical explanations of the Eucharistic presence ("Luther's Stake in the Lord's Supper Controversy," 50, 53).

61. *That These Words of Christ,* 29.

62. Quoted in Stone, *A History of the Doctrine of the Holy Eucharist,* vol. 2, 21; also in A. von Harnack, *History of Dogma,* 7 vols. (Boston, MA: Little, Brown, 1900), vol. 7, 264.

63. Fischer, "Luther's Stake in the Lord's Supper Controversy," 54.

64. *That These Words of Christ,* 88.

65. Ibid., 104–5.

Yet Luther polarized the issues much as Aquinas did.[66] In his view, the "sacramentarians" were guilty of teaching that the elements are "bare symbols," while he taught a real presence. The Eucharist is *either* bare sign of an absent Christ *or* the substantial and "physical" presence of Christ's body. He excluded the possibility of a real presence that is not "substantial" in a physical sense and made "substance" a touchstone of Eucharistic orthodoxy. Thus, McCue is right to conclude that Luther maintained the doctrine of the real presence by an "emphatic reiteration of the most traditional medieval vocabulary."[67]

---

66. Sasse writes that there is no middle ground in Lutheran thought between *est* and *significat* ("A Lutheran Contribution," 37). This also denies the possibility that a doctrine can affirm both *est* and *significat*.

67. McCue, "The Doctrine of Transubstantiation from Berengar through Trent," 413. Althaus explains Luther's emphasis on the bodily presence of Christ as an implication of Luther's stress on the historicity of redemption. Luther feared that the Swiss "spiritualization" of the Eucharist implied a docetic Christology (*The Theology of Martin Luther,* 393–94). See the similar comments of Fischer, "Luther's Stake in the Lord's Supper Controversy," 55–56; and Fischer, "Introduction," in *Luther's Works*, vol. 37, xix. Luther was certainly correct to insist that God communicates himself through created means, but this does not, it seems to me, explain the way he insisted on the bodily and substantial presence of Christ in the Supper. There are, in short, other ways to protect the historicity of salvation and the reality of Christ's presence. For example, Luther insisted that the feeding on Christ's body and blood was a "spiritual" eating because the body and blood is offered through the Holy Spirit (Althaus, *The Theology of Martin Luther,* 396). Had Luther refrained from his insistence that the body of Christ is "substantially" present, his doctrine would have

Robert Fischer has suggested that Luther's intent was simply to affirm the reality of the body and blood of Christ. Thus, he offered philosophical argumentation only to prove that his doctrine was not philosophically absurd; he never raised his speculations to the level of dogma.[68] While Fischer's is an attractive and to a certain extent accurate interpretation of Luther—and one that brings his doctrine very close to Calvin's—it is difficult to avoid the conclusion that Luther's Eucharistic doctrine was more deeply indebted to late medieval philosophical conceptions of "substance" than Fischer admits.

Several lines of evidence support this conclusion. Luther's notion of "substance," though hardly precise, was much more definitely physical than Thomas's. In this respect, Luther's doctrine is quite consistent with late medieval conceptions. At the same time, however, Luther denied that Christ's bodily presence was a local presence.[69] Even more strongly than with Thomas's doctrine, Luther's forces the question of how a substantial *bodily* presence can be anything but a local presence. To answer this question, Luther appealed to Ockham's three modes

---

protected the real presence without being forced into an affirmation of the ubiquity of Christ's body. As we shall see below, this was precisely what Calvin did.

68. Fischer, "Luther's Stake in the Lord's Supper Controversy," 53.

69. Sasse, "A Lutheran Contribution," 37.

of presence.[70] What interests us here is not the theory itself, but the fact that Luther defended his doctrine by an appeal to late scholastic theories of space. It is also telling that Luther recognized that a doctrine of the ubiquity of Christ's body was necessary to defend his teaching.[71] This suggests that Luther wanted to affirm something more than the presence of Christ through the Spirit, and that he was not satisfied simply to affirm the mysterious reality of Christ's presence.

Luther's interpretation of the words of institution suggest, moreover, that he presupposed the medieval "substantialist" framework. For Luther, the words of institution were both self-explanatory and definitive. "The sum and substance of all this is that we have on our side the clear, distinct Scripture which reads, 'Take, eat; this is my body.'"[72] In his *Confession Concerning the Lord's Supper* (1528), he discourses for several pages on "the identical predication of diverse natures."[73] Even in this later treatise, he claimed that the controversy over transubstantiation is "unnecessary," because "it is of no great

---

70. Stinson, "'Substantia Corporis,'" 621.

71. Sasse, *This Is My Body,* 155–60; Althaus, *The Theology of Martin Luther,* 398–99.

72. *That These Words of Christ,* 33.

73. *Confession Concerning Christ's Supper,* in *Luther's Works,* vol. 37, 294ff.

consequence whether the bread remains or not."[74] Still, he preferred to say that there are two substances, which in reality and name are one substance. The incarnation again provided a ready analogy. There is, to be sure, a difference between the personal union of God and man in the incarnate Son and the "sacramental" union of the elements and Christ's body. Yet, it is this sacramental union that permits one to say that the bread is Christ's body and the wine Christ's blood.[75] Fischer points out that Luther insisted on a physical (*leiblich*) eating because the words of institution promised Christ's body and blood.[76]

This interpretation raises several hermeneutical questions. On what basis does Luther assume that a "simple" and "literal" interpretation of the words of institution requires a "physical" or "substantial" presence?

---

74. Ibid., 296.

75. Ibid., 297–300. At times in the argument, Luther appeared to be claiming that the sacramental union permits nothing more than a verbal *communicatio idiomatum*. "What one does to the bread is rightly and properly *attributed* to the body of Christ by virtue of the sacramental union" (ibid., 300). Grammar provides "a rule of expression" by which two things can be embraced by a single expression (ibid., 301). Elsewhere, of course, he went further to affirm a real communication of divine attributes.

76. "Luther's Stake in the Lord's Supper Controversy," 57. Also, "Luther emphasizes the material element or Sacrament because Christ commanded us to receive him there, and God always comes to us through created means" (ibid.). See also Fischer, "Introduction," in *Luther's Works*, vol. 37, xviii–xix.

Does a predication of a subject require the presence of the "substance" of that subject? Does this question itself arise from biblical exegesis, or philosophical speculation? What, indeed, does it mean to give a "literal" interpretation? Has not Luther himself interpreted the text to arrive at his position? That is, is not a "literal" interpretation still an *interpretation?* And, if Luther has interpreted the text, what has happened to the appeal to simple faith in the straightforward words of Jesus?

Luther's treatment of the adoration of the Eucharistic elements leads to a similar conclusion. In a 1523 treatise, *On the Adoration of the Sacrament,* Luther argued that the purpose of the sacrament was communion with Christ, not adoration of the consecrated elements. Christ ascended into heaven to be adored, but is present in the Supper to help and minister to his people. In making this argument, Luther broke decisively with the medieval obsession with the Eucharistic elements themselves. It is in the *eating* of bread and *drinking* of wine, not in the mere presence of consecrate bread and wine, that the church meets with her Savior. Despite this refreshing emphasis, however, Luther concluded that there was nothing heretical about the adoration of the host; nothing forbids the church to bow before a raised host. Luther only urged that adoration not be required.[77]

77. Stone, *A History of the Doctrine of the Holy Eucharist,* vol. 2, 18. Luther's reformed Mass retained the elevation of the host until 1544,

We should in all charity sympathize with Luther's pastoral concern on this issue. For centuries, the central rite of Christendom had been the adoration of the consecrated host. Luther knew that the religious habits of men cannot be changed overnight and avoided a violent sundering of the fabric of medieval religious life. Yet, it is difficult to avoid the conclusion that Luther's easy acceptance of adoration shows that his sacramental theology was not completely liberated from the medieval "substantialist" paradigm.

Luther's response to the doctrine of transubstantiation and his doctrine of the real presence may be summarized under these points.

1. Luther's main emphasis in his doctrine of the real presence was that the Supper is a gift of real communion with the body and blood of Christ.

2. In seeking to explain how this communion takes place, Luther accepted certain elements of the late scholastic framework, focusing especially in later writings on the substantial presence of Christ.

3. Luther's handling of the words of institution assumed, with Thomas, that Christ was speaking

---

though it was explained as a Hebraic rite (Stone, 19).

about the "substance" of the elements. Luther understood "substance" in a physical sense.

4. Luther's pastoral concern for freedom of conscience was prominent in his attack on the Roman doctrine of transubstantiation.

5. Luther claimed to base his doctrine on the simple and literal sense of the words of institution.

6. Like Thomas, Luther sharply contrasted "substance" and "figure."

Calvin

Tracing the lines of influence in Reformation sacramental theology yields some surprising results. Though Calvin's doctrine of the real presence is popularly associated with Zwingli's, Calvin considered himself more at home in Luther's world of thought.[78] Indeed, upon reading Luther's

---

78. For general treatments of Calvin's doctrine, see Stone, *A History of the Doctrine of the Holy Eucharist*, vol. 2, 50–56; Hans Grass, *Die Abendmahlslehre bei Luther und Calvin;* J. Beckmann, *Vom Sakrament bei Calvin: Die Sakramentenlehre Calvins in ihren Beziehungen zu Augustin* (Tübingen: Verlag von J. C. B. Mohr, 1926); J. Codier, *La Doctrine Calviniste de la Sainte Cene* (Montpellier: Faculté de Théologie Protestante, 1951); Ronald S. Wallace, *Calvin's Doctrine of the Word and Sacrament* (1953; repr., Tyler, Texas: Geneva Divinity School, 1982); Wilhelm Niesel, *Calvins Lehre vom Abendmahl* (Munich: Kaiser, 1930); B. A. Gerrish, "The Lord's Supper in the Reformed Confessions," *Theology Today* 23 (1966), 224–43; Gerrish, "John Calvin and the Reformed Doctrine of the Lord's Supper," *Mc-*

sharp attacks on Zwingli, Calvin refrained for many years from reading the works of the reformer of Zurich.[79] Brian Gerrish has suggested that Luther, Calvin, and Bullinger may be classed as three representatives of one school of Eucharistic thought, while Zwingli represents an entirely

Cormick Quarterly, 22:2 (1969), 85–98; Joseph N. Tylenda, "Calvin and Christ's Presence in the Supper—True or Real," *Scottish Journal of Theology* 27:1 (1974), 65–75; Boniface Meyer, "Calvin's Eucharistic Doctrine: 1536–39," *Journal of Ecumenical Studies* 4 (1967), 47–65; and Wilhelm Niesel, "The Sacraments," in *Readings in Calvin's Theology*, ed. D. K. McKim (Grand Rapids, MI: Baker, 1984), 244–59. See also the brief discussions in François Wendel, *Calvin: Origins and Development of His Religious Thought*, trans. Philip Mairet (Durham, NC: Labyrinth, 1987), 329–55; Benjamin Charles Milner Jr., *Calvin's Doctrine of the Church*, in Studies in the History of Christian Traditions, vol. 5 (Leiden: Brill, 1970), 110–33; and Geddes MacGregor, *Corpus Christi: The Nature of the Church According to the Reformed Tradition* (Philadelphia, PA: Westminster, 1958), 176–96. A fine summary of Calvin's doctrine and a detailed study of his role in the production of the *Consensus Tigurinis* (1549) may be found in Paul Rorem, "Calvin and Bullinger on the Lord's Supper," *Lutheran Quarterly* 2 (1989), 155–84, 357–89.

79. Gerrish writes that "Calvin found Zwingli's position no less defective than the Roman, for Zwingli (like Carlstadt) seemed to turn the sacrament into a religious exercise, in which the devout communicant concentrated his thoughts on what the dying Christ had done for him centuries ago. Against this, Calvin insists that we do not merely recall Christ's benefits in the supper: we actually receive them. The supper is a gift, it does not merely remind us of a gift" ("John Calvin and the Reformed Doctrine Lord's Supper," 93). On these points, Calvin's doctrine contained nothing that Luther had not already said. (See also Wendel, *Calvin*, 330, 333, 340.)

different theological type.[80] Like Luther, Calvin closely associated the words of institution with the gospel and emphasized that the Supper is a gift,[81] and even preferred the Thomistic doctrine to the Zwinglian illusion that Christ did not mean what he said.[82] Yet, despite similarities of emphasis, Calvin's critique of transubstantiation moved along quite different lines from Luther's, and his own doctrine was defended on a very different basis.

Calvin strongly affirmed that Christ's body and blood were truly present in the sacrament:[83] "Our souls are fed by the flesh and blood of Christ in the same way that bread and wine keep and sustain physical life. For the analogy of the sign applies only if souls find their nourishment in Christ—which cannot happen unless Christ truly grows into one with us, and refreshes us by the eating of his flesh and the drinking of his blood" (*Inst.* 4.17.10). Calvin was indeed much more comfortable us-

---

80. Gerrish, *John Calvin*, 97.

81. Wendel, *Calvin*, 336–37.

82. Rorem, "Calvin and Bullinger on the Lord's Supper," 175.

83. Tylenda argues that Calvin avoided describing Christ's presence as "real," a term that suggested to him a corporeal presence. In his first reply to the Lutheran Joachim Westphal (1555), Calvin conceded that, if "real" means nothing more than true, as opposed to fallacious and imaginary, it was admissible; Calvin professed that he would "rather speak barbarously than afford material for strife" (quoted in Tylenda, "Calvin and Christ's Presence in the Supper," 70).

ing the Augustinian language of "sign" than either Luther or Aquinas, yet he insisted at the same time that in the presentation of the symbol the reality is also offered and received. Like Luther, Calvin stressed that the Lord's promise is not false: "when we have received the symbol of the body, let us no less surely trust that the body itself is also given to us" (ibid.). He denied that Christ is received only by the "understanding and imagination." Through the symbols of bread and wine, Christ's "very body and blood" are shown, so that believers might "grow into one body with him" and "be made partakers of his substance" (4.17. II).[84] Calvin here adopted his familiar formula, "distinct, but not separate," in relation to the sacramental signs and their accompanying reality.

Calvin even used the term "substance" to describe what is communicated in the Supper: "I confess that our souls are truly fed by the substance of Christ's flesh," and "those who exclude the substance of vivifying flesh from the communion defraud themselves of the use of the supper."[85] Calvin did not, however, use "substance" in

---

84. Though it is beyond the scope of our concern, Calvin's characteristic blurring of Eucharistic and ecclesiological language is significant.

85. Quoted in Wallace, *Calvin's Doctrine of the Word and Sacrament,* 199. It should be noted that Calvin's stress is on the reception of the elements, not on the elements as such. It is in the communion and eating through which Christ communicates the substance of his flesh to his people.

its technical Aristotelian sense nor, in most cases, in the physicalist sense that seems to dominate Luther's thought. Instead, Calvin used the term in the sense employed by the church fathers, for whom "substance" was simply a way of emphasizing the reality of Christ's self-communication.[86] To say that the Supper effects a union with Christ's substance is to say that there is a *real* union and communion with Christ in the Supper.

Calvin's overall approach to the question of "substance" becomes clearer as we begin to examine his treatment of transubstantiation. He admitted, for example, that the church fathers sometimes spoke of a conversion of the elements. In employing such language, however, the fathers "do not mean that the elements have been annihilated, but rather that they now have to be considered of a different class from common foods intended solely to feed the stomach, since in them is set forth the spiritual food and drink of the soul. This we do not deny" (4.17.14). There is a change in the elements, but this change has nothing to do with "substance," if that means a material reality: "There is no one of the ancient writers who does not admit in clear words that the sacred symbols of the Supper are bread and wine, even though, as has been said, they sometimes distinguish them with var-

---

86. Some church fathers, like the prudent Augustine, avoided the term altogether (Stinson, "'Substantia Corporis,'" 580). In many respects, this is also the fundamental motivation of Thomas and Luther.

ious titles to enhance the dignity of the mystery" (ibid.). There is a change in the meaning and use, but not the material substance.

Calvin's larger purpose was not so much to deny transformation of the elements as to remove the issue of conversion from the framework of the scholastic concept of "substance." This strategy permitted him to follow the Fathers in using titles "to enhance the dignity of the mystery" and explains his often strikingly realistic language. Calvin used this language because it is the language of Scripture. There is no reason to think that Calvin was privately hedging on the truth of his words, as later Lutherans charged. Instead of hiding a pure symbolism under the language of substance, Calvin was rejecting the centuries-old separation of figure and reality; he attempted to get out of the dead end and ambiguities of medieval and early Reformation Eucharistic debates by affirming that the Eucharist was *both* symbolic *and* real, or, perhaps better, by offering a new understanding of the nature of religious symbols. His Lutheran opponents, still operating with the polarizations inherited from Luther himself, simply could not escape the conclusion that Calvin was being evasive.

In fairness, it must be admitted that Calvin's use of "substance" could be ambiguous and confusing. Wendel notes that Calvin sometimes used "substance" in its scholastic sense, sometimes in the sense of "foundation," and at other times with reference to spiritual gifts.[87] The very fluidity of Calvin's usage, while liable to misunderstanding, shows that he was not operating on scholastic assumptions and models. Thus, while employing realistic language, Calvin refused to permit a philosophical notion of substance to determine his doctrine of the real presence. Instead, his Eucharistic doctrine and his objections to transubstantiation and Luther's doctrine were determined by several theological considerations.

It is true, of course, that Calvin scorned transubstantiation as a doctrine "which they [i.e., the Roman Catholics] neither understand themselves nor can explain to others" (4.17.13). The core of the doctrine is that "through consecration, what was previously bread is made Christ, so that thereupon Christ lies hidden under the appearance of bread." Whatever qualifications are introduced by Roman Catholic theologians are just so many sophistries (ibid.). The Roman Catholic denial that its doctrine requires a local presence of Christ's body is, said Calvin, absurd. Calvin initiated his attack upon the Roman doctrine with an appeal to reason. There seems, at this point, a certain amount of truth to the Lutheran and Roman charges that Calvin was rationalizing away the mystery of the Eucharist. If this is the foundation of Calvin's critique, Rome has a built-in answer: Believe that

---

87. Wendel, *Calvin,* 341–42.

God can do what he wills; lay aside reason, and hold to Christ's words in faith.

Calvin also expressed pastoral concerns. Transubstantiation led both common folk and church leaders into great superstition. Fixation on the transformed elements blinded the church to the real value of the sacrament, and its relation to faith: "They are little concerned about true faith by which alone we attain fellowship with Christ and cleave to him. Provided they have a physical presence of him, which they have fabricated apart from God's Word, they think that they have presence enough" (ibid.).

Several important Calvinistic themes come to light in these sentences. First, Calvin denied, against both Rome and Luther, the *communicatio infidelium*. Believers alone partake of Christ in the sacrament. He did not mean to deny that Christ is truly and objectively offered, but to stress that grace is always received *sola fide*. Only by faith does a sinner take hold of Christ, in the sacrament or anywhere else. Second, Calvin observed that in any case Christ's physical presence does not guarantee fellowship with him. Finally, we find in Calvin, as also in Luther, the objection that transubstantiation is an extra-biblical construction.

Most importantly, this argument reveals Calvin's teaching that the Supper is a communion with the whole Christ, both his divinity and his humanity, not with a portion of Christ: "He is both God and man in us, for, in the first place, He makes us alive by the power of His Holy Spirit: then He is man within us, for He makes us participate in the sacrifice He offered for our salvation, and declares to us that it is not without cause that He has appointed His flesh to be our food indeed, and His blood our drink indeed."[88] It is through participation in Christ's flesh and blood that we receive life.

As Berkouwer points out, Calvin's insistence on communion with the whole Christ was a protest, largely implicit, against the depersonalizing tendencies inherent in any fascination with the "substance" of the elements. For Calvin, "it was precisely the communion with 'substantial physicality' in the Lutheran doctrine of the Lord's Supper that threatened the *praesentia Christi realis* in the Supper."[89] Calvin was challenging, in a more fundamental way than Luther had done, the liturgical and religious straightjacket in which the scholastic framework had bound Eucharistic theology. That framework had developed from and reinforced a fixation on the Eucharistic elements. For Calvin, the Supper is not a theatrical miracle at which the people of God are spectators, but a living encounter with the glorious person of the ascended Christ; the elements are given not to gaze upon but to consume.

---

88. Quoted in Wallace, *Calvin's Doctrine of the Word and Sacrament*, 200.

89. G. C. Berkouwer, *The Sacraments* (Grand Rapids, MI: Eerdmans, 1981), 228.

Calvin also objected to transubstantiation because it cuts the very root of the nature of a sacrament. The sacrament is intended to provide a parallel between an "earthly" and a "heavenly" reality. Just as we feed on bread and wine to sustain our bodies, so Christ invites us to feed on him to the nourishment of our souls. This analogy breaks down if only the accidents of bread and wine are present, because "the whiteness"—the accidents of bread and wine—do not nourish us (4.17.14).[90]

At the heart of Calvin's critique of both transubstantiation and the Lutheran doctrine, however, were Christological and redemptive-historical arguments. Those who teach transubstantiation claim that their doctrine ensures the comforting nearness of Christ. Calvin was sympathetic with this concern, but objected that Christ's

---

90. Roman Catholic theologian Christopher Kiesling accuses Calvin of philosophical speculation in this argument. Are bread and wine signs by virtue of their appearance or their substance, or is the question even valid? To answer this question at all, as Calvin does, is pure speculation (*The Eucharist in Ecumenical Dialogue*, ed. Leonard Swindler [New York, NY: Paulist Press, 1976], 82). In response to this criticism, two points can be made. First, even if Kiesling is correct, this criticism does not address Calvin's most central challenges to transubstantiation. Second, it might be argued that his criticism misses Calvin's essential insight. Calvin is not speculating on the nature of signs, but insisting on the parallel that Christ himself established in John 6. If we do not feed on the bread in its wholeness, then it is not analogous to say that we feed on Christ in his wholeness. The common element in the two is food; if food is absent from the symbol, then it is an inappropriate symbol.

nearness does not force one to affirm transubstantiation. In fact, transubstantiation implies a second humiliation of the Son; it accepts the presence of a Christ who has not yet risen and ascended. Unable to leap beyond heaven to reach Christ, Rome has brought him down from heaven: "What nature denied to them they tried to correct by a more harmful remedy, so that by remaining on earth we may need no heavenly nearness of Christ" (4.17.15). Calvin agreed with his opponents that Christ draws near in the Supper, but he refused to affirm this in a way that undermines the reality of Christ's heavenly enthronement.

Much has been made of Calvin's insistence that Christ is bodily and locally present in heaven. Calvin's spatial understanding of heaven seems rather simplistic at first blush, but his position should not be understood to imply that Christ is a prisoner on his own throne, unable to meet intimately with his people. Rather, Calvin's basic concern was to emphasize that there has been real progress in redemptive history; Christ is no longer in a state of humiliation, but in a state of exaltation, having ascended and risen to the heavenlies. A Eucharistic doctrine that brings Christ from his throne is, in effect, a throwback to the Old Covenant. Calvin insisted that however subtly it may be explained, the Thomistic doctrine tends to carry precisely this implication.

How is the church united to an ascended Savior? As in his explanation of the Eucharistic presence, Calvin offered a doctrine of the Eucharistic communion that was consistent with the progressive character of redemption. Calvin explained Christ's presence in a variety of ways. Sometimes, he spoke of the church's presence in heaven with Christ: "To them Christ does not seem present unless he comes down to us. As though, if he should lift us to himself, we should not just as much enjoy his presence! The question is therefore only of the manner, for they place Christ in the bread, while we do not think it lawful for us to drag him from heaven" (4.17.31).[91]

In other places, Calvin argued that the Spirit communicated the body and blood of Christ to the faithful. Though he denied that the believer's communion is with the Spirit alone (that is, apart from communion with the body and blood of Christ), Calvin taught that the Spirit is the "bond of connection" (4.17.12). He used the analogy of the sun and its beams to illustrate the point. Just as the sun "casts its substance" by shedding its beams upon the

---

91. It cannot seriously be suggested by anyone who has read this passage that Calvin rationalized away the mystery of the Eucharist. The mystery, however, is not the transformation of the substance of the elements, but rather that the Spirit unites the church on earth with all the company of heaven, and carries the church to heaven to commune in table fellowship with the exalted Christ. The mystery of the Eucharist is the mystery of the gospel: that we, separated from a holy God, yet intimately commune with him.

earth, the Spirit's "radiance" imparts the "communion of his flesh and blood" (ibid.).[92]

In his insistence on the spiritual presence, Calvin's purpose was again to underscore the progress of redemptive history. Christ's presence among his New Covenant people is always spiritual, that is, by the personal agency of his Spirit. If Christ's ascension were merely a "change of mortal state," he would not have had to send his Spirit. But "the coming of the Spirit and the ascent of Christ are antithetical; consequently, Christ cannot dwell with us according to the flesh in the same way that he sends his Spirit" (4.17.26). Any doctrine that tends to affirm a "fleshly" presence of Christ implicitly denies that Christ is now known according to and through his Spirit. Calvin's insistence on the "spiritual" presence of Christ in the Eucharist was thus not inconsistent with the reality of the presence, as the Lutherans suggested. Because he was not operating within a "substance" framework, Calvin did not oppose "Spirit" and "reality" in such a fashion; working within a redemptive-historical framework, he could affirm a "spiritual" presence without "spiritualizing."[93]

---

92. It is obvious that this analogy does not fit any Lutheran or Roman idea of substance; "substance" instead refers to the power of Christ's flesh and blood offered to the believer in the Eucharist through the Spirit.

93. According to Fischer, this was the same connotation that Luther gave to "spiritual." Against Zwingli's dualism of flesh and spirit,

Calvin's fundamental motivation in these passages was to articulate a doctrine of the real presence consistent with the full, eschatological reality of the resurrection, ascension, and Pentecost. From the time of Pentecost, the enthroned Christ is personally present among his people through the Spirit.[94] Calvin's argument was that what is true in general about the NT era is true in particular about the presence of Christ in the Supper.

Christological considerations were also prominent in Calvin's doctrine.[95] Transubstantiation and even more explicitly Luther's teaching posit that Christ's body is in some way ubiquitous. Christ's body (or, for Thomas, the substance of that body) is present on every altar in every

---

Luther insisted that all of life is spiritual, that is, under the government of the Spirit ("Luther's Stake in the Lord's Supper Controversy," 55–56). Luther's doctrine, however, fails to recognize that the fleshly and spiritual presence of Christ are redemptive-historically (not ontologically) antithetical.

94. Richard B. Gaffin Jr., writes that "Pentecost is Christ's personal coming to the church as the life-giving Spirit" (*Perspectives on Pentecost: Studies in New Testament Teaching on the Gifts of the Holy Spirit* [Phillipsburg, NJ: Presbyterian and Reformed, 1979], 19). This provides an answer to the frequent charge that Calvin depersonalizes the Holy Spirit, or collapses the Spirit's personality into Christ's. For Calvin, as for Paul, Christ and the Spirit are, after Pentecost, economically (redemptive-historically), not ontologically, identical. See also Gaffin, *Resurrection and Redemption: A Study in Paul's Soteriology*, 2nd ed. (Phillipsburg, NJ: Presbyterian and Reformed, 1987), 78–92.

95. Wendel, *Calvin*, 350.

celebration of the Eucharist. Calvin objected to this line of thinking not because it is unreasonable, but because it endangers the true humanity of Christ; it is a theological, not a philosophical, absurdity. The notion that Christ's body was invisibly present in the elements likewise does violence to the reality of the humanity of Christ. Calvin feared that Gnosticism would follow "if Christ's body seemed mortal and lowly in this one place, but in another was considered immortal and glorified" (4.17.17).

Calvin summarized his teaching in this manner:

> Let us never (I say) allow these two limitations to be taken away from us: (1) Let nothing be withdrawn from Christ's heavenly glory—as happens when he is brought under the corruptible elements of this world, or bound to any earthly creatures. (2) Let nothing inappropriate to human nature be ascribed to his body, as happens when it is said either to be infinite or to be put in a number of places at once [4.17.19].

Several aspects of this remarkable statement should be noted. First, Calvin's method was to set limits to the doctrine of the Eucharistic presence, instead of seeking to define with technical precision the nature of that presence. By doing this, Calvin was able to maintain the mystery of the real presence without reducing his doctrine to sheer irrationality. Second, these limiting statements do not depend on the interpretation of any single passage, not even on the crucial words of institution. They are clear teachings of the NT and are acknowledged by all orthodox Christians.

Finally, these limiting statements are thoroughly theological, not philosophical, in character. What is remarkable in all of his discussions of the real presence is Calvin's resolute resistance to the temptation to speculate *philosophically* about the Eucharistic presence. Thomas and Luther said in effect, "Let nothing detract from the substantial presence of Christ in the Eucharist." But such a formulation employs a (vague) philosophical concept to delimit the boundaries of the doctrine. Calvin, by contrast, enclosed his doctrine within Christological and eschatological boundaries. We can set theological boundaries to our understanding, but beyond those boundaries, all is mystery.

Within these limits, Calvin allowed for a great variety of expression, much of it of a very "high sacramental" character. Once the true humanity of Christ and the progress of redemptive history have been firmly established,

> I freely accept whatever can be made to express the true and substantial partaking of the body and blood of the Lord, which is shown to believers under the sacred symbols of the Supper—and

so to express it that they may be understood not
to receive solely by imagination or understanding
of mind, but to enjoy the thing itself as nourishment of eternal life. [4.17.19]

Clearly, Calvin taught much more than a "memori-
alism" or a "virtualism."[96] Christ is objectively present and
offered to the believer; even the language of "substance"
and "change" is permissible, as long as it is not understood in a way that undermines fundamental Christological and eschatological truths.

---

96. Against MacGregor, *Corpus Christi,* 178. It is wholly foreign
to Calvin's thought to suggest that one can receive the "virtue" of
Christ's work without receiving Christ himself. My conclusion is precisely the same as that of Gerrish, who characterizes Calvin's position
as a "symbolic instrumentalism," Christ's flesh and blood being received by the believer *through* the instrument of the signs (Gerrish,
"The Lord's Supper in the Reformed Confessions"). See also Rorem's
comment that Calvin "went to great lengths to express the fullness
and completeness of the communion not only with the virtue or
power of Christ, but with Christ's very body and blood. He drew
the line only at a transfusion or mixture of substances or natures"
("Calvin and Bullinger on the Lord's Supper," 158). In fact, Calvin
explicitly rejected a "virtualistic" interpretation in his commentary
on 1 Corinthians 11:24: "Jesus Christ offers us not only the benefits
of his death and resurrection, but also his own body in which he suffered and was resurrected" (quoted in Wendel, *Calvin,* 340).

Thus, to summarize Calvin's doctrine:

1. Calvin's dominating concerns were biblical-theological, rather than philosophical or pastoral.

2. Calvin did not deny the "substantial" or "true" presence of Christ. Instead, he affirmed Christ's "substantial" presence only in the context of more fundamental theological considerations and used "substance" in a fluid way.

3. Calvin wanted especially to protect the reality of Christ's human nature and of progress in redemptive history.

4. Calvin insisted that Christ's body and blood are offered and received in the sacrament through the Spirit. It is not "merely" the Spirit who is present, nor simply the virtue of Christ's death, but Christ himself.

5. Calvin's doctrine did not stand and fall on a particular interpretation of the words of institution.

6. Calvin affirmed that the Eucharist was both symbol *and* reality.

7. Calvin's emphasis was on the presence of Christ in the communion, rather than the presence of Christ in the elements.

Conclusion

In several respects, Thomas, Luther, and Calvin all displayed the same concerns with regard to the Eucharistic presence of Christ. All wanted to avoid both a mere symbolism, and (with the partial exception of Luther) a crass physicalism. All agreed that Christ himself is truly present and offered in the Supper, and all based this belief on the words of institution. All agreed that in the Supper believers are united to Christ. All agreed that the presence of Christ in the Supper is a great mystery. When they attempted to explain the mystery, however, their paths diverged. Thomas relied explicitly on Aristotelian philosophical categories; despite his protests to the contrary, Luther retained much of the scholastic framework; Calvin's contribution was to insist on a *theological* explanation of the Eucharistic presence.

In this sense, Calvin's doctrine of the Eucharist is a case study in theological "paradigm shift." When the doctrine of the real presence stalled and deadlocked on the philosophical question of substance and on the antithesis of "figure" and "reality," Calvin challenged the terms of the debate and offered a formulation of the real presence that is both consistent with orthodox Christology and satisfying to the pastoral concerns of other theologians. Calvin did not offer a "mediating" doctrine. Instead, Calvin's achievement was, in George Weigel's happy phrase, to "stake out ground ahead of the barricades."[97]

Unfortunately, Reformed theologians have often been more Zwinglian than Calvinistic on the doctrine of the real presence and so have missed the genius of Calvin's achievement. (Indeed, some Reformed theologians are actually more Zwinglian than Zwingli!) We may briefly examine the views of Robert L. Dabney as representative of this anti-Calvinist strain within the Reformed tradition of Eucharistic teaching. Dabney explicitly rejected Calvin's doctrine, charging that "it is not only incomprehensible, but impossible."[98] In particular, he argued that Calvin's notion that believers receive the body and blood of the Christ who is in heaven is "contrary to the laws of extension." Dabney complained that Calvin's doctrine is as offensive to reason as transubstantiation.[99] Positively, Dabney taught a "virtualist" view, arguing that Christ's "operations are present, through the power of the Holy Ghost employing the elements as means of grace," and expresses appreciation for Zwingli's liberation from superstition.[100]

---

97. George Weigel, *Catholicism and the Renewal of American Democracy* (New York, NY: Paulist Press, 1989).

98. Robert L. Dabney, *Lectures on Systematic Theology* (1878; repr., Grand Rapids, MI: Zondervan, 1972), 811.

99. Ibid., 812.

100. Ibid., 808–9.

Our understanding of Calvin's doctrine may be sharpened by speculating on his response to Dabney's arguments. First, Calvin would point to the NT teaching that believers participate in the body and blood of Christ in the Supper (1 Cor 10:16), and would remind Dabney that Christ has promised to give us his body and blood as food and drink. That is to say, Scripture itself places emphasis on partaking of and union with the *man,* Jesus Christ. Moreover, Calvin would refuse to reduce this participation to a participation in the "benefits" or "operations" of Christ; the idea that one could receive benefits without union with the benefactor was nonsensical to Calvin.[101]

Given the fact of participation in the body and blood, how is this participation in the body and blood of Christ to be explained? How can it be made consistent with the "laws of extension"? Calvin's answer to this question is twofold. Ultimately, this participation *cannot* be fully explained; the presence of Christ in the Supper

---

101. Gerrish emphasizes that Calvin's understanding of the Eucharistic presence was of a piece with his understanding of the gospel. The purpose of the gospel is not merely that we should enjoy the benefits of Christ's work, but that we should commune with God in Christ. Thus, as Gerrish comments, "we are already using Eucharistic language before we come to speak directly about the Lord's Supper" ("John Calvin and the Reformed Doctrine of the Lord's Supper," 87–89).

is something more felt than explained.[102] Calvin would likely have felt no need to make his doctrine consistent with the "laws of extension," but like Thomas and Luther would have insisted that God performs a miracle in the Supper (though he disagreed with them about the character of that miracle). Calvin's admission that the Supper awes and overpowers him shows that Calvin operated with very different conceptions of the Eucharist than Dabney, who can justly be charged with a rationalistic tendency.

Yet, Calvin would continue, though the Eucharist is a mystery, explanations may be offered, so long as they do not violate the fundamental teachings of NT Christology and eschatology. Among the relevant NT doctrines are: Christ is enthroned in heaven; he is present among his people by his Spirit; he is true man. In the light of these considerations, it is difficult to see how Calvin could have come to any other conclusion than he did.

Reformed theologians of Dabney's persuasion have forced Eucharistic debate back into a pre-Reformation deadlock and replayed continually the tragedy of Marburg. A recovery of Calvin's basic insights and approach

---

102. *Inst.* 4.17.7

would help to achieve a genuinely ecumenical orthodoxy on the doctrine of the real presence.[103]

103. Barth commented that Calvin "spoke the *Yes* and *But*" to Luther's doctrine, and that Calvin's doctrine "points to the tragedy of this historical cul-de-sac—perhaps also the *way out* and *hope*" ("Luther's Doctrine of the Eucharist," 111).

BIBLIOGRAPHY

Adam, Karl. *Saint Augustine: The Odyssey of His Soul*. London: Sheed and Ward, 1932.

Adams, Jeremy Duquesnay. *The Populus of Augustine and Jerome: A Study in the Patristic Sense of Community*. New Haven, CT: Yale University Press, 1971.

Adang, Camilla. "Ibn Hazm's Criticism of some 'Judaizing' Tendencies among the Malikites." In *Medieval and Modern Perspectives on Muslim-Jewish Relations*. Edited by Ronald Nettler. Psychology Press, 1995.

Althaus, Paul. *The Theology of Martin Luther*. Translated by Robert C. Schultz. Philadelphia, PA: Fortress, 1966.

Ando, Clifford. "Signs, Idols and the Incarnation in Augustinian Metaphysics." In *Representations, 73*. 2001.

Aquinas, Thomas. *Summa Theologiae*. Translated and edited by Thomas Gilby. Volumes 58–59. New York, NY: Blackfriars and McGraw-Hill, 1975.

Arthur, Ross G. *Medieval Sign Theory and Sir Gawain and the Green Knight*. Toronto: University of Toronto Press, 1987.

Asad, Talal. *Genealogies of Religion: Discipline and Reasons of Power in Christianity and Islam.* Baltimore, MD: Johns Hopkins, 1993.

Attridge, Harold W. "The Uses of Antithesis in Hebrews 8–10." In *Christians among Jews and Gentiles Essays in Honor of Krister Stendahl on his Sixty-fifth Birthday.* Edited by George W. E. Nickelsburg with George W. Mac Rae. Philadelphia, PA: Fortress Press, 1986.

Attridge, Harold W. *The Epistle to the Hebrews.* Hermeneia. Philadelphia, PA: Fortress Press, 1989.

Augier, Barnabé. "Le Sacrifice" [The Sacrifice]. In *Revue thomiste,* 34/n.s. 12. (1929).

Augustine. *On Christian Doctrine.* Translated by D. W. Robertson. Indianapolis, IN: Bobbs-Merrill, 1958.

Augustine. *Letters.* 6 vols. Translated by Sister Wilfrid Parsons. New York: Fathers of the Church, 1951-56.

Augustine. *The Fathers of the Church: A New Translation.* Translated by Robert P. Russell. Washington, D.C.: Catholic University of America Press, 1968.

Augustine. *The Trinity.* The Fathers of the Church. Translated by Stephen McKenna. Washington: Catholic University of America Press, 1963.

Austin, John L. *How to Do Things with Words.* Oxford: Oxford University Press, 1962.

Babcock, William S. "*Caritas* and Signification in *De doctrina Christiana* 1-3." In *De Doctrina Christiana: A Classic of Western Culture*. Edited by Duane W. H. Arnold and Pamela Bright. Notre Dame, IN: University of Notre Dame Press, 1995.

Bachli, Otto. *Das Alte Testament in der Kirchlichen Dogmatik von Karl Barth* [The Old Testament in the Church Dogmatics of Karl Barth]. Neukirchener, 1987.

Baciocchi, J. de "Le Mystere eucharistique dans les perspectives de la Bible" [The Eucharistic Mystery in Biblical Perspectives]. *Nouvelle revue theologique*, no. 6 (1955).

Barth, Karl. *Church Dogmatics IV/4: The Christian Life (Fragment): Baptism at the Foundation of the Christian Life*. Translated by G.W. Bromiley. Edinburgh: T&T Clark, 1969.

Barth, Karl. "Luther's Doctrine of the Eucharist." In *Theology and Church: Shorter Writings (1920–1928)*. New York: Harper & Row, 1962.

Barth, Karl. *The Teaching of the Church Regarding Baptism*. Translated by Ernest A. Payne. London: SCM, 1948.

Barth, Markus. *Die Taufe—Ein Sakrament? Ein exegetischer Beitrag zum Gespräch über die kirchliche Taufe* [Baptism—A Sacrament? An Exegetical Contribution to the Discussion on Church Baptism]. Zürich: Evangelischer A.G. Zollikon, 1951.

BeDuhn, Jason David. *Augustine's Manichaean Dilemma*. Philadelphia: University of Pennsylvania Press, 2010.

BeDuhn, Jason David. *The Manichaean Body: In Discipline and Ritual*. Baltimore: Johns Hopkins, 2000.

Beckmann, J. *Vom Sakrament bei Calvin: Die Sakramentenlehre Calvins in ihren Beziehungen zu Augustin* [On the Sacrament in Calvin: Calvin's Doctrine of the Sacraments in its Relationship to Augustine]. Tübingen: Verlag von J. C. B. Mohr, 1926.

Bell, Catharine. *Ritual Theory, Ritual Practice*. New York: Oxford University Press, 1992.

Berkouwer, G.C. *The Conflict with Rome*. Translated by David H. Freeman. Philadelphia, PA: Presbyterian and Reformed Publishing, 1958.

Berkouwer, G.C. *The Sacraments*. Grand Rapids, MI: Eerdmans, 1981.

Best, Ernest. "Spiritual Sacrifice: General Priesthood in the New Testament." *Int* 14 (1960).

Bobik, Joseph. *Aquinas on Being and Essence: A Translation and Interpretation*. Notre Dame, IN: University of Notre Dame, 1965.

Bonner, Gerald. "Augustine's Concept of Deification." *Journal of Theological Studies* 37 (1986).

Borg, Marcus. *Conflict, Holiness, and Politics in the Teaching of Jesus*. Studies in Bible and early Christianity, no. 5. Lewiston: Edwin Mellen, 1984.

Borg, Marcus. *Jesus: A New Vision*. London: SPCK, 1993.

Bourassa, F. "Theologie trinitaire chez saint Augustin"[Trinitarian Theology in Saint Augustine]. *Gregorianum* 58 (1977).

Bouyer, Louis. *Eucharist: Theology and Spirituality of the Eucharistic Prayer*. Translated by Charles Underhill Quinn. Notre Dame, IN: University of Notre Dame Press, 1968.

Bray, Gerald. *The Doctrine of God*. Contours of Christian Theology. Downers Grove: InterVarsity Press, 1993.

Brown, John. *An Exposition of Hebrews*. London: Banner of Truth Trust, 1961.

Brown, Peter. *Augustine of Hippo*. London: Faber and Faber, 1967.

Bruce, F. F. *Commentary on the Epistle to the Hebrews*. The New London Commentary on the New Testament. London: Marshall, Morgan & Scott, 1964.

Brunner, Emil. *Truth as Encounter*. Philadelphia, PA: Westminster Press, 1964.

Bultmann, Rudolf. "The Significance of the Old Testament for the Christian Faith." In *The Old Testament and Christian Faith: A Theological Discussion*. Edited by Bernhard W. Anderson. New York: Herder and Herder, 1964.

Burns, J. Patout. "Christ and the Holy Spirit in Augustine's Theology of Baptism." In *Augustine: From Rhetor to Theologian*. Edited by Joanne McWilliam. Ontario: Wilfrid Laurier University Press, 1992.

Burrows, Eric. *The Gospel of the Infancy, and Other Biblical Essays*. Bellarmine Series, no. 6. London: Burns Oates & Washbourne, 1940.

Caird, G.B. *The Language and Imagery of the Bible*. Grand Rapids, MI: Eerdmans, 1980.

Calvin, John. *Commentaries on the Epistle of Paul the Apostle to the Hebrews*. Translated by John Owen. Edinburgh: Calvin Translation Society, 1853.

Calvin, John. *Institutes of the Christian Religion*. 2 vols. Edited by John T. McNeill. Translated by Ford Lewis Battles. Philadelphia: Westminster, 1960.

Camberon, Averil. "Jews and Heretics – A Category Error?" In *The Ways That Never Parted: Jews and Chris-*

tians in Late Antiquity and the Early Middle Ages, edited by Adam H. Becker and Annette Yoshiko Reed. Minneapolis: Fortress, 2007.

Casel, Odo. *The Mystery of Christian Worship and Other Writings*. Edited by Burkhard Neunheuser. Westminster, MD: Newman Press, 1962.

Cavadini, John. "The Quest for Truth in Augustine's *De Trinitate*," *Theological Studies* 58 (1997).

Chauvet, Louis-Marie. *Symbol and Sacrament: A Sacramental Reinterpretation of Christian Existence*. Translated by Patrick Madigan and Madeleine Beaumont. Collegeville, MN: Liturgical Press, 1995.

Chemnitz, Martin. *Examination of the Council of Trent, Part II*. Translated by Fred Kramer. St. Louis, IL: Concordia, 1978.

Chenu, Marie-Dominique. *Nature, Man, and Society in the Twelfth Century: Essays on New Theological Perspectives in the Latin West*. Translated by Jerome Taylor and Lester K. Little. Chicago: University of Chicago Press, 1968.

Codier, J. *La Doctrine Calviniste de la Sainte Cene* [The Calvinist Doctrine of the Lord's Supper]. Montpellier: Faculté de Théologie Protestante, 1951.

Cohen, Shaye J. D. *The Beginnings of Jewishness: Bound-aries, Varieties, Uncertainties*. Berkeley: University of California Press, 1999.

Congar, Yves. *Lay People in the Church: A Study for a Theology of Laity*. rev. ed. London: Geoffrey Chapman, 1985.

Congar, Yves. *L'Église de saint Augustin à l'époque moderne* [The Church of Saint Augustine in the Modern Era]. Histoire de Dogmes 3. Paris: Éditions du Cerf, 1970.

Congar, Yves. "The Idea of the Church in St. Thomas Aquinas." *The Thomist* 1 (1939).

Conzelmann, Hans and Martin Dibelius. *The Pastoral Epistles*. Hermeneia. Philadelphia, PA: Fortress Press, 1972.

Cooke, Bernard J. *The Distancing of God: The Ambiguity of Symbol in History and Theology*. Minneapolis, MI: Fortress, 1990.

Cowdrey, H. E. J. "The Dissemination of St. Augustine's Doctrine of Holy Orders during the Later Patristic Age." *Journal of Theological Studies* 30 (1969).

Cramer, Peter. *Baptism and Change in the Early Middle Ages, c. 200–c. 1150*. Cambridge Studies in Medieval Life and Thought. Cambridge: Cambridge University Press, 1992.

Crouter, Richard. "Introduction." In *On Religion: Speeches to its Cultured Despisers* by Friedrich Schleiermacher. Cambridge: Cambridge University Press, 1988.

Cuervo, Manuel. "La transubstanciación según Santo Tomás y las nuevas teorías físicas" [Transubstantiation According to Saint Thomas and the New Physical Theories]. *Ciencia tomista* 84 (1957).

Cullmann, Oscar. *Baptism in the New Testament*. Translated by J. K. S. Reid. London: SCM, 1950.

Dabin, Paul. *Le sacerdoce royal des fidèles dans la tradition ancienne et moderne* [The Royal Priesthood of the Faithful in Ancient and Modern Tradition]. Brussels: L'Editions Universelles, 1950.

Dabney, Robert L. *Lectures on Systematic Theology*. Grand Rapids, MI: Zondervan, 1972. First published 1878.

Dahl, Nils A. "A New and Living Way: The Approach to God According to Hebrews 10:19–25." *Int* 5 (1951).

D'Argenlieu, B. Thierry. "La doctrine de Saint Thomas d'Aquin sur le caractère sacramentel dans les 'Sentences'" [The Doctrine of Saint Thomas Aquinas on the Sacramental Character in the 'Sentences']. *Revue thomiste* 34/n.s. 12 (1929).

D'Argenlieu, B. Thierry. "La doctrine du caractère sacramentel dans la 'Somme'" [The Doctrine of the Sacramental Character in the 'Summa']. *Revue thomiste* 34/n.s. 12 (1929).

Denzinger, Henricus. *Enchiridion Symbolorum: Definitionum et Declarationum de Rebus Fidiei et Morum* [Encyclopedia of Symbols: Definitions and Declarations on Matters of Faith and Morals]. 33rd ed. Freiburg: Herder, 1965.

Didier, J. C. "Saint Augustine et le baptême des enfants" [Saint Augustine and the Baptism of Children]. *Revue des études augustiniennes* 2 (1956).

Dittoe, John T. "Sacramental Incorporation into the Mystical Body." *The Thomist* 9 (1946).

Douglas, Mary. *Natural Symbols: Explorations in Cosmology*. New York: Vintage, 1973.

Due, Antonio. "Las especies eucarísticas y las teorías modernas" [The Eucharistic Species and Modern Theories]. *Pensamiento* 13 (1957).

Duffey, Eamon. *The Stripping of the Altars: Traditional Religion in England, c.1400–c.1580*. New Haven, CT: Yale University Press, 1992.

Dulles, Avery. *A Church to Believe in: Discipleship and the Dynamics of Freedom*. New York: Crossroad, 1983.

Dunnill, John. *Covenant and Sacrifice in the Letter to the Hebrews.* Cambridge: Cambridge University Press, 1992.

Dunn, James D. G. *Baptism in the Holy Spirit: A Re-Examination of the New Testament Teaching on the Gift of the Spirit in Relation to Pentecostalism Today.* Studies in Biblical Theology. 2nd series, no. 15. London: SCM Press, 1970.

Dunn, James D. G. *Jesus, Paul and the Law.* London: SPCK, 1990.

Early Medieval Theology. Translated and edited by George E. McCracken and Allen Cabaniss. Library of Christian Classics. vol. 9. London: SCM, 1957.

Eco, Umberto. "The Theory of Signs and the Role of the Reader." *Bulletin of the Midwest Modern Language Association* 14:1 (1981).

Eire, Carlos M. N. *War Against the Idols: The Reformation of Worship from Erasmus to Calvin.* Cambridge: Cambridge University Press, 1986.

Engels, J. "La doctrine du signe chez saint Augustin" [The Doctrine of the Sign in Saint Augustine]. *Studia Patristica* 6 (1962).

Erickson, Millard J. *Introducing Christian Doctrine.* 2nd ed. Grand Rapids: Baker, 2001.

Evans, Robert F. *One and Holy: The Church in Latin Patristic Thought.* London: SPCK, 1972.

Fahey, John F. *The Eucharistic Teaching of Ratramn of Corbie.* Mundelein, IL: St. Mary of the Lake Seminary, 1951.

Fahey, Michael A. "Augustine's Ecclesiology Revisited." In *From Rhetor to Theologian.* Edited by McWilliam.

Farrell, Walter. *A Companion to the Summa.* vol. 4. New York: Sheed & Ward, 1942.

Ferretter, Luke. "The Trace of the Trinity: Christ and Difference in Augustine's Theory of Language." *Literature and Theology* 12:3 (1998).

Finn, Thomas M. *Early Christian Baptism and the Catechumenate.* 2 vols. Message of the Fathers of the Church 5–6. Collegeville, MN: Liturgical Press, 1992.

Firth, Raymond. *Symbol: Public and Private.* London: George Allen Unwin, 1973.

Fischer, Robert H. "Introduction." *Luther's Works.* 55 vols. Edited by Helmut T. Lehmann. Philadelphia, PA: Muhlenberg, 1961.

Fischer, Robert H. "Luther's Stake in the Lord's Supper Controversy." *Dialog* 2:4 (1963).

FitzPatrick, P. J. *In Breaking of Bread: The Eucharistic Ritual.* Cambridge: Cambridge University Press, 1993.

Flemington, W. F. *The New Testament Doctrine of Baptism.* London: SPCK, 1948.

Floor, L. "The General Priesthood of Believers in the Epistle to the Hebrews." *Neotestamentica* 5 (1971).

Frame, John. *Cornelius Van Til: An Analysis of His Thought.* Phillipsburg, NJ: Presbyterian and Reformed Publishing, 1995.

Frame, John. *Doctrine of the Knowledge of God.* Phillipsburg, NJ: Presbyterian and Reformed, 1987.

Fredriksen, Paula. *Augustine and the Jews: A Christian Defense of Jews and Judaism.* New York: Doubleday, 2008.

Gaffin, Richard B., Jr. *Perspectives on Pentecost: Studies in New Testament Teaching on the Gifts of the Holy Spirit.* Phillipsburg, NJ: Presbyterian and Reformed, 1979.

Gaffin, Richard B., Jr. *Resurrection and Redemption: A Study in Paul's Soteriology.* 2nd ed. Phillipsburg, NJ: Presbyterian and Reformed, 1987.

Geiselmann, Josef Rupert. *Die Abendmahlslehre an der Wende der christlichen Spatantike zum Frühmittelalter: Isidor von Sevilla und das Sakrament der Eucharistie* [The Doctrine of the Lord's Supper at the Turn of

Christian Late Antiquity to the Early Middle Ages: Isidore of Seville and the Sacrament of the Eucharist]. Munich: Max Hueber, 1933.

Geiselmann, Josef Rupert. *Die Eucharistielehre der Vorscholastik* [The Eucharistic doctrine of pre-scholasticism]. Paderborn, 1926.

Gennep, Arnold van. *The Rites of Passage*. Translated by Monika B.Vizedom and Gabrielle L. Caffee. London: Routledge & Kegan Paul, 1960.

Gerrish, B. A. "Discerning the Body: Sign and Reality in Luther's Controversy with the Swiss." *JR* 68 (1988).

Gerrish, B. A. *Grace & Gratitude: The Eucharistic Theology of John Calvin*. Minneapolis, MN: Fortress, 1993.

Gerrish, B.A. "John Calvin and the Reformed Doctrine of the Lord's Supper." *McCormick Quarterly*, 22:2 (1969).

Gerrish, B. A. "The Lord's Supper in the Reformed Confessions." *Theology Today* 23 (1966).

Ghellinck, Joseph de. "Eucharistie du XIIe siècle en occident" [12th century Eucharist in the West]. *DTC*, vol. 5 (1913).

Ghysens, G. "Présence réelle eucharistique et transsubstantiation dans les définitions de l'Eglise Catholique"

[Eucharistic Real Presence and Transubstantiation in the definitions of the Catholic Church. *Iren* 2 (1959).

Grabmann, Thomas. *Thomas Aquinas: His Personality and Thought.* New York: Longmans, Green, and Co. 1928.

Grass, Hans. *Die Abendmahlslehre bei Luther und Calvin: Eine Kritische Untersuchung* [The Doctrine of the Lord's Supper in Luther and Calvin: A Critical Study]. Gütersloh: C. Bertelsmann Verlag, 1954.

Grimes, Ronald. *Beginnings in Ritual Studies.* rev. ed. Studies in Comparative Religion. Columbia, SC: University of South Carolina Press, 1995.

Grislis, Egil "The Manner of Christ's Eucharistic Presence in the Early and Medieval Church." *Consensus* 6 (October 1980).

Gunton, Colin. *The One, the Three and the Many: God, Creation and the Culture of Modernity.* The Brampton Lectures, 1992. Cambridge: Cambridge University Press, 1993.

Gunton, Colin. *The Promise of Trinitarian Theology.* London: T. & T. Clark, 1991.

Guthrie, G. H. "The Structure of Hebrews: A Textlinguistic Analysis." PhD diss., Southwestern Baptist Theological Seminary, 1991.

Gutwenger, E. "Substanz und Akzidens in der Eucharistielehre" [Substance and Accident in the Doctrine of the Eucharist]. *ZKT* 83 (1961).

Gutwenger, Engelbert. "Transubstantiation." In *Sacramentum Mundi: An Encyclopedia of Theology*. vol. 6. New York: Herder and Herder, 1970.

Hafemann, Scott J. *Paul, Moses, and the History of Israel: The Letter/Spirit Contrast and the Argument from Scripture in 2 Corinthians 3*. Peabody, Massachusetts: Hendrickson Publishers Inc., 1995.

Han, S. J. "An Investigation into Calvin's Use of Augustine." *Acta Theologica Supplementum* 10 (2008).

Haran, Menahem. "Priests and Priesthood." In *Encyclopaedia Judaica*. Jerusalem: Keter Publishing House, 1972.

Haring, N. M. "The Augustinian Axiom: *Nulla Sacramento Injuria Facienda Est*." *Mediaeval Studies* 16 (1954).

Haring, N. M. "Berengar's Definitions of *Sacramentum* and their Influence on Mediaeval Sacramentology." *Medieval Studies* 10 (1948).

Haring, N. M. "One Baptism: An Historical Study of the Non-Repetition of Certain Sacraments." *Mediaeval Studies* 10 (1948).

Harnack, Adolf von. *History of Dogma.* 7 vols. Boston, MA: Little, Brown, 1900.

Harnack, Adolf von. *Marcion: The Gospel of the Alien God.* 2nd ed. Translated by John E. Steely and Lyle D Bierma. 1924; Durham, NC: Labyrinth, 1990.

Harnack, Adolf von. *What Is Christianity?* 5th ed. Translated by Thomas Bailey Saunders. London: Ernest Benn, 1958.

Harris, Horton. *The Tubingen School.* Oxford: Clarendon, 1975.

Hart, D. G. and John R. Muether. *With Reverence and Awe: Returning to the Basics of Reformed Worship.* Phillipsburg, NJ: P&R Publishing, 2002.

Hauerwas, Stanley. *The Peaceable Kingdom: A Primer in Christian Ethics.* Notre Dame: University of Notre Dame Press, 1983.

Heppe, Heinrich. *Reformed Dogmatics.* rev. ed. Edited by Ernst Bizer. Translated by G. T. Thomson. London: Wakeman Great Reprints, 1950.

Hodge, Charles. *Systematic Theology.* 3 vols. Grand Rapids, MI: Eerdmans, 1986.

Hofmann, Fritz. *Die Kirchenbegriff des hl. Augustinus: In Seinen Grundlagen und in Seiner Entwicklung* [St. Augustine's Concept of the Church: Its Foundations and Its Development]. Munich: Max Huber, 1933.

Holifield, E. Brooks. *The Covenant Sealed: The Development of Puritan Sacramental Theology in Old and New England, 1570–1720*. New Haven, CT: Yale University Press, 1974.

Horton, Michael. *A Better Way: Rediscovering the Drama of God-Centered Worship*. Grand Rapids, MI: Baker, 2002.

Houssiau, A. "L'engagement baptismal" [Baptismal Commitment]. *Revue théologique de Louvain* 9 (1978).

Hughes, P. E. *A Commentary on the Epistle to the Hebrews*. Grand Rapids, MI: Eerdmans, 1977.

Hugh of St. Victor. *On the Sacraments of the Christian Faith*. Translated by Roy J. Deferrari. Cambridge, Mass.: Mediaeval Academy of America, 1951.

Jackson, B. Darrell. "The Theory of Signs in St. Augustine's *De doctrina christiana*." *Revue etudes augustiniennes* 15 (1969).

Jenson, Philip Peter. *Graded Holiness: A Key to the Priestly Conception of the World*. JSOT Supplement Series no. 106. Sheffield: JSOT Press, 1992.

Jenson, Robert. *Visible Words: The Interpretation and Practice of Christian Sacraments.* Philadelphia, PA: Fortress, 1978.

Jeremias, Joachim. *The Eucharistic Words of Jesus.* New Testament Library. 3rd ed. Translated by Norman Perrin. London: SCM Press, 1966.

Jewett, Paul K. *Infant Baptism and the Covenant of Grace.* Grand Rapids, MI: Eerdmans, 1978.

Jones, David. *Epoch and Artist: Selected Writings.* Edited by Harman Grisewood. London: Faber and Faber, 1959.

Jones, Paul Henry. *Christ's Eucharistic Presence: A History of the Doctrine.* American University Studies. New York: Peter Lang, 1994.

Jones, Paul Henry. "The Mode of Christ's Eucharistic Presence: An historical archaeology and ecumenical proposal." PhD diss., Vanderbilt, 1988.

Jordan, Mark D. "Words and Word: Incarnation and Signification in Augustine's *De Doctrina Christiana.*" *Augustinian Studies* 11 (1980).

Jorissen, Hans. *Die Entfaltung der Transsubstantiationslehre bis zum Beginn der Hochscholastik* [The development of the doctrine of transubstantiation up to the beginning of high scholasticism]. Münster: Aschen-dorff, 1965.

Jorissen, Hans. "Materie und Forme der Sakramente in Verstandnis Albertus des Grossen" [Matter and Form of the Sacraments in the Understanding of Albert the Great]. *ZKT* 80 (1958).

Jourjon, Maurice. "L'évêque et le peuple de Dieu selon saint Augustin" [The Bishop and the People of God according to Saint Augustine]. In *Saint Augustin parmi nous* by Henri Rondet, Charles Morel, Maurice Jourjon, and Jules Lebreton. Paris: Xavier Mappus, 1954.

Jungmann, Josef. *The Mass: An Historical, Theological, and Pastoral Survey.* Collegeville, MN: Liturgical Press, 1972.

Kant, Immanuel. *Religion Within the Limits of Reason Alone.* 2nd ed. Translated by Theodore M. Greene and Hoyt H. Hudson. LaSalle, IL: Open Court, 1960.

Karant-Nunn, Susan C. *The Reformation of Ritual: An Interpretation of Early Modern Germany.* London: Routledge, 1997.

Kattenbusch, E. "Transubstantiation." In *The New Schaff-Herzog Encyclopedia of Religious Knowledge.* vol. 11. New York: Funk and Wagnalls, 1911.

Kavanagh, Aidan. *The Shape of Baptism: The Rite of Christian Initiation*. Collegeville, MN: Liturgical Press, 1978.

Kerr, Fergus. *Theology after Wittgenstein*. Oxford: Blackwell, 1986.

Kiesling, Christopher. *The Eucharist in Ecumenical Dialogue*. Edited by Leonard Swindler. New York: Paulist Press, 1976.

Kiesling, Christopher. "The Sacramental Character and Liturgy." *The Thomist* 27 (1963).

King, Peter. "Augustine on the Impossibility of Teaching." *Metaphilosophy* 29:3 (1998).

Klingbeil, Gerard A. "Between Law and Grace: Ritual and Ritual Studies in Recent Evangelical Thought." *Journal of the Adventist Theological Society*, vol. 13, iss. 2, no. 4 (2002).

Kloos, Kari. "History as Witness: Augustine's Interpretation of the History of Israel in *Contra Faustum* and *De trinitate*." In *Augustine and History*. Edited by Christopher T. Daly, John Doody, and Kim Paffenroth. Lanham: Lexington Books, 2008.

Kostlin, Julius. *The Theology of Luther in its Historical Development and Inner Harmony*. 2nd ed. vol. 2. Philadelphia, PA: Lutheran Publishing Society, 1897.

Lakoff, George and Mark Johnson. *Philosophy in the Flesh: The Embodied Mind and Its Challenge to Western Thought*. New York: Basic, 1999.

Lamirande, Émilien. "Un siècle et demi d'études sur l'ecclésiologie de saint Augustin: Essay bibliographique" [A Century and a Half of Studies on the Ecclesiology of Saint Augustine: A Bibliographic Essay]. *Revue des ètudes Augustiniennes* 8 (1962).

Landgraf, Artur. "Die Gnadenökonornie des Alten Bundes nach der Lehre der Frühscholastik" [The economy of grace of the Old Testament according to the teachings of early scholasticism]. *ZKT* 57 (1933).

Lane, WIlliam. *Hebrews 1–8*. WBC, 47A. Dallas, TX: Word, 1991.

Lane, William. *Hebrews 9–13*. WBC, 47B. Dallas, TX: Word, 1991.

Laporte, Jean. "Models from Philo in Origen's Teaching on Original Sin." In *Living Water, Sealing Spirit: Readings on Christian Initiation*. Edited by Maxwell E. Johnson. Collegeville, MN.: Liturgical Press, 1995.

Lash, Nicholas. *Easter in Ordinary: Reflections on Human Experience and the Knowledge of God*. London: SCM, 1988.

Laurentin, René. *Structure et théologie de Luc I–II* [Structure and Theology of Luke I–II]. Etudes Bibliques. Pans Gabalda, 1957.

Lawler, Michael G. *Symbol and Sacrament: A Contemporary Sacramental Theology*. New York: Paulist Press, 1987.

Lecuyer, Joseph. "Le sacrifice selon saint Augustin" [Sacrifice according to Saint Augustine]. *Augustinus Magister*. Paris: Etudes Augustiniennes, 1954.

Lecuyer, Joseph. "Les étapes de l'enseignement thomiste sur l'épiscopat" [The stages of Thomistic teaching on the episcopate]. *Revue thomiste* 57 (1957).

Leeming, Bernard. *Principles of Sacramental Theology*. London: Longmans, Green and Co., 1956.

Levering, Matthew. *Christ's Fulfillment of Torah and Temple: Salvation according to Thomas Aquinas*. Notre Dame: University of Notre Dame Press, 2002.

Lieu, Judith. *Image and Reality: The Jews in the World of Christians in the Second Century*. Edinburgh: T&T Clark, 2003.

Lieu, Judith. *Neither Jew Nor Greek? Constructing Early Christianity*. Edinburgh: T&T Clark, 2005.

Lindbeck, George. "The Gospel's Uniqueness: Election and Untranslatability." *Modern Theology 13:4* (1997).

Lindbeck, George. *The Nature of Doctrine: Religion and Theology in a Postliberal Age.* London: SPCK, 1984.

Lohse, Bernhard. *Martin Luther: An Introduction to his Life and Work.* Translated by Robert C. Schultz. Philadelphia, PA: Fortress Press, 1986.

Lonergan, Bernard J. *Verbum: Word and Idea in Aquinas.* Notre Dame, IN: University of Notre Dame, 1967.

Lubac, Henri De. *Catholicism: A Study of Dogma in Relation to the Corporate Destiny of Mankind.* London: Burns, Oates, and Washbourne, 1950.

Lubac, Henri De. *Catholicism: Christ and the Common Destiny of Man.* Translated by Lacelot Sheppard and Sister Elizabeth Englund. San Francisco: Ignatius, 1988.

Lubac, Henri De. *Corpus Mysticum: L'eucharistie et l'eglize au moyen age: Etude historique* [Mystical Body: The Eucharist and the Church in the Middle Ages: Historical study]. 2nd ed. Paris: Aubier, 1949.

Lubac, Henri De. *The Mystery of the Supernatural.* Translated by Rosemary Sheed. London: Geoffrey Chapman, 1967.

Lubac, Henri De. *The Splendour of the Church.* Translated by Michael Mason. London: Sheed and Ward, 1966.

Luck, Ulrich. "Himmlisches und irdisches Geschehen im Hebräerbrief" [Heavenly and earthly events in the Epistle to the Hebrews]. ▨▨*um Testamentum* 6 (1963).

Luther. "The Babylonian Captivity of the Church." In *Luther's Works.* 55 vols. Edited by Helmut T. Lehmann. Gen. ed. Translated by A.T.W. Steinhäuser. Philadelphia, PA: Muhlenberg Press, 1959.

MacCulloch, Diarmaid. *The Reformation: A History.* New York: Viking, 2003.

MacDonald, Allan John. *Berengar and the Reform of Sacramental Doctrine.* 1930; repr., Merrick, NY: Richmond, 1977.

MacGregor, Geddes. *Corpus Christi: The Nature of the Church According to the Reformed Tradition.* Philadelphia, PA: Westminster, 1958.

MacIntyre, Alasdair. "Virtues, the Unity of a Human Life, and the Concept of a Tradition." In *Why Narrative?,Readings in Narrative Theology*, edited by Hauerwas and Jones. Grand Rapids, MI: Eerdmans, 1989.

Macquarrie, John. *A Guide to the Sacraments.* London: SCM, 1997.

Macy, Gary. *The Theologies of the Eucharist in the Early Scholastic Period: A Study of the Salvific Function of the Sacrament According to the Theologians, c. 1080–c. 1220*. Oxford: Clarendon, 1984.

Mahoney, John. "The Church of the Holy Spirit in Aquinas." *Heythrop Journal* 15 (1974).

Manetti, Giuovanni. *Theories of the Sign in Classical Antiquity*. Translated by Christine Richardson. Bloomington, IN: Indiana University Press, 1993.

Mangenot, E. "Eucharistie du XIIe au XVe siècle" [Eucharist from the 12th to the 15th century]. *DTC*, vol. 5 (1913).

Markus, R. A. *Signs and Meanings: World and Text in Ancient Christianity*. Liverpool: Liverpool University Press, 1996.

Markus, R. A. "St. Augustine on Signs." In *Augustine: A Collection of Critical Essays*. Edited by R. A. Markus. Garden City, NY: Doubleday, 1972.

Martha, Jules. *Les sacerdoces athéniens* [The Athenian priesthoods]. Bibliothèque des Écoles Françaises d'Athènes et de Rome. no. 26. Paris: Ernest Thorin, 1882.

Mascall, E. L. *Corpus Christi: Essays on the Church and the Eucharist*. London: Longmans, Green and Co., 1953.

Mathison, Keith. *Given For You: Reclaiming Calvin's Doctrine of the Supper*. Phillipsburg, NJ: P&R Publishing, 2002.

McCabe, Herbert. *The New Creation*. London: Continuum 2010. First published 1964.

McCabe, Herbert. "The Real Presence." *CR* 49 (1964).

McCormack, Stephen. "The Configuration of the Sacramental Character." *The Thomist* 7 (1944).

McCue, James F. "The Doctrine of Transubstantiation from Berengar through Trent: The Point at Issue." *HTR*, vol. 61 (1968).

McGrath, Alister E. *Iustitia Dei: A History of the Christian Doctrine of Justification*. 2 vols. Cambridge: Cambridge University Press, 1986.

McKim, Donald. *Dictionary of Major Biblical Interpreters*. Downers Grove: InterVarsity Press, 2007.

Medieval Jewish Civilization: An Encyclopedia. Edited by Norman Roth. Taylor & Francis, 2003.

Meer F. Van der. *Augustine the Bishop*. London: Sheed and Ward, 1961.

Mersch, Emile. *Le Corps Mystique du Christ: Études de théologie historique* [The Mystical Body of Christ:

Studies in Historical Theology]. 2nd ed. Paris: Desclèe de Brouwer et Cie, 1936.

Meyer, Boniface. "Calvin's Eucharistic Doctrine: 1536–39." *Journal of Ecumenical Studies* 4 (1967).

Meyers, Jeffrey. *The Lord's Service*. Moscow, ID: Canon Press, 2003.

Milbank, John. *The Suspended Middle: Henri de Lubac and the Debate Concerning the Supernatural*. Grand Rapids, MI: Eerdmans, 2005.

Milbank, John. *Theology and Social Theory: Beyond Secular Reason*. Oxford: Blackwell, 1990.

Milbank, John. *The Word Made Strange: Theology, Language, Culture*. Oxford: Blackwell, 1997.

Milner, Benjamin Charles, Jr. *Calvin's Doctrine of the Church*. In Studies in the History of Christian Traditions. vol. 5. Leiden: Brill, 1970.

Mitchell, Leonel. *Baptismal Anointing*. Notre Dame, IN: University of Notre Dame Press, 1978.

Moffatt, James. *A Critical and Exegetical Commentary on the Epistle to the Hebrews*. ICC. Edinburgh: T. & T. Clark, 1924.

Molloy, Noel. "Hierarchy and Holiness: Aquinas on the Holiness of the Episcopal State." *The Thomist* 39 (1975).

Moloney, Raymond. "Eucharist." In *A New Dictionary of Theology*. Edited by J. A. Komonchak, Mary Collins, O.S.B., and Dermot A. Lane. Wilmington: Glazier, 1987.

Mondos, Jean de. *Lanfranc et Berengar: La controverse eucharistique du XIe siècle* [Lanfranc et Berengar: The Eucharistic controversy of the 11th century]. Louvain: Spicilegium Sacrum Lovaniense, 1971.

Mueller, John Theodore. *Christian Dogmatics*. St. Louis, IL: Concordia Publishing Company, 1955.

Muir, Edward. *Ritual in Early Modern Europe*. 2d ed. Cambridge: Cambridge University Press, 2005.

Muller, Richard. *Dictionary of Latin and Greek Theological Terms: Drawn Principally from Protestant Scholastic Theology*. Grand Rapids, MI: Baker, 1985.

Nicolas, R. P. Marie-Joseph. "La doctrine de S. Thomas sur le sacerdoce" [The doctrine of St. Thomas on the priesthood]. *Studitomistici*. Rome: Pontificia Accademia Romana di S. Thomasso d'Aquino, 1974.

Neill, Stephen and Tom Wright. *The Interpretation of the New Testament, 1861–1986*. Oxford: Oxford University Press, 1988.

Neunheuser, Burkhard. *Eucharistie in Mittelalter und Neuzeit* [Eucharist in the Middle Ages and Modern Times]. Handbuch der Dogmengeschichte; Freiburg: Herder, 1963.

Newman, Louis Israel. *Jewish Influence on Christian Reform Movements*. Columbia University Press, 1925.

Niesel, Wilhelm. *Calvins Lehre vom Abendmahl* [Calvin's doctrine of the Lord's Supper]. Munich: Kaiser, 1930.

Niesel, Wilhelm. "The Sacraments." In *Readings in Calvin's Theology*. Edited by D. K. McKim. Grand Rapids, MI: Baker, 1984.

Nietzsche, Friedrich. *The Antichrist*. Translated by H.L. Mencken. Costa Mesa, CA: Noontide Press, 1988.

Oberman, Heiko A. *Luther: Man between God and the Devil*. New Haven, CT: Yale University Press, 1989.

Oden, Thomas C. *Systematic Theology: Life in the Spirit*. vol. 3.1994; Peabody, MA: Prince Press, 1998.

O'Donovan, Oliver. "*Usus* and *fruitio* in Augustine, *De doctrina Christiana* I." *Journal of Theological Studies* n. s. 33 (1982).

O'Neill, Colman E. "St. Thomas on Membership of the Church." *The Thomist* 27 (1963).

O'Neill, J. C. "The Study of the New Testament." In *Nineteenth Century Religious Thought in the West.* Edited by Ninian Smart, John Clayton, Steven Katz, and Patrick Sherry. 3 vols. Cambridge, 1985.

Osborne, Kenan B. "Methodology and the Christian Sacraments." *Worship* 48 (1974).

Ozment, Steven. *The Age of Reform: 1250–1550: An Intellectual and Religious History of Late Medieval and Reformation Europe.* New Haven, CT: Yale University Press, 1980.

Pagan Priests. Edited by Mary Beard and John North. London: Gerald Duckworth, 1990.

Pak, G. Sujin. *The Judaizing Calvin: Sixteenth-Century Debates over the Messianic Psalms.* Oxford, 2009.

Pannenberg, Wolfhart. *Systematische Theologie, Band 3* [Systematic Theology, Volume 3]. Göttingen: Vandenhoeck & Ruprecht, 1993.

Pelikan, Jaroslav. *The Growth of Medieval Theology (600–1300).* Chicago: University of Chicago Press, 1978.

Pelikan, Jaroslav. *Obedient Rebels: Catholic Substance and Protestant Principle in Luther's Reformation.* New York, NY: Harper & Row, 1964.

Pelikan, Jaroslav. *Spirit versus Structure: Luther and the Institutions of the Church*. London: Collins, 1968.

Pellegrino, Cardinal Michele. *The True Priest: The Priesthood as Preached and Practiced by Saint Augustine*. Langley, UK: St Paul Publications, 1968.

Pelser, G. M. M. "A Translation Problem Heb 10:19–25." *Neotestamentica* 8 1974.

Perinelle, J. "La doctrine de S. Thomas sur le sacrement de l'ordre" [The doctrine of St. Thomas on the sacrament of orders]. *Revue des sciences philosophiques et théologiques* 19:2 (1930).

Peters, Albrecht. *Realpräsenz: Luthers Zeugnis von Christi Gegenwart im Abendmahl* [Real Presence: Luther's Testimony of Christ's Presence in the Lord's Supper]. Berlin: Lutherisches Verlagshaus, 1960.

Peterson, David. *Hebrews and Perfection: An Examination of the Concept of Perfection in the Epistle to the Hebrews*. Cambridge: Cambridge University Press, 1982.

Power, David N. *Unsearchable Riches: The Symbolic Nature of Liturgy*. A PuebloBook. Collegeville, MN: Liturgical Press, 1984.

Prenter, R. "Metaphysics and Eschatology in the Sacramental Theology of St. Augustine." *Studia Theologica* 1 (1948).

Pursiful, Darrell J. *The Cultic Motif in the Spirituality of the Book of Hebrews.* Lewiston, NY: Mellen Biblical Press, 1993.

Quinot, Bernard. "L'influence de L'Épître aux Hébreux dans la notion augustinienne du vrai sacrifice" [The influence of the Epistle to the Hebrews on the Augustinian notion of true sacrifice]. *Revue des etudes augustiniennes* 8 (1962).

Rahner, Karl. *Schriften zur Theologie* [Writings on theology].vol. 4. Einsiedeln: Benziger, 1967.

Rahner, Karl. "Theology of Symbol." In *Theological Investigations, Volume IV: More Recent Writings.* Translated by Kevin Smyth. Baltimore: Helicon Press, 1966.

Rahner, Karl. *The Trinity.* Translated by Joseph Donceel. New York: Crossroad, 1997.

Redmond, R. P. "The Real Presence in the Early Middle Ages." *CR* 8 (1934).

Reinhold, G. *Die Lehre der örtlichen Gegenwart Christi in der Eucharistie bei Thomas von Aquin* [The doctrine of the local presence of Christ in the Eucharist in Thomas Aquinas]. Vienna, 1893.

Reveillard, Michel. "Le Christ-Homme, tête de l'Eglise: Étude d'ecclèsiologie selon les *Enarrationes in Psalmos* d'Augustin" [Christ the Man, Head of the Church:

A Study of Ecclesiology According to Augustine's *Enarrationes in Psalmos*]. *Recherches augustiniennes* 5 (1968).

Reventlow, Henning Graf. *The Authority of the Bible and the Rise of the Modern World*. Translated by John Bowden. Philadelphia: Fortress Press, 1985.

Reymond, Robert L. *A New Systematic Theology of the Christian Faith*. 2nd ed. Nashville, TN: Thomas Nelson, 1998.

Ringer, Jeffrey. "Faith and Language: Walter Hilton, Augustine, and Poststructural Semiotics." *Christianity and Literature* 53:1 (2003).

Rorem, Paul. "Calvin and Bullinger on the Lord's Supper." *Lutheran Quarterly* 2 (1989).

Rublack, Ulinka. *Reformation Europe*. Cambridge: Cambridge University Press, 2005.

Rupprecht, P. R. "Der heilige Thomas und das Leidensgedächtnis in der Eucharistie" [Saint Thomas and the Memory of the Passion in the Eucharist]. *TQ*, vol. 118 (1937).

Sabourin, Leopold. *Priesthood: A Comparative Study*. Supplements to Numen, Studies in the History of Religions, no. 25. Leiden: E. J. Brill, 1973.

Sabra, George. *Thomas Aquinas' Vision of the Church: Fundamentals of an Ecumenical Ecclesiology*. Mainz: Matthias-Grunewald Verlag, 1987.

Saebo, Magna. *Hebrew Bible/Old Testament: The History of Its Interpretation*. Candenhoeck & Ruprecht, 2008.

Salvesen, Alison. "A Convergence of the Ways? The Judaizing of Christian Scripture by Origen and Jerome." In *The Ways That Never Parted: Jews and Christians in Late Antiquity and the Early Middle Ages*. Edited by Adam H. Becker and Annette Yoshiko Reeds. Minneapolis: Fortress, 2007.

Sanders, E. P. *Jesus and Judaism*. Philadelphia, PA: Fortress Press, 1985.

Sasse, Hermann. "A Lutheran Contribution to the Present Discussions on the Lord's Supper." *CTM* 30 (1959).

Sasse, Hermann. *This Is My Body: Luther's Contention for the Real Presence in the Sacrament of the Altar*. Minneapolis, MN: Augsburg, 1959.

Schaff, Philip. *History of the Christian Church: Volume V: The Middle Ages, AD 1049–1294*. 1907; Grand Rapids, MI: Eerdmans, 1981.

Schildgen, Brenda Deen. "Augustine's Answer to Derrida in the De Doctrina Christiana." *New Literary History* 25:2 (1994).

Schillebeeckx, Edward. *Christ, the Sacrament of Encounter with God.* Translated by Paul Barrett and N. D. Smith. London: Sheed and Ward, 1963.

Schillebeeckx, Edward. *The Eucharist.* Translated by N. D. Smith. London: Sheed and Ward, 1968.

Schleiermacher, Friedrich. *The Christian Faith.* 2nd. ed. Translated by H.R. MacIntosh and J. S. Stewart. Edinburgh: T&T Clark, 1928.

Schleiermacher, Friedrich. *The Life of Jesus.* Translated by S. Maclean Gilmour. Edited by Jack E. Verheyden. Philadelphia: Fortress, 1975.

Schleiermacher, Friedrich. *On Religion: Speeches to its Cultured Despisers.* Translated by John Oman. New York: Harper Torchbooks, 1958.

Schmemann, Alexander. *For the Life of the World.* Crestwood, NY: St. Vladimir's Seminary Press, 1973.

Scholer, John M. *Proleptic Priests: Priesthood in the Epistle to the Hebrews.* JSNT Supplement Series, no. 49. Sheffield: JSOT Press, 1991.

Schoonenberg, P. "Transubstanciación: ¿hasta qué punto está determinada históricamente esta doctrina?" [Transubstantiation: To what extent is this doctrine historically determined?]. *Concilium* 24 (1967).

Scribner, R. W. *Popular Culture and Popular Movements in Reformation Germany.* London: The Hambledon Press, 1987.

Searle, John. *Speech Acts: An Essay in the Philosophy of Language.* Cambridge: Cambridge University Press, 1969.

Selvaggi, Filippo. "Il concetto di sostanza nel dogma eucaristico in relazione alla fisica moderna" [The concept of substance in the Eucharistic dogma in relation to modern physics]. *Gregorianum* 30 (1949).

Selvaggi, Filippo. "Ancora intorno ai concetti di 'sostanza sensible' e 'realtà fisica'" [Still on the concepts of 'sensible substance' and 'physical reality']. *Gregorianum* 38 (1957).

Sheedy, Charles E. *The Eucharistic Controversy of the Eleventh Century Against the Background of Pre-Scholastic Theology.* 2nd series, no. 4. S. T. D. diss., Catholic University of America Studies in Sacred Theology. New York: AMS Press, 1980.

Silva, Moises. "Perfection and Eschatology in Hebrews." *WTJ* 39:1 (1976–1977).

Smith, James K. A. "Between Predication and Silence: Augustine on How (Not) to Speak of God." *Heythrop Journal* 41 (2000).

Smits, Luchesius. *Saint Augustine dans l'oeuvre de Jean Calvin* [Saint Augustine in the work of John Calvin]. Assen: Van Gorcum, 1956.

Spicq, Ceslas. *Les Epîtres Pastorales* [The Pastoral Epistles]. Etudes Bibliques. Paris: Gabalda, 1969.

Stendahl, Krister. "The Apostle Paul and the Introspective Conscience of the West." *HTR* 5 (1963).

Stinson, Charles Herbert. "'Substantia Corporis': A Study of the Philosophical Semantics and Terminology in Latin Christian Dogma with Special Reference to the Eucharist: From Tertullian's Time to the Berengarian Controversy." PhD diss., Columbia University, 1971.

Stone, Darwell. *A History of the Doctrine of the Holy Eucharist.* vol. 1. London: Longmans, Green, 1909.

Strathmann, H. "λατρεύω, λατρεία" [I Worship, Worship]. *TDNT.*

Stroup, George W. *The Promise of Narrative Theology.* London: SCM, 1981.

Swetnam, James. "Form and Content in Hebrews 7–13" *Biblica* 55:3 (1974).

Sykes, Stephen. *Frederich Schleiermacher.* Makers of Modern Theology. London: Lutterworth, 1971.

Sykes, Stephen. *The Identity of Christianity: Theology and the Essence of Christianity from Schleiermacher to Barth*. London: SPCK, 1984.

Taylor, Charles. *A Secular Age*. Cambridge, MA: Belknap, 2007.

Taylor, Charles. *Sources of the Self: The Making of Modern Identity*. Cambridge: Cambridge University Press, 1989.

Teske, Roland. *Answer to Faustus, A Manichean*. The Works of Saint Augustine, a Translation for the 21st Century. Hyde Park: New City Press, 2007.

Thils, G. "Le pouvoir cultuel du baptisé" [The cult power of the baptized]. *Ephemerides Theologicae Lovanienses* 15 (1938).

Thurian, Max. *The Eucharistic Memorial*. 2 vols. Translated by J. G. Davies. Ecumenical Studies in Worship no. 7–8. London: Lutterworth Press, 1960–1961.

Thurian, Max. "Toward a Renewal of the Doctrine of Transubstantiation." In *Christianity Divided*. Edited by D. J. Callahan, Heiko A. Obermann, and Daniel J. O'Hanlon. New York, NY: Sheed & Ward, 1961.

Todorov, Tsvetan. *Theories of the Symbol*. Translated by Catherine Porter. Ithaca, NY: Cornell University Press, 1982.

Torrance, T. F. *The Doctrine of Grace in the Apostolic Fathers*. Edinburgh: Oliver and Boyd, 1948.

Trelcatius, Lucas. *Scholastica, et Methodica, Locorum communium, S. Theologiae Institutio* [Scholasticism and Methodism, Common Places, Sacred Theology Instruction].1610.

Turner, Victor. *The Ritual Process: Structure and Anti-Structure*. Chicago, IL: Aldine Publishing Company, 1969.

Turretin. *Institutes of Elenctic Theology*. 3 vols. Phillipsburg, NJ: P&R Publishing, 1997.

Tylenda, Joseph N. "Calvin and Christ's Presence in the Supper—True or Real." *Scottish Journal of Theology* 27:1 (1974).

Uberoi, J. P. S. *Science and Culture*. Delhi: Oxford University Press, 1978.

Vanhoye, Albert. "Longue marche ou acces tout proche? Le context biblique de Hébreux 3, 7–4, 11" [Long Walk or Close Access? The Biblical Context of Hebrews 3:7–4:11]. *Biblica* 49:1 (1968).

Volf, Miroslav. *After Our Likeness: The Church as the Image of the Trinity*. Grand Rapids, MI: Eerdmans, 1998.

Vollert, Cyril. "The Eucharist: Controversy on Transubstantiation." *TS* 22 (1961).

Wainwright, Geoffrey. *Doxology: The Praise of God in Worship, Doctrine, and Life: A Systematic Theology.* New York, NY: Oxford University Press, 1980.

Wallace, Ronald S. *Calvin's Doctrine of the Word and Sacrament.* Tyler, TX: Geneva Divinity School, 1982.

Walsh, Liam G. "Liturgy in the Theology of St. Thomas." *The Thomist* 38 (1974).

Wandel, Lee Palmer. *Voracious Idols & Violent Hands: Iconoclasm in Reformation Zurich, Strasbourg, and Basel.* Cambridge: Cambridge University Press, 1994.

Warfield, B. B. *Calvin and Augustine.* Phillipsburg, NJ: P&R, 1980.

Warfield, B. B. *The Plan of Salvation.* rev. ed. Grand Rapids, MI: Eerdmans, 1984.

Webber, Robert. *Worship Is a Verb.* Waco, Texas: Word Books, 1985.

Wedderburn, A. J. M. *Baptism and Resurrection Studies in Pauline Theology against its Graeco-Roman Background.* WUNT, no. 44. Tubingen: J. C. B. Mohr, 1987.

Weigel, George. *Catholicism and the Renewal of American Democracy.* New York, NY: Paulist Press, 1989.

Welker, Michael. *What Happens in Holy Communion?* Translated by John F. Hoffmeyer. Grand Rapids, MI: Eerdmans, 2000.

Wendel, François. *Calvin: Origins and Development of His Religious Thought.* Translated by Philip Mairet. Durham, NC: Labyrinth, 1987.

Why Narrative? Readings in Narrative Theology. Edited by Stanley Hauerwas and Gregory L. Jones. Grand Rapids, MI: Eerdmans, 1989.

Wilken, Robert L. *John Chrysostom and the Jews: Rhetoric and Reality in the Late Fourth Century.* University of California Press, 1983.

Wilken, Robert L. *Judaism and the Early Christian Mind: A Study of Cyril of Alexandria's Exegesis and Theology.* 1971; Eugene, OR: Wipf & Stock, 2004.

Williams, Rowan. "Language, Reality and Desire in Augustine's *De doctrina.*" *Literature and Theology* 3 (1989).

Williams, Rowan. "The Nature of a Sacrament." In *Signs of Faith, Hope and Love: The Christian Sacraments Today,* edited by John Greenhalgh and Elizabeth Russell. London: St. Mary's Bourne Street, 1987.

Williams, Rowan. "The Paradoxes of Self-Knowledge in the *De Trinitate.*" In *Collectanea Augustiniana.* Edited by Joseph T. Lienhard, Earl C. Muller, and Roland J. Teske. New York: Peter Lang, 1993.

Williams, Rowan. "Sacraments of the New Society." In *Christ: the Sacramental Word*. Edited by David Brown and Ann Loades. London: SPCK, 1996.

Williams, Rowan. "*Sapientia* and the Trinity: Reflections on the *De Trinitate*." In *Collectanea Augustiniana*. Edited by B. Bruning. Leuven University Press, 1990.

Winkler, Gabriele. "The Original Meaning of the Prebaptismal Anointing and Its Implications." In *Living Water, Sealing Spirit: Readings on Christian Initiation*. Edited by Maxwell E. Johnson. Collegeville, MN: Liturgical Press, 1995.

Worgul, George S. *From Magic to Metaphor: A Validation of the Christian Sacramentsa*. New York: Paulist, 1980.

Wright, N. T. *Jesus and the Victory of God*. London: SPCK, 1996.

Wright, N. T. *The New Testament and the People of God*. London: SPCK, 1993.

Wright, N. T. *Who Was Jesus?* London: SPCK, 1992.

Young, Frances. "From Analysis to Overlay: A Sacramental Approach to Christology." In *Christ the Sacramental Word: Incarnation, Sacrament and Poetry*. Edited by David Brown and Ann Loades. London: SPCK, 1996.

Zizioulas, John. *Being As Communion: Studies in Personhood and the Church*. 1985; Crestwood, NY: St. Vladimir's Seminary Press, 1993.